Grounding Religion

D0148886

How do religion and the natural world interact with one another? *Grounding Religion* introduces students to the growing field of religion and ecology, exploring a series of questions about how the religious world influences and is influenced by ecological systems.

Grounding Religion examines the central concepts of "religion" and "ecology" using analysis, dialogical exchanges by established scholars in the field, and case studies. The first textbook focused on encouraging critical thinking about the relationships between the environment and religious beliefs and practices, it also provides an expansive overview of the academic field of religion and ecology as it has emerged in the past forty years.

The contributors introduce students to new ways of thinking about environmental degradation and the responses of religious people. Each chapter brings a new perspective on key concepts such as sustainability, animals, gender, economics, environmental justice, globalization, and place. Discussion questions and contemporary case studies focusing on topics such as Muslim farmers in the US and Appalachian environmental struggles help students apply the perspective to current events, other media, and their own interests.

Whitney A. Bauman is Assistant Professor of Religion and Science at Florida International University. He is the author of *Theology, Creation, and Environmental Ethics* (Routledge, 2009) and Assistant Editor for the *Encyclopedia of Sustainability: Spirituality* (Berkshire, 2009).

Richard R. Bohannon II teaches in the Environmental Studies and Theology departments at the College of St. Benedict and St. John's University, and is a Ph.D. candidate in Religion and Society at Drew University. His publications include "Constructing Nature at a Chapel in the Woods," in *Ecospirit: Religion and Philosophies for the Earth* (Fordham, 2007).

Kevin J. O'Brien is Assistant Professor of Christian Ethics at Pacific Lutheran University. He is the author of *An Ethics of Biodiversity: Christianity, Ecology, and the Variety of Life* (Georgetown, 2010).

Grounding Religion

A Field Guide to the Study of Religion and Ecology

Edited by
Whitney A. Bauman, Richard R.
Bohannon II, and Kevin J. O'Brien

Routledge
Taylor & Francis Group

LONDON AND NEW YORK

First edition published 2011
by Routledge
2 Park Square, Milton Park, Abingdon, OX14 4RN

Simultaneously published in the USA and Canada
by Routledge
270 Madison Avenue, New York, NY 10016

Routledge is an imprint of the Taylor & Francis Group, an informa business

Typeset in Times New Roman by Taylor & Francis Books
Printed and bound in Great Britain by
CPI Antony Rowe, Chippenham, Wiltshire

British Library Cataloguing in Publication Data
A catalogue record for this book is available from the British Library

Library of Congress Cataloging in Publication Data
Grounding religion : a field guide to the study of religion and ecology / edited
by Whitney A. Bauman, Richard Bohannon II, Kevin J. O'Brien. – 1st ed.
p. cm.
Based on a colloquium held Feb. 26-Mar. 1, 2009 at Florida International
University, Miami, Fla.
Includes bibliographical references and index.
1. Human ecology – Religious aspects. I. Bauman, Whitney. II. Bohannon,
Richard (Richard R.) III. O'Brien, Kevin J.
GF80.G76 2010
201'.77 – dc22
2010006037

ISBN13: 978-0-415-78016-2 (hbk)
ISBN13: 978-0-415-78017-9 (pbk)
ISBN13: 978-0-203-84603-2 (ebk)

Contents

Notes on contributors   vii
Acknowledgments   xii

Introduction   1
WHITNEY A. BAUMAN, RICHARD R. BOHANNON II,
AND KEVIN J. O'BRIEN

PART I
Religion   11

1 Religion: what is it, who gets to decide, and why does
   it matter?   13
   WHITNEY A. BAUMAN, RICHARD R. BOHANNON II,
   AND KEVIN J. O'BRIEN

2 Religion: a dialogue   27
   REBECCA GOULD AND MARK I. WALLACE

3 Case study: "religion" in Appalachian environmental
   struggles   41
   JOSEPH WITT

PART II
Ecology   47

4 Ecology: what is it, who gets to decide, and why does
   it matter?   49
   WHITNEY A. BAUMAN, RICHARD R. BOHANNON II,
   AND KEVIN J. O'BRIEN

5 Ecology: a dialogue   64
   CELIA DEANE-DRUMMOND AND LISA SIDERIS

6 Case study: images of "land" among Muslim farmers
   in the US   73
   ELEANOR FINNEGAN

PART III
Key issues   79

7 Intellectual and organizational foundations of religion
   and ecology   81
   JOHN GRIM AND MARY EVELYN TUCKER

8 Sustainability   96
   WILLIS JENKINS

9 Animals and religion   113
   DAVE AFTANDILIAN

10 Gender   130
   AMANDA BAUGH

11 Economics   147
   LAURA M. HARTMAN

12 Environmental justice and eco-justice   163
   RICHARD R. BOHANNON II AND KEVIN J. O'BRIEN

13 Globalization   181
   LOIS ANN LORENTZEN

14 Place   203
   BRIAN G. CAMPBELL

   Afterword: teaching indoors, but not business as usual   222
   LAUREL KEARNS

   Glossary   228
   Index   236

Contributors

Dave Aftandilian is Assistant Professor of Anthropology at Texas Christian University and co-chair of the American Academy of Religion's Animals and Religion Consultation. From 2003 to 2008, he served as lecturer, preceptor, and program coordinator for the Environmental Studies Program at the University of Chicago. He co-founded the University of Chicago Religion and Environment Initiative, and coordinated it until 2008. His research and teaching interests include animals and religion, agriculture and religion, Native American religions and ethnohistory, and interpretive archaeology. He is the editor of a book on multidisciplinary and interdisciplinary approaches to the meaning of real animals in human worlds entitled *What Are the Animals to Us?* (University of Tennessee, 2007).

Amanda Baugh is a doctoral candidate in American Religions at Northwestern University. Her research focuses on interfaith religious environmentalism and the Green Cities movement, and she teaches in the areas of American religion and gender studies. Amanda is a co-chair for the Religion, Ecology, and Culture section of the Midwest American Academy of Religion.

Whitney A. Bauman is Assistant Professor of Religion and Science at Florida International University in Miami, FL, USA. He is the author of *Theology, Creation, and Environmental Ethics: From* Creatio ex Nihilo *to* Terra Nullius (Routledge, 2009) and the Assistant Editor for volume 1 of the *Berkshire Encyclopedia on Sustainability: The Spirit of Sustainability* (Berkshire, 2009). He also serves as Book Review Editor for *Worldviews: Global Religions, Culture and Ecology.*

Richard R. Bohannon II teaches in the Environmental Studies and Theology departments at the College of St. Benedict and St. John's University (Collegeville, MN), and is a Ph.D. candidate in Religion and Society at Drew University. He also worked with a small architecture firm in Boston for two years. His publications include "Constructing Nature at a Chapel in the Woods," in *Ecospirit: Religion and Philosophies for the Earth*

(Fordham, 2007), and entries on architecture and evangelicalism in the *Spirit of Sustainability* (Berkshire, 2009). He is a steering committee member for the Religion and Ecology Group at the American Academy of Religion.

Brian G. Campbell is a doctoral student in American Religious Cultures at Emory University. His research and teaching have focused on the history of race and environmental justice in Atlanta and on Emory's place in this social and ecological context. He is currently working on a cultural history of American hermits and solitaries, exploring their significance for notions of spirituality, their performance of gender, and their relationships with particular places and regions in the American landscape. Brian has a Masters of Divinity from Pacific School of Religion in Berkeley, California.

Celia Deane-Drummond holds a chair in theology and the biological sciences at the University of Chester, UK, is Director of the Centre for Religion and the Biosciences that she founded in 2002, and in 2009 was elected Vice Chair of the European Forum for the Study of Religion and Environment. She has a doctorate in plant physiology from Reading University and a doctorate in theology from Manchester University, and has focused her research on the engagement of theology and the biological sciences, with a particular interest in the practical, ethical implications of this work. Her recent books include *Creation through Wisdom* (T & T Clark, 2000), *ReOrdering Nature* (Continuum, 2003), *The Ethics of Nature* (Blackwells, 2004), *Wonder and Wisdom: Conversations in Science, Spirituality and Theology* (Templeton Foundation Press, 2006), and *Christ and Evolution: Wonder and Wisdom* (Fortress/SCM Press, 2009).

Eleanor Finnegan is a Ph.D. candidate in Religion at the University of Florida. Her scholarly interests include American Islam and Muslims, the impact of the Islamic tradition on environmental ethics and practices, and Muslim hip-hop music. The recipient of several Foreign Language and Area Studies (FLAS) fellowships, Eleanor is a contributor to *Environmental Ethics* and the *Encyclopedia of Environment and Society*. She has presented research on American Muslims at national conferences, such as the American Academy of Religion Annual Meeting, the UNC/Duke Islamic Studies Conference, and the Florida State Graduate Student Symposium. Her dissertation focuses on farming among American Muslim communities.

Rebecca Gould is Associate Professor of Religion at Middlebury College in Middlebury, VT. She is the author of (among other things) *At Home in Nature: Modern Homesteading and Spiritual Practice in America* (University of California Press, 2005). She is currently engaged in a research project entitled "Religion on the Ground: The New Environmentalism of Religious Institutions," funded by the Louisville Institute.

She is a fellow in the Young Scholars Program of the Center for American Religion at Indiana University—Purdue University Indianapolis. She is also a Board Member of two national non-profit initiatives: the Simplicity Forum and Take Back Your Time.

John Grim is a Senior Lecturer and Research Scholar at Yale University, teaching courses that draw students from the School of Forestry and Environmental Studies, Yale Divinity School, the Department of Religious Studies, the Institution for Social and Policy Studies, and Yale College. With Mary Evelyn Tucker he edited the 10-volume series "World Religions and Ecology," from the Harvard Center for the Study of World Religions and distributed by Harvard University Press. In that series he edited *Indigenous Traditions and Ecology: The Interbeing of Cosmology and Community* (Harvard, 2001). John is also President of the American Teilhard Association. Recently, he and Mary Evelyn Tucker edited Thomas Berry's last collection of essays, titled *The Christian Future and the Fate of Earth* (Orbis, 2009).

Laura M. Hartman teaches in the Religion department at Augustana College in Rock Island, IL. She researches applied ethics and Christian ethics, with a concentration in environmental ethics and feminist ethics. Her special interests include: economics and the environment, consumption, transportation, food, and gender. She has written articles about food ethics and the Eucharist, and Sabbath-keeping and the environment. Her first book, about consumption, will soon be published by Oxford University Press.

Willis Jenkins is Margaret Farley Assistant Professor of Social Ethics at Yale Divinity School, with a secondary appointment to the Yale School of Forestry and Environmental Studies. He is author of *Ecologies of Grace: Environmental Ethics and Christian Theology* (Oxford, 2008) and editor, with Whitney A. Bauman, of *The Spirit of Sustainability* (Berkshire, 2009).

Laurel Kearns is Associate Professor of Sociology of Religion and Environmental Studies at Drew University in Madison, NJ. Her research is focused on religious involvement, particularly Christian involvement in ecological issues and movements in the US and Australia, nature spirituality, and religious responses to global warming. She is co-editor of *EcoSpirit: Religions and Philosophies for the Earth* (Fordham, 2007) and author of dozens of articles dealing with various aspects of religion and the environment.

Lois Ann Lorentzen is Chair of the Theology and Religious Studies Department and Director of the Center for Latino Studies in the Americas (CELASA) at the University of San Francisco. Lois's research and teaching interests include religion and the environment, environmental ethics, and immigration. She is the author of *Etica Ambiental* (Universidad Iberoamericana, 2000) and *Raising the Bar* (Jossey-Bass 2004) and co-editor of numerous texts, including *On the Corner of Bliss and Nirvana: The Intersection of Religion, Politics, and Identity in New Migrant Communities* (Duke, 2009) and *Ecofeminism and Globalization: Exploring Culture, Context, and Religion* (Roman and Littlefield, 2003). She is a former wilderness guide and misses it desperately.

Kevin J. O'Brien is Assistant Professor of Christian Ethics at Pacific Lutheran University in Tacoma, WA. His research focuses on the intersections between natural science and Christian ethics and between social justice and environmental concern. He is the author of *An Ethics of Biodiversity: Christianity, Ecology, and the Variety of Life* (Georgetown, 2010). He is also a board member at Earth Ministry, a non-profit organization committed to engaging the Christian community in environmental stewardship.

Lisa Sideris is Associate Professor of Religious Studies at Indiana University. Her areas of research include environmental ethics and the science–religion interface, including evolution controversies. She is author of *Environmental Ethics, Ecological Theology, and Natural Selection* (Columbia, 2003) and co-editor (with Kathleen Dean Moore) of *Rachel Carson: Legacy and Challenge* (SUNY, 2008). Her current research interests include scientific and religious perspectives on wonder and enchantment, as well as nineteenth-century and contemporary nature study movements for children. In 2010 Sideris was a fellow at the Rachel Carson Center for Environmental Studies in Munich, Germany.

Mary Evelyn Tucker is a Senior Lecturer and Senior Scholar at Yale University, where she has appointments in the School of Forestry and Environmental Studies as well as the Divinity School and the Department of Religious Studies. She is a co-founder and co-director with John Grim of the Forum on Religion and Ecology. Together they organized a series of 10 conferences on "World Religions and Ecology" at the Center for the Study of World Religions at Harvard Divinity School. She is also Research Associate at the Reischauer Institute of Japanese Studies at Harvard. She is the author of *Worldly Wonder: Religions Enter Their Ecological Phase* (Open Court, 2003), *Moral and Spiritual Cultivation in Japanese Neo-Confucianism* (SUNY, 1989), and *The Philosophy of Qi* (Columbia University Press, 2007).

Mark I. Wallace, graduate of the University of Chicago, is Professor of Religion and member of the Interpretation Theory Committee and the Environmental Studies Committee at Swarthmore College, Pennsylvania. His teaching and research interests focus on the intersections between

Christian theology, critical theory, and environmental studies. His books include *Green Christianity: Five Ways to a Sustainable Future* (Fortress, 2010), *Finding God in the Singing River: Christianity, Spirit, Nature* (Fortress, 2005), and *Fragments of the Spirit: Nature, Violence, and the Renewal of Creation* (Continuum, 1996; Trinity, 2002). He is a member of the Constructive Theology Workgroup, active in the educational reform movement in the Philadelphia area, and received in 2004 an Andrew W. Mellon New Directions Fellowship for a research sabbatical in Costa Rica.

Joseph Witt is a Ph.D. candidate in the University of Florida's graduate program in Religion and Nature. His research focuses on the environmental and religious histories and contemporary issues of environmental justice in the southern United States. His current research examines the religious dimensions of activism against mountaintop removal coal mining in Appalachia, focusing especially upon the place of religious values in periods of cooperation and conflict between various stakeholders surrounding the issue. He is the recipient of a Kentucky Historical Society research grant and also currently works as Senior Assistant Editor for the *Journal for the Study of Religion, Nature and Culture*.

Acknowledgments

Preparing an introductory textbook for an interdisciplinary field of study is no easy task, and this is particularly true for the field of religion and ecology. While this academic pursuit only began to surface explicitly in the 1960s, its roots extend back millennia, into the origins and prehistory of human religion and human cultures and their interactions with the land and world around them. The task of this book is to draw upon parts of that history in order to help students think critically about the ways religious beliefs and practices intersect with the natural world and environmental issues.

A book like this would be absolutely impossible without over 40 years of work by scholars in religious studies, ethics, theology, philosophy, history, sociology, and anthropology who have developed the case that religions *matter* in and to the rest of the natural world. Thanks to these scholars, there is now an array of resources on world religions and ecology and a growing body of scholarly work on religious practices and belief systems that fall outside of the traditional list of "world religions": e.g. neo-pagan traditions, religious naturalism, and other earth-based spiritualities. As the bibliographies throughout this book demonstrate, we build on that work here, and could not have conceived or written this without the scholars who produced it.

However, this text fills a gap the editors observed in the existing literature: a book about religion and ecology that takes "religion," "ecology," and the ideas with which they most prominently intersect as its primary topic rather than studying particular religious traditions and comparing their approaches to environmental issues. This book, then, is not about a comparative understanding of how various world religions shape environmental attitudes and human self-understanding within the rest of the natural world. Instead, it is concerned with how to think about the world from within the field of "religion and ecology." We intend it to complement the work of the scholars who have come before us, and hope that they will find in it compliment and gratitude for their accomplishments.

We would also like to thank some specific people and organizations directly related to the publication of this book. First, *Grounding Religion* would not be possible without the authors of each chapter, dialogue, and case study. Their voices represent so well the richness, diversity, and insights that we were anxious to capture from the field of religion and ecology. We are deeply grateful for their willingness to work with us.

We are also grateful to the American Academy of Religion for a Collaborative Research Grant, which enabled the editors to host a colloquium at Florida International University (FIU) in Miami from February 26 to March 1, 2009 entitled, "Inherited Land: The Changing Grounds of Religion and Ecology." Though the contributors to this volume were not all present, the interactions at that conference led to the emergence of this book. Thanks are also due to all those who contributed papers for that colloquium: Eleanor Finnegan, Luke Johnston, Sam Snyder, Joseph Witt, Laura M. Hartman, Evan Berry, Greg Zuschlag, Brian Campbell, Forrest Clingerman, Tovis Paige, Sarah Fredericks, Gavin van Horn, Eilzabeth McAnally, Sam Mickey, David Wright, Greg Hitzhusen, and Willis Jenkins. Thanks also go to the Religious Studies Department and College of Arts and Sciences at Florida International University for hosting the colloquium and to the graduate students at FIU who helped make this meeting a success: Sandra Rios, Gudny Rosen, Andrea Eggebeen, and Liz Perez.

Three other scholarly habitats have enabled and encouraged us to develop our thinking around religion and ecology. First are all of our friends, mentors, and colleagues in the Religion and Ecology Group at the American Academy of Religion. Through paper sessions, conversations, and informal gatherings, this group has helped to foster future generations of scholars. Second, we thank the Forum on Religion and Ecology, especially Mary Evelyn Tucker and John Grim, for the meetings, publications, leadership, and mentorship that made space for an academic field of religion and ecology to emerge. Third, we would like to thank the International Society for the Study of Religion, Nature, and Culture (SSRNC), especially Bron Taylor. It was at the organizational meeting for the SSRNC in Cocoa Beach, Florida, that the three editors began to seriously discuss ideas that led to this book, and where we first met many of the authors who appear in these pages.

Finally, we thank our editorial contacts at Routledge, Lesley Riddle, Amy Grant and Andrew Watts. Their faith in this project and help in building a set of ideas into a collection of essays and then a text have been invaluable.

Introduction

Whitney A. Bauman, Richard R. Bohannon II,
and Kevin J. O'Brien

Religion matters. In our world today, this is difficult to deny. The majority of the world's people still identify themselves as belonging to or shaped by a religious belief system; questions about the public role of religious morality in democratic societies remain hugely controversial; and threats of terrorism and violent extremism motivated by religious belief are increasingly becoming a part of contemporary life.

It is also difficult to deny that the nonhuman natural world matters. Modernity is in part defined by the biological assertion that human beings are a species like all others, emerging from and dependent on natural systems. For the last 50 years, we have also become increasingly aware that these systems are influenced by our choices, and that the air, the soil, the water, and the climate can all be changed—and degraded—by human beings.

This book is about religion and the natural world, but more specifically it is about the ways they matter to one another, about how the religious world influences and is influenced by ecological systems. The chapters that follow are meant to inspire questions about the relationship between religion and ecology and to help you think critically about the role of each in shaping one another and the world. Each one investigates the intersections of religion and ecology, introduces ongoing debates within the academic field that studies these intersections, and raises some of the important questions yet to be answered within the field.

Connecting religion and ecology in a context of environmental degradation

We will begin by examining two assumptions that are shared throughout the book: (1) There is an important connection between religion and ecology, and (2) this connection is particularly important and in flux today because of the reality of environmental degradation.

The connection between religion and ecology is quite unfamiliar for many, partly because of a widespread assumption that those who are devoutly religious focus their attention exclusively on a narrow set of cultural rules, on a heaven beyond this reality, or on a nirvanistic salvation from the cycle of rebirth in nature. At its extreme, this understanding of religion leads some to believe that people of faith must be antagonistic to ecological science and the natural environment. In a more moderate sense, this understanding leads many to assume that religion is simply a different sphere that does not interact with science and public policy, and so is not connected to studies of the natural world or claims to environmental responsibility.

However, when one looks closely at any religious tradition, one finds considerations of and connections to the natural world. The Buddha's enlightenment took place outdoors, under a bodhi tree; the Muslim Qur'an and the Hebrew Bible both repeatedly stress the importance of land in shaping and defining a community; the most sacred site on earth for many Hindus is the River Ganges, and many indigenous religious traditions are similarly centered on particular features of their local ecosystems; the parables of Jesus in the Christian scriptures frequently draw on images from the natural world, with mustard seeds, trees, seas, and wildlife featuring prominently. These brief examples are just a small taste of the many ways in which recognized, mainstream religions have long been concerned with and related to the natural world.

There is also evidence of relationships between religion and ecology outside these faith traditions. Many people, both within and outside of traditional religious structures, experience a profound sense of something spiritual and holy in the natural world: Gardeners, campers, anglers, and surfers frequently describe their activities and passions in spiritual terms. The outdoors and the wilderness feel sacred to many people, whether they define this sacredness as a connection to a transcendent divine creative force or the immanent reality of ecological interdependence. While many might describe such experiences as "spiritual" rather than religious, we are less interested in this distinction than in the fact that this is further evidence of a relationship between the religious realm of human cultures and the nonhuman world that forms the context for all cultures.

This book thus assumes that religion and ecology are interrelated, and so that the scholarly study of religion must include attention to the ways religious and spiritual traditions relate their beliefs and practices to environmental issues and priorities. The authors of the following chapters understand religions, and the cultures of which they are a part, as emerging from and related to the natural world. Religions do not simply appear and exist on their own, *sui generis*, but evolve in conversation with other social and natural forces. Religions and other cultural systems, in turn, shape how human beings choose to think about, relate to, and treat the natural world. In sum, human cultures matter greatly to how the very concept of "nature" gets constructed, and the natural world itself matters in how the concept of "religion" is constructed.

The second basic assumption of this book concerns a set of social and natural forces which are particularly influential upon and potentially influenced by religion in the twenty-first century: environmental degradation.

The most widely publicized example of this degradation is climate change, which is considered by many to be the most urgent and negative impact of human industrial activity and agriculture on the world around us. The technology upon which our society depends and the ways we have decided to grow our food and transport ourselves emit tons of gases like carbon dioxide and methane, which then persist in the atmosphere. These gases trap heat energy, thereby changing the interconnected and wildly complex climate system: the temperature in the atmosphere affects the temperature in the oceans, which affects the currents, which affect the breeding of fish, which affects the health of bears, which affects the health of forests. Scientific experts who study climate systems and their ecological impacts assert without controversy that human industrial activity is changing the climate, and that the climate will inevitably change more severely and unpredictably in the near future.

Another example of environmental degradation is the destruction of biodiversity: As human beings in industrial cultures develop land and extract resources, we decimate ecosystems and habitats, leading to a rate of species extinction that is as much as 1,000 times faster than it would be without us. Biodiversity is threatened in rainforests as we use and burn trees, in prairies as we introduce invasive species that compete with natives, in rivers as we build dams and divert water, and in crop fields as we choose to grow only one species for cash and kill off all others as weeds.

The environment is also degraded by the pollution of air, water, and land as human beings create and distribute toxic chemicals and substances. While they may be less publicized than climate change and biodiversity loss, problems like acid rain and air pollution persist throughout the world, and the dumping of waste in rivers and oceans remains a dangerous and largely unmonitored problem. These trends also serve as a reminder that when the environment is degraded the people who depend upon it suffer: Fishers and those who eat fish are endangered by the mercury that enters the oceans from coal-fired power plants; urban populations suffer increased rates of asthma and other respiratory illnesses as they breathe more car and industrial exhaust; developing countries are increasingly treated as a dumping ground for the waste and wasteful industries of the developed world. Environmental degradation is a problem not only for distant environments and for exotic species, but for human beings and all of the earth.

This book assumes not only that environmental degradation is a real and complicated set of problems, but also that these problems form a vital context for discussing religion. If religion is to be relevant to our time, it needs to respond to the reality of environmental degradation. If faith traditions and spiritual practices are to fulfill their role as moral guides, they need to reflect on the ethical implications of these trends and to lead people of faith to more just and sustainable lives. Religion must respond to the reality of environmental degradation.

The academic field of religion and ecology

These two assumptions—that religious traditions are related to the natural world and that this contemporary relationship is particularly shaped by environmental degradation—are not unique to this book, but rather emerge from an academic field: religion and ecology.

This field has developed over the last 40 years as scholars of religious studies, ethics, philosophy, environmental history, and environmental sciences began to pay attention to the ways studies of the environment and of religion can be mutually informative. Within and alongside this academic field, scholars have developed new ethical models for relationships between human beings, other animals, and the rest of the natural environment, and have explored the implications of several philosophical and theological approaches for making sense of the natural world, many of which are discussed in this book.

Religion and ecology as an academic field is deeply interdisciplinary, incorporating the work of philosophers, ethicists, theologians, sociologists, historians, and many others. In addition, scholars in this field frequently draw upon the natural sciences, incorporating the findings of environmental and ecological scientists, as well as physicists, cosmologists, geneticists, and ethologists, all of whom offer important lessons about the interconnectedness of reality, the origins of human cultural systems, and the character of the world to which religion responds and relates.

Partly because it is always learning from developments in other disciplines, religion and ecology is a constantly evolving field of study. As scholars understand more about the natural world, study the history and range of religious ideas and practices, and expand our views of what counts as "religion" and "ecology," the academic study of these topics changes. Even more importantly, the field develops as the world itself changes: Environmental degradation is an ongoing process, and human understanding of it continues to develop, greatly influencing the academic study of religion and ecology.

Related processes are also changing religions in important ways, with globalization as the most prominent example. Connections between economies and cultures have made the world a much smaller place, as more and more of the world's human population moves to urban areas and can increasingly connect through faster transportation, the proliferation of cell phones and the internet, and markets that cross all boundaries. Religious traditions and human relationships to the natural world are changed by these developments, and so the field of religion and ecology must change alongside them.

Like all scholarly fields, religion and ecology has developed classic books and articles, a set of challenging questions which scholars debate and discuss, and a range of acceptable methods of analysis used to consider those questions. Most of the classic texts in the field are referenced throughout this book and included in the bibliographies. Even these bibliographies cannot be considered comprehensive, however, because the list of classics continually expands as the field incorporates and responds to new questions, questions that add new perspectives, challenge earlier assumptions, and open up new lines of thought. Those questions are the primary subject of this book, and will be considered throughout.

One question in the background of all the others is what to name this academic field. The editors of this book have chosen "religion and ecology," but this is not an easy or clear choice, partly because the words "religion" and "ecology" themselves are so complicated and controversial. Thinking about distinct religious traditions has become increasingly difficult in a world where evangelical Christians read their daily horoscope, strands of Judaism have been influenced by Buddhism, and indigenous traditions mix with Islam and Christianity in the global South. Thinking about a static "environment" has also become impossible as scientists have chronicled both the inevitability of evolutionary change and the incredibly rapid changes caused by contemporary human societies. We must therefore understand both the world of religion and the world of nature as evolving, hybrid realities, which will be discussed in detail in Chapters 1 and 4.

Many of our colleagues refer to this field as "religion and nature." These scholars assert—with many good reasons—that religion and nature is a broader category than religion and ecology and allows for more two-way reflection (from sciences/nature to religion and from religion to nature). They also argue that religion and ecology has focused too exclusively on a static list of world religions. "Religion and nature" signals, for some, a more inclusive perspective that studies these traditions but also attends to less-recognized religious movements such as neo-paganism or spiritual environmentalism and minority viewpoints within all traditions.

However, we editors nevertheless chose "religion and ecology" for three reasons. First, as discussed in Chapter 8, this name has the longest-standing history and institutional structure: The group that studies these issues within the American Academy of Religion, the premier organization for scholars of religion in North America, calls itself "Religion and Ecology," with the support of the highly influential Forum on Religion and Ecology. The second reason is more philosophical: While we appreciate the breadth of the term "nature," we value the specificity of "ecology" even more. Ecology calls particular attention to systems of interconnection, to the energy and material exchange between organisms, and to the relationships between the living and non-living worlds (minerals, rocks, and other organisms; or atmosphere, oceans, and land, for example).

Third and finally, we worry that too many people in the western world have unhelpful and misleading understandings of "nature." On one hand, nature is frequently contrasted with culture, which problematically suggests that human beings are somehow separate from the rest of the world. At the same time, "nature" is often thought of as a pristine and perfect reality looked upon with an unhealthy nostalgia. Thus, we hope that naming our field "religion and ecology" will emphasize the interconnections between human cultures and the rest of the world, and the ever-changing nature of both. Nevertheless, many of the authors we cite in this book refer to the field as "religion and nature," and we learn from them about the importance of broadening our attention and bringing as many voices into this scholarly pursuit as possible.

The methodologies of religion and ecology

In order to delve into the chapters that follow and the ways they raise and wrestle with difficult questions, it is important to understand how scholars in this field work with ideas and discuss their findings. It is important, in other words, to analyze the academic methodologies of religion and ecology, which we define here primarily as synthetic and activist.

Perhaps the core methodological commitment of religion and ecology is a synthesis of scholarly attention to religious worldviews and to lived religions. In other words, this field studies both the broad intellectual traditions of religions (the attitudes and views of religious leaders, sacred texts, and traditions) and the everyday reality of religion on the ground (the practices and actions of religious people in their day-to-day lives). Religion and ecology attends both to the intellectual frameworks for human life provided by religious beliefs and to the ways religious adherents express these ideas.

Some scholars of religion understand "worldviews" and "lived religions" as oppositional, and many suggest that we must choose between them, deciding whether we want to pay primary attention to ideas or practices. There is ancient precedent for such a choice in debates between Platonic ideals and Aristotelian natural philosophy, and more recent roots in the tension between Hegelian idealism and Marxist materialism. This division separates the world of ideas from the material world, and demands that scholars make a choice about which world they prefer.

Religion and ecology is a field that refuses to make this choice, a field based on a commitment to understand theory and practice, ideas and actions, worldviews and lived religion together, as complementary and mutually informative.

Worldviews are deeply important, and one cannot study religion without paying attention to them. Religious people have spent thousands of years developing intricate cosmologies, involved stories about how things came to be and why, and hugely controversial belief systems about the future of humanity in relation to the world around us and the gods and/or God structuring it. Worldviews also have vital environmental implications: How we understand the relationship between human beings and the rest of the world will shape our decisions about how to treat other beings and one another. Whether we see the human species as a product of an evolutionary process or as a unique and distinct creation has implications for how responsible and related we will feel to the rest of the world.

However, the lived experience of religious people cannot always be explained by the broad worldviews of their tradition. The daily life of a devout Buddhist in contemporary China cannot be reduced to the Four Noble Truths and the sermons of the Buddha, but rather needs to be studied and appreciated on its own terms, in its own context. The attitudes of evangelical Christians toward environmental issues should not be derived solely by reading the Bible and their leaders' sermons, but should be discerned through talking to them one on one and paying attention to their behavior. Furthermore, a study of the environmental impacts of religious belief cannot focus only on attitudes and beliefs, but must also focus on practices and behaviors, on what people do in addition to what they say.

To study only worldviews would allow religious leaders and powerful spokespeople to exclusively define religion, ignoring the perspectives and practices of the marginalized within and outside traditional religions. At the same time, to study only lived religion, the "on the ground" practices and ideas of individual believers, would make it impossible to connect people within and across faiths. Some generalizations about worldviews are necessary in order to bring together the ways various people make sense of reality, in order to observe meaningful trends and distinctions in the stories people tell about the place of human beings within the world. Observations of lived religions need the connections made possible by worldviews, and worldviews need the attention to details and difference provided by a lived religions approach. Thus, the methodology of religion and ecology is synthetic: Scholars establish and build connections between thought and action, between ideas and practices.

A related aspect of religion and ecology's methodology is a commitment that activists need scholars and scholars need activists. This may surprise some people, particularly those who distinguish the "academic" world of ideas from the "real" world of practical concerns outside it. Just as there is a reason to distinguish worldviews and lived religion, there is some validity to this separation of scholarship from practicality. The academic world is designed to develop intellectual skills, to provide space and time for students to nurture the habits of lifelong, self-critical thinkers. In this sense, it is important that academia be somewhat distinct from other parts of the world.

However, this separation should not and cannot be absolute. The academic world is not just abstract and separate; it is also a key place for generating worldview-changing ideas. It is a community that asks you to question every assumption and provides the tools of analysis needed for creative solutions to ecological and social problems. Furthermore, the academic world itself is a space of lived experiences: Students and their teachers develop very specific habits of action and habitats for thinking, which can be instruments for social and environmental change in positive or negative directions, both on and off campus. In other words, the academic world is part of the real world, and so it has the chance to make a practical difference. This is particularly true if academics can train and inspire others to think critically about their actions and beliefs.

Scholars in the field of religion and ecology seek to make a practical difference in the world. This field exists not just to develop theories and ideas, but also to contribute to the activist cause of building a more sustainable world. Scholars of religion and ecology help people to think critically about how religion has been shaped by the natural world and can be shaped by environmental degradation, and to imaginatively consider how religion and/ or the study of religion might positively impact the future of our species and our planet. This book, as a product of that field, is no exception: You are invited here to enter into a methodology that studies religious worldviews and environmental practices in the hope that it might help you to clarify and perhaps change the ways you shape your world.

Format of the book

There are many excellent texts that discuss the field of religion and ecology. Some take comparative approaches by analyzing the contributions of world religions, some develop constructive environmental proposals from a single religious tradition, and some focus on a particular environmental issue. This book is an attempt to complement that literature by offering a single volume that takes "religion and ecology" itself as the central topic and works through a series of intersecting issues in order to nurture critical thinking about the intersection between religious and spiritual life, on the one hand, and nature and environmental degradation, on the other. This book is a "field guide" to religion and ecology because it is designed to help you more actively recognize and participate in this academic project.

Parts I and II, "Religion" and "Ecology," feature an introductory overview of what these terms might mean, followed by dialogues between two established scholars in the field who address these questions from their own perspectives in a more conversational and personal style. Each part then concludes with a case study, offering the chance to apply relevant ideas and tools to a specific situation. Part III begins with a reflective, historical, and institutional account of the field from two of its founders, and continues with seven chapters focused on some of the central issues relevant to religion and ecology: sustainability, animals, gender, economics, justice, globalization, and place. Each of the seven topical chapters also concludes with a case study, again offering a chance to apply the ideas therein. This part ends with an afterword about the interplay of scholarship and activism. Finally, the book concludes with a glossary, which you can consult as you work through the key terms in each chapter.

No field guide can possibly include everything you will encounter out in the world, and so this book cannot hope to cover every relevant issue, idea, or term in religion and ecology. Instead, the editors and authors have aimed to offer an introduction for students and a pedagogical tool for teachers, and we expect those who use it to continue thinking and applying the ideas here to other issues, to other terms. Above all, we hope that readers will continue the questioning and thinking essential for an academic study of religion and ecology.

Part I

Religion

Chapter 1

Religion

What is it, who gets to decide, and why does it matter?

Whitney A. Bauman, Richard R. Bohannon II, and Kevin J. O'Brien

Max Weber, an early and influential sociologist, started his major treatise on *The Sociology of Religion* (1978) by noting that the term "religion" cannot be defined at the beginning of a study, but only after one's research is complete. He then proceeded to write the equivalent of over five books on the subject, but never achieved enough clarity or completion to reach a definition.

"Religion," it turns out, is a tricky word.

This chapter does not attempt to do what Weber neglected, and will not offer a single, authoritative definition. Instead, it will explore the range of ways in which this tricky word is used by a variety of scholars in order to prepare the way for critical thinking about religion and ecology. We will explore a series of different ways religion is defined, studied, and critiqued, paying particular attention to the debates and tensions inherent in these choices. The overarching question is: Who gets to decide what religion is and who gets left out of each approach to religion?

While the focus here is on the ways scholars think about the word "religion," our most important argument is that careful thought about this term and the reality it represents does not just matter in classrooms and books, but is very important to many people's lives. Religion has shaped human cultures, and through them has shaped the entire planet on which we live. Religion is deeply and personally important to billions of people on the planet, and religious institutions play instrumental roles in most people's lives in the world today. Religion literally changes the bodies and minds of human beings; through those people and the institutions of which they are a part, religion changes the face of the entire planet. What religion is and how it functions in the lives of human beings and in cultural institutions matters deeply.

While religion matters, it is important to be careful not to assume too much about it. The term itself has its origins in Latin, and so emerges from western history and carries western baggage. In other words, when we talk about religion we are having a discussion with parameters set in a particular (largely European) cultural context, and we cannot assume that all the assumptions made in such a discussion will apply to all cultures. For example, reference to traditions like Japanese Shinto and Indian Hinduism as religions is the result of a western classification system that is now, through physical and economic colonization, globalized. Shinto and Hinduism can helpfully be understood as religions, but we cannot assume that they will fulfill all the expectations Westerners bring to that term. Many Hindus do not think of themselves as Hindu (itself a Western term), but instead primarily affiliate with their geographic region of origin and its ritual traditions. Many practitioners of Shinto are also active Buddhists, and feel no requirement to choose between these two religions.

In light of these complexities and in hopes of developing a view of religion that is not applicable only in the West, the prominent contemporary scholar of religion Jonathan Z. Smith critiques lists of "major world religions," arguing that "It is impossible to escape the suspicion that a world religion is simply a religion like ours ... that has achieved sufficient power and numbers to enter our history to form it, interact with it, or thwart it" (2004: 191–92). So, in this chapter and in this book, when we write about "religion," we are not only referring to world religions, but rather to a broad range of meaning-making practices, institutions, rituals, belief systems, sacred texts, moral norms, taboos, and even philosophical reflection upon religion as a whole. As will be clear the more you reflect on the definitions below, one can find religion in many phenomena and institutions that are rarely recognized as religions, one can find religious dimensions in many structures and systems which may not themselves be religions, and one can find practitioners of religions who are not particularly religious in their approach to their tradition.

Five definitions of religion

Not all scholars of religion have been as reluctant as Max Weber to present a definition, but a quick review of their offerings shows that, as a group, they have reached no more clarity than he did. What follows is a discussion of five distinct definitions—just a sample of the many available—which emphasizes the different choices scholars have made in their approaches to the term. As a group, these definitions clearly demonstrate the complexity of what it is we talk about when we talk about religion, and attention to the differences between them reveals many of the questions and considerations that students of religion must take seriously.

1   Religion is the state of being grasped by an ultimate concern.

—Paul Tillich

Paul Tillich (1886–1965) was a Christian theologian who understood religion primarily in terms of that to which believers devote themselves: Religion is about one's "ultimate concern," whatever one is willing to give one's life for, the most important thing in reality, that against which all else is measured (1988 [orig. pub. 1958]: 42). Influenced by his own Lutheran Christian tradition, Tillich believed that there is a truly Ultimate reality, an Ultimate concern that is most worthy of such devotion, based on the idea of God revealed and incarnate in Jesus Christ. However, his definition sought to be more general than this by acknowledging that non-Christians also experience and are shaped by the mystery of the Ultimate. Tillich assumed that all people have a real experience of something beyond themselves, and that this experience is what characterizes religion.

Considered a "theologian of culture," Tillich found insight in the society around him, learning from secular philosophers, artists, and thinkers, as well as from religious people. He therefore sought a single characteristic of religious life common to all; he wanted to articulate a definition of religion that was not dependent upon any specific tradition. To achieve this goal, Tillich placed his emphasis upon the more philosophical and theological aspects of religion. So, his definition focuses on what people believe most deeply, assuming that everyone is religious because everyone has an ultimate faith in something.

Tillich's definition is an important insight and contribution to the study of religion, but of course it is not a comprehensive account of all religious experience. In his definition, cultural particularities, sacred texts, rituals, and day-to-day choices and practices take a back seat to the singular experience of ultimate reality. Tillich's definition helps to reveal common ground between Muslims and Christians, who might both name a supreme and singular deity as their ultimate concern. However, this definition does not shed light on the many vital differences between these religious traditions and the different cultures and contexts in which they are expressed.

This limitation of Tillich's definition demonstrates the perennial tension between the universal and the particular. To which should we pay primary attention: the universal, ultimate, beyond, and eternal; or the particular, everyday life in the material world? Tillich's definition clearly emphasizes the universal, but the third and fourth definitions on pp. 17 and 18 will demonstrate more of a focus on the particularities of religion, on the details and expressions of religious traditions in particular contexts.

The distinction between universality and particularity is deeply important in discussions of religion and ecology because it raises a basic question for the scholar: How should one both recognize common ground as well as articulate differences in the ways religious people and institutions respond to environmental degradation? Is it the job of religion and ecology scholars to demonstrate that the major religions universally call for environmental responsibility—that the "ultimate concerns" of most of the world's religious leaders are compatible with environmental ethics? Or is it the job of religion and ecology scholars to parse the distinctions and differences in the ways those calls for environmental responsibility are articulated and justified, to observe and categorize the particularities of religions?

2 Religion is the inmost voice of the human heart that under the yoke of a seemingly finite existence groans and travails in pain.

—D.T. Suzuki

D.T. Suzuki (1870–1966), a Japanese Zen Buddhist, defines religion as the universally human response of "groans and travails" in the face of the world's suffering (1963: 24). Like Tillich, Suzuki articulates a definition not explicitly tied to any particular tradition, developing a view of religion that crosses cultural and denominational boundaries. Also like Tillich, however, one can clearly detect the influence of the author's religious background: In Suzuki's case, the core Buddhist teaching of *dukkha*, the reality of suffering, is evident. Religion, for Suzuki, is a response to the troubling reality that all things suffer and all things die.

Unlike Tillich, Suzuki never appeals to anything beyond human beings themselves; he sees religion as something created by "the human heart," something internal. In this definition, there is no "Ultimate" that gives human life purpose or meaning. What is most real and most important for Suzuki is the very natural and common experience of *suffering*, not the supernatural and distant reality of God or the Holy.

The difference between this approach and that of Tillich raises the important distinction between transcendence and immanence, between religious approaches that find meaning and value beyond the world and those that find meaning and value within it. For Suzuki, whose approach is purely immanent, religion is a direct response to the reality of this world. For Tillich, in contrast, there is something Ultimate beyond the world, something transcendent that deserves human faith.

In general, the more a religion focuses on transcendence, the more it will tend to stress that this world is valuable for the sake of something else, a reality beyond it. The more a religion's focus is on immanence, the more it will tend to stress the value of this world and the lives we are given for their own sake. Obviously, this has great implications for thinking about religion and ecology, because transcendent and immanent belief systems might result in different ways of acting toward the natural world.

IA

Is an approach like Suzuki's—which views religion as a response to earthly, material realities—the best way to respond to the environmental crisis earth is undergoing? Or is the moral power of an external authority, a distinct and divine Ultimate, a better motivator for reform and transformation?

3 A religion is a unified system of beliefs and practices relative to sacred things, that is to say, things set apart and forbidden—beliefs and practices which unite into one single community all those who adhere to them.

—Emile Durkheim

This definition from French sociologist Emile Durkhiem (1858–1917) emphasizes two aspects of religion: (1) It separates some aspects of life from others, marking off "the sacred" from the rest of "profane" reality, and (2) it serves the social function of uniting a community (1995 [orig. pub. 1912]: 46). In the first part of his definition, Durkheim sounds a bit like Tillich, noting that religion is about a special kind of devotion. However, while Tillich thought of "the Ultimate" as something real and outside of human control, Durkheim understands "the sacred" as something human beings create: We make sense of the world by splitting the sacred from "the profane," and create religious traditions to unite a community around those things that are sacred.

The second part of Durkheim's definition explains *why* human beings create religion: to nurture unity, to bring people together. He often referred to such united communities as "churches," and even wrote, "in history we do not find religion without Church" (Durkheim 1995: 41). This is commonly and justifiably cited as too provincial a definition of religion, skewing the category toward things that look like Christianity (even though Durkheim himself was raised in a Jewish family). Despite the fact that he wrote his most influential work on religion about aboriginal religion in Australia, for instance, Durkheim's study drew not on his own observations, but rather on the notes of another researcher, and his definition looks to many critics like a veiled description of French Christianity. The Australian aborigines he studied would almost certainly never have described their spiritual community as a "church," nor did they have any form of congregational organization like that found in modern Christian communities.

Despite the limits of Durkheim's perspective, however, the particular time and place from which he wrote led him to notice something important about religion. Europe was in great social upheaval during Durkheim's life, and he had a genuine concern about the disintegration of his society. Religion's role in uniting people was, for Durkheim, a vitally important source of order and community, a way to preserve society. He understood religion as a way to establish and maintain cohesion, and so presents religion as a force to nurture stable societies.

Durkheim's approach to defining religion is fundamentally different from Tillich's and Suzuki's in an important way. He does not address the substance of religion—the supernatural (Ultimate) or natural (groans and travails) reality to which it responds. Instead, he asks how religions function to keep societies cohesive. Durkheim took a social scientific approach to understanding religion, seeking to observe and explain it rather than to find truth within it. This distinction raises still more important questions for the study of religion and ecology. Scholars in this field who focus on the substance of religion tend to talk about the incredible potential of religion in response to environmental degradation, identifying underappreciated texts and traditions and calling people to recognize their value and embrace their potential in our time. Other scholars, however, study the actions and beliefs of existing religious practices, observing religion as it currently is rather than arguing for what it should be.

4   A religion is (1) a system of symbols which acts to (2) establish powerful, pervasive, and long-lasting moods and motivations in men [and women] by (3) formulating conceptions of a general order of existence and (4) clothing these conceptions with such an aura of factuality that (5) the moods and motivations seem uniquely realistic.

—Clifford Geertz

Here we have a definition of religion that draws from sociology, anthropology, and a field known as semiotics (Geertz 1973: 90). For Clifford Geertz (1926–2006), symbols are of primary importance: Formulated over long periods of time, passed down from generation to generation, re-constructed and revitalized by each passing generation, symbols live and evolve. They represent the continuing presence of a community's collective history. Thus, Geertz defines religion first and foremost as a system of symbols.

Like Durkheim's, Geertz's definition focuses on the place of religion in a social context, and so he further explains that religious symbols formulate "conceptions of a general order of existence" that justify and explain a set of "moods and motivations." In other words, religion establishes a consistency between a community's worldview and ethos, between its understanding of how reality works and of what human beings are expected to do within that reality. Religion is a means of establishing consistency between beliefs and practices, of maintaining a set of cultural ideas and morals in the face of a changing world. This definition argues that symbols are constructed by communities of people, which then guide how people in those communities act in everyday life and thereby become habitual or "natural."

These views of religion as something that evolves to *sustain* cultures raises an important question about how religions can *change*. The history of religions in the world shows impressive periods of consistency as a tradition endures (such as the Catholic Church in medieval Europe or Chan Buddism in China), but also great periods of schism and change (the Reformation and Counter-Reformation, or the splitting of Buddhism into many schools, for example). A Geertzian view of religion raises the question of how this happens: How does a system of symbols change, and, when it does, what happens to the community and to the community's worldview and ethos? Another way of asking this question makes the power dynamics inherent in it explicit: Who gets to decide which symbols become central in a culture, how a worldview and ethos are articulated? What happens if a system of symbols is used by those in power to marginalize or disempower others? How can such a religion be changed? A constructive approach must wrestle with this question of how a religion can and should change.

This is, of course, a central task in religion and ecology. Scholars in this field must continually ask: Are existing religious traditions flexible enough to deal with contemporary environmental and social crises, or do we need new symbolic systems, new religious perspectives to deal with these crises? If something new is necessary, who has the authority and the power to develop it? How will religious symbols change and evolve in an era of environmental degradation?

5 Religion is the sigh of the oppressed creature, the heart of a heartless world, just as it is the spirit of a spiritless situation. It is the opium of the people. The abolition of religion as the illusory happiness of the people is required for their real happiness.

—Karl Marx

For Karl Marx (1818–83) and his co-author Friedrich Engels (1820–95), religion is an ideology, which for them specifically means that it is a mindset born out of oppressive social relations (1964 [orig. pub. 1844]: 42). Religion soothes and comforts the poor masses, but in doing so legitimates the economic imbalances that keep them poor. This is part of Marx's "materialist" perspective on society—that is, he understands religion and other social structures as arising out of material conditions (how we work, where we live, how we get our food). This perspective leaves little room for viewing religion as a catalyst for change. Unlike Tillich and Suzuki, Marx did not seek to appreciatively clarify the content of religion. While he was like Durkheim and Geertz insofar as he was concerned about the role religion plays within a society, among our five definitions Marx's is unique in viewing religion as a negative phenomenon tied to economic oppression.

Marx's critique of religion and the critique of economic and political structures overarching it have inspired liberationists, feminists, racial minorities, people with disabilities, GLBTQ (gay, lesbian, bisexual, transgender, and queer) advocates, and many others who organize for radical social change. A key idea that these movements all share with Marx is a condemnation of hierarchical structures, a critique of the way contemporary society values the rich over the poor, men over women, whites over people of color, etc. The assumption in Marx's definition is that religion is part of this oppressive hierarchical system; he never considered that religion could be a force opposing oppression (though Engels was able to see this possibility). Religion, as Marx understood it, creates the illusion of heart and spirit in a heartless and spiritless society; it gives people hope for an immaterial salvation and so prevents them from seeking real, material change. This critique has become common since Marx's articulation, with many advocates of progress arguing that religion is inherently backwards, an obstacle to positive change.

Interestingly, despite the fact that Marx writes about "the abolition of religion," he opposed some of his radical peers who sought to make religion illegal in a socialist society. Instead, he believed religion would simply fade into irrelevancy over time. If religion is "the sigh of the oppressed creature," it will become unnecessary when oppression ends. This prediction of a secular, communist future has not occurred in the timescale Marx seemed to expect, but his critique of religion nevertheless remains vitally important, and raises vital questions for religion and ecology. Is it possible for religion to be a force for positive social change, or is religion inevitably only concerned with spiritual, immaterial matters and completely a product of oppressive and destructive systems? Will a study of religion focused on its relationship to ecological issues demonstrate the validity of Marx's critique, or will it serve as a counterexample?

IB

The definitions of Tillich, Suzuki, Durkheim, Geertz, and Marx shed light not only on the complexity of religion, but also on the important questions a critical perspective on the term raises for the project of this book: How should religion and ecology balance universality and particularity? Transcendence and immanence? Substantive and descriptive views? How does religious change happen, and how should it happen? Can religions be a force for positive social change, or are they inherently problematic?

Why defining religion matters

It may be tempting to argue that if five intelligent and insightful thinkers could have such divergent definitions of religion the term has become meaningless—it can apparently be defined any way one wants. However, Jonathan Z. Smith draws a hopeful conclusion from this reality: What we learn from the diversity of definitions is that religion *can* be defined (Smith 2004). The job of the student or researcher is to choose which definition will be most fruitful for his or her particular project, with an awareness of how much is at stake in this choice.

Definitions of religion matter to scholars of religion because they work as filters through which we see things: If you believe that all religions are about an ultimate concern, as did Tillich, or that they demarcate the sacred, as did Durkheim, then you will start asking religious people what they consider sacred or most worthy of concern, and you will likely assume that this is central to their religious experience. If, on the other hand, you assume that religion is a response to suffering—as do both Marx and Suzuki, in different ways—then you will look at any spiritual system to see how it addresses, mitigates, or disguises the key sources of suffering in human life. Different definitions highlight different aspects of religion.

Perhaps the primary example of this is the question raised by Marx's definition: Is religion most likely to be a problematic or a promising force in developing a response to environmental degradation? If we adopt Marx's perspective and view religion as a coping mechanism that inevitably solidifies the status quo, we will be skeptical about the capacity of religious groups to respond constructively to environmental crises. According to Marx's definition, religion is fundamentally opposed to any real social change, and so people concerned with environmental degradation would seek to understand and study religion only as part of the problem to be solved.

If, on the other hand, we follow thinkers like Tillich and Suzuki in seeing religion as a universal and healthy human response to reality, then it is much easier to imagine faith communities and commitments playing a constructive role in addressing environmental challenges. Tillich believed that life only has meaning when it is centered on an "ultimate concern," that this is a fundamental and inevitable part of being human. So, from a Tillichian perspective it would be counterproductive to try to address the problem of environmental degradation without engaging it religiously. Suzuki offers an even clearer case, and would see the perils of climate change, biodiversity loss, and pollution as clear examples of the "groans and travails" that characterize human life. According to Suzuki's definition, any authentically human response to those challenges is itself a kind of religion, and so it is impossible to imagine an environmentalism that it is not in some sense religious. From these perspectives, there is a clear, even necessary, role that religion must play in responding to environmental degradation.

Many activists and scholars have nevertheless found a use for Marx. His central concern is about social conflict—specifically, the conflict between the haves and the have-nots in a society built upon economic injustice and the transformation of that society to one in which all people are free to realize their fullest potential. Thus Marx's theory helps point toward social change, while theories such as those of Durkheim and Geertz are often seen to point toward social stasis.

Some scholars apply this Marxist understanding of social conflict to environmental issues—noting that our current social structures value humans over the rest of the natural world in the same way as the rich are valued over the poor—but do not follow Marx in dismissing religion as a force for change. Such prophetic, socially engaged approaches present religion as more than simply an opiate; they see religion as "the heart of a heartless world" in a way that nurtures action rather than complacency. In this view, religion can speak for the poorest of the earth, and in some cases the earth itself, and can call for radical change. These perspectives understand the role of religion as that which trips up ideologies, which challenges systems of injustice, and which deconstructs the ways in which humans dominate the rest of the natural world.

Another question posed by these definitions concerns what counts as a religion. If we assume with Durkheim that religion is a unifying social force that demarcates the "sacred" from the profane, then we will start looking for organized groups of people who clearly distinguish one category of things as special and holy and separate from the rest of the world. When seeking out religious responses to environmental degradation, we will likely look to organized structures like the Roman Catholic Church, the Religious Society of Friends, the Rabbinical Assembly, or the World Union for Progressive Judaism. These are important groups, and it is valuable to research how each of these institutions has developed a response to environmental degradation in light of what their leaders consider most sacred. However, not all religious activities are reflected in such organizational structures. The diversity of Native American spiritualities, Hindu communities, and Christian house churches, for instance, is not well represented in institutional structures, and yet each demonstrates interesting and important religious responses to environmental degradation.

Clifford Geertz's more inclusive definition of religion offers a helpful corrective, freeing us to see as religious *any* social system that creates and combines a view of the world with a call to action. It is easy to see how many communities—some formally organized and others not—could be recognized as "religious" from this perspective, and so the field of religion and ecology becomes much broader. Indeed, a Geertzian definition can be used to characterize the environmental movement itself as religious: By developing a factual set of stories about the destruction of the natural world, environmentalism creates strong moods and motivations toward conservation and social change (e.g. Gottlieb 2006: 147ff). The potential downside of the Geertzian approach, of course, is that when religion is defined so broadly it is possible to see *anything* as religious, which might pose the challenge of expanding religion and ecology beyond a manageable scope.

IC

Is environmentalism religious? According to which definitions might this claim make sense, and which definitions preclude it? What difference might it make to the goals and cause of environmentalism to see this movement as religious?

Studying religion inside and out

Scholars argue not just about what religion is, but also about how to study it. The most common question is whether we should think and teach about religion primarily from within or outside of religious communities. At its most basic, the question might be phrased this way: Do you place more trust in a scholar of religion working from a personal faith, or one working from a scholarly approach that is not overtly influenced by particular faith commitments?

A comparison to other disciplines might help to clarify—if not answer—this question: Would you trust a professor of criminology more or less if you knew she had herself worked as a police officer, or committed a crime, or served time in jail? Would you value the insights of a professor of elementary education more or less if you knew he had studied educational theory for years but had never himself taught elementary-age students? Would you rather learn from an economics professor who had spent years in the financial industry, or one who had spent that time in the academy developing tools with which to analyze that industry? The basic question is: Does more insight come from being inside or outside the object of our study?

In the simplest terms, scholars who work from inside a religious tradition, assuming its importance and working to carry on the traditions of a faith, practice "theology." Scholars who view religion from the outside, applying objective or comparative tools to religious traditions without assuming that they contain special insight, practice "religious studies." Religious studies is about understanding the relationship between religion and society and making sense of the ways religious people organize themselves. By contrast, theologians frequently prioritize the traditions, practices, and texts of a community; they understand religion from within the experience of a particular faith.

Some theologians claim that religion cannot be understood unless one is personally invested and participating in it, and note that it insults and marginalizes believers and practitioners to believe that religion can be understood and categorized *without* the insights that come from commitment to a faith community. Some scholars of religious studies, on the other hand, claim that the critical distance of an outsider is vital, arguing that theology gives too much authority and power to a single tradition, privileging the view of religion adopted by one community rather than appreciating religion as a diverse global reality. These two approaches reflect important, and sometimes heated, disagreements about where and how it is *legitimate* to study religion.

In the United States, public universities and secular private colleges tend to teach religious studies, assuming no validity for any particular tradition and approaching religion as a social phenomenon. Religiously affiliated private colleges and universities, on the other hand, tend to teach theology,

---

ID

Is scholarship on religion more reliable if it emerges from religious people, or if it emerges from an academic study of such people that does not assume the validity of their beliefs and claims?

---

working from within a particular faith community, assuming that there is wisdom in the texts and traditions of that community. Some evangelical Christian colleges, interestingly, teach "Bible" courses rather than theology because of a core assumption everything of crucial importance can be learned directly from the Christian Bible. In the terms we have introduced, however, this emphasis on scripture is clearly "theological" in that it studies religion based on the internal standards and categories of a tradition which asserts that its scriptures are divinely inspired.

Having drawn the distinction between religious studies and theology, it is important to note that theologians can do religious studies and scholars of religious studies can do theology. Moreover, some theologians work *outside* of specific religious traditions and/or use sources from a variety of traditions, while some religious studies scholars work *within* traditions (e.g. sociologists who study the growth and development of a particular church of which they also are members). There is a great deal of crossover between these two areas of study and a lot of confusion about "who's who" within the study of religion.

As will become increasingly clear throughout this book, the distinction between "theology" and "religious studies" is too simple: Many scholars cross between these categories, and many approaches to religion do not fit well into either. For example, Divinity Schools, such as are found at Yale, Harvard, and Vanderbilt, train ministers and priests while also offering degrees and courses in religious studies. Furthermore, referring to insider perspectives on religion as "theological" shows a bias toward monotheistic, western religions, because theology is traditionally understood as thought about God. It is, however, possible to work from inside a religion without an emphasis on God or gods. Many Buddhists, for example, believe that the question of divinity is irrelevant or secondary to their religious faith. Thus, a Buddhist scholar might be reluctant to label herself "theological" even though she studies her tradition from the inside. Clearly, the distinction between religious studies and theology is not perfect.

However limited it may be, though, this distinction illustrates a real difference in how religion is taught and thought about by many scholars and students today, a difference that has important implications within the field of religion and ecology. Many scholars in this field have worked in a "theological" context, seeking to understand and represent a particular tradition in order to identify and encourage its environmental aspects. For example, the Islamic anthropologist and philosopher Nawal Ammar works from within her tradition to offer "a Muslim response to the ecological crisis," deriving a set of principles from the Qur'an and Islamic history to call for a more careful and more just distribution and use of earth's resources. Ammar highlights the Arabic virtue of *hay'a*, a "respect and reverence" that "reflects balance, honorable manners, and protection of God's glory including his creatures and other creation" (2004: 287). Her discussion of an environmental ethics based on *hay'a* is an articulation of religious duty to the environment from *within* a religious tradition, clearly a theological argument.

Other religion and ecology scholars specialize in religious studies, identifying and observing trends in religious communities rather than advocating particular approaches from within. For instance, Richard Foltz is a prominent scholar in the field who has, like Nawal Ammar, paid careful attention to how Muslims respond to environmental degradation. Foltz edited the volumes *Islam and Ecology* (2003) and *Environmentalism in the Muslim World* (2005), and so helped to define the place of Islam in the field of religion and ecology. However, Foltz's authority for doing this work does not come from his own religious affiliation, but instead from his scholarship as an historian of comparative religion. He studies Islam from the outside, and has also published analyses of Zoroastrianism, Judaism, and Mormonism. This is the work of religious studies, which allows for more easy comparison between traditions and makes it possible to attend to the wide range of ways to be religious in our world rather than speaking exclusively from one single tradition.

The field of religion and ecology is better because it includes both of these scholars, and because it includes a wide range of outsiders and insiders studying a wide range of religious traditions. However, no guide to this field can ignore that each scholar is making important choices about how much they will identify with and work within the traditions they study and how much they will value a critical distance that allows for more objectivity and comparison.

Conclusion

Debates about how to study religion matter because it is vital that we understand religion as well as possible. Religion has been important, though also at times stifling, to the transmission of information from generation to generation. In addition, religion and the results of studying religion have been important shapers of economics, law, art, and almost every other facet of human life. To pretend that religion doesn't matter in and to the world would be to ignore a huge part of human histories and experiences.

As this chapter has made clear, religion can mean many different things. Nevertheless, however we understand and frame it, the religious world is a major force in shaping how we interact with our environment, and it is continually being reshaped by new encounters with the nonhuman world. Amidst all the disagreements, this idea unites all the definitions discussed here, it unites scholars of religion and ecology, and it unites the contributors to this book: However we define and debate it, religion matters.

References

Ammar, N. (2004) "An Islamic Response to the Manifest Ecological Crisis: Issues of Justice," in R. Gottlieb (ed.) *This Sacred Earth*, New York: Routledge.

Durkheim, E. (1995) *The Elementary Forms of Religious Life*, trans. K.E. Fields, New York: Free Press.

Foltz, R.C. (ed.) (2003) *Islam and Ecology: A Bestowed Trust*, Cambridge, MA: Harvard University Press.

——(ed.) (2005) *Environmentalism in the Muslim World*, New York: Nova Science Publishers.

Geertz, C. (1973) *The Interpretation of Cultures*, New York: Basic Books.

Gottlieb, R.S. (2006) *A Greener Faith: Religious Environmentalism and Our Planet's Future*, New York: Oxford University Press.

Marx, K. and F. Engels. (1964) *On Religion*, ed. Reinhold Niebuhr, New York: Schocken.

Smith, J.Z. (2004) *Relating Religion: Essays in the Study of Religion*, Chicago: University of Chicago Press.

Suzuki, D.T. (1963) *Outlines of Mahayana Buddhism*, New York: Schocken.

Tillich, P. (1988) *The Spiritual Situation in our Technical Society*, ed. J.M. Thomas, Macon, GA: Mercer University Press.

Weber, M. (1978) "The Sociology of Religion," in *Economy and Society*, ed. G. Roth and C. Wittich, Berkeley: University of California Press.

Further reading

Beckford, J.A. (2003) *Social Theory and Religion*, Cambridge: Cambridge University Press.

Boff, L. (1995) *Ecology and Liberation: A New Paradigm*, trans. J. Cumming, Maryknoll, NY: Orbis.

Gould, R.K. (2005) *At Home in Nature: Modern Homesteading and Spiritual Practice in America*, Berkeley: University of California Press.

Masuzawa, T. (2005) *The Invention of World Religions: Or, How European Universalism Was Preserved in the Language of Pluralism*, Chicago: University of Chicago Press.

Chapter 2

Religion

A dialogue

Rebecca Gould and Mark I. Wallace

Mark Wallace:

I have been captivated by the question of religion since childhood, and ever since then I have been fascinated with the possibility of a reality alternative to the everyday that I could inhabit.

My first encounter with the sacred occurred along the banks of the Singing River in Pascagoula, Mississippi. As a boy I spent summers in coastal Mississippi, where I heard stories about how the indigenous people in this area, generations ago, made a pact not to fight one another as long as there was no intermarriage between neighboring communities. But a young man from the Biloxi people and a young woman from the Pascagoula clan fell in love. In order to avoid conflict, according to the legend, the Pascagoula walked down into the river and perished singing their tribal anthem. I was told that when you sit nearby or swim in the river you can hear the voices of the lost people—and so the name of the river, the Singing River. I spent a lot of time in and around this body of water and often heard, as was my experience at that time, the haunting and beautiful lament of the river's original human inhabitants. This was my first and most enduring meeting with something outside normal life which I was drawn to experience again, understand better, and somehow explain to others.

At Swarthmore College I often teach introductory courses about the study of religion. In this context many thinkers have been major influences on my thinking, but I will mention just one: Paul Tillich, a twentieth-century German émigré to the United States during World War II, defines religion as orienting one's life toward whatever one regards as her "ultimate concern" (1957: 1).

Whether we acknowledge this fact or not, we all have basic loyalties toward those ideas, relationships, or activities in our lives that we find to be fundamentally fulfilling and worthwhile. These realities, imaginary or real, are the objects of our ultimate concern. For Tillich, this means that any idea or activity, in principle, is a type of religious (or, as I would say, spiritual) enterprise insofar as any such idea or activity serves a grounding or purposeful role in our lives. This means, then, that the study of religion is not primarily about doctrines or rituals *per se*, but about whatever a person or a community considers to be her tacit or explicit ultimate concern. In this vein, for example, saving Earth from environmental degradation can be a spiritual act even when the actors themselves do not think of themselves as conventionally religious. Tillich continues to open up to my students the possibility of uncovering the profoundly spiritual and moral dimensions of their commitments to social and political change.

Rebecca Gould:

Like Mark, some of my earliest memories of what might be called a "spiritual experience" were always deeply connected to the natural world. Because I left California before I turned seven, my memories of the many places we lived are patchwork at best: the announcement of Martin Luther King's assassination over the radio, a few peace marches in Berkeley—complete with teargas—and the makeshift Starship Enterprise that my siblings created in the woods near our house and never, ever let me enter! But the memories that stick with me the most, in near-tangible form, are memories of the natural world: starlit campfires on the beaches of Rio Del Mar, playing in the field of sunflowers that my grandfather had planted in Woodside, watching my grandmother—a biologist—lovingly tend her snapdragons. From where I am now, a remembered place in nature isn't so much "called to mind" as it is called to body and spirit. I can smell pine sap and feel it stick to my fingers; I can hear the suck and tumble of the Pacific surf on giant cliffs.

So what do these personal memories and reflections have to do with religion? In comparing, Mark, your reflections with my own, it is interesting—and not surprising—to find the common theme of early childhood experiences in the natural world that were profound, sacred occasions. As I discussed in my book *At Home in Nature* (2005), experiencing the sacredness of nature does not require formal religiosity at all, and if one's reverence for nature *is* grounded in religion, elevating one particular religious orientation over others is inaccurate and unwise.

Mark and I share childhood experiences of reverence for nature that have shaped our contemporary ecological concerns as well as our religious identities. That Mark is a Christian and I am a Jew (from a multi-religious, sometimes agnostic, family) makes little difference in the grand scale of nature's sacredness. Both of these traditions—as well as Hinduism, Buddhism, and Islam—have sacred texts, rituals, and social structures that emphasize the sacrality of the human–nature relationship. At the same time, each of these traditions certainly contains "nature-denying" strands, and at certain points in history (more often than not) these strands have been the dominant ones.

It is not surprising, then, that many who feel a strong connection to the natural world—and who have grown up in religious contexts where the "nature-denying" aspects of a tradition were prominent—have turned to nature as part of a "spiritual, but not religious" orientation. Given that spirituality is itself a part of religious practice (as in prayer, chant, and Bible study), this distinction between spiritual and religious is not always useful. Rather, I think it is helpful to see these categories placed on a continuum, with institutional religion on one pole and private forms of spirituality on the other. As I think about religion and nature and religion in general, my tendency is to pitch a large tent and to welcome many forms of religiosity and spirituality under it. At the same time, I recognize that the five great "world religions"—Judaism, Christianity, Islam, Hinduism, and Buddhism—occupy a special place in that tent.

With these caveats and approaches in mind, how do I, how do we, think about religion in general? The word "religion" scarcely seems big enough to hold the myriad worldviews, histories, geographies, charismatic figures, teachers and devotees, artistic expressions, social structures, economic shifts, and countless narratives of personal experience, all of which may invite, or even demand, our attention. In the largest sense, *one* meaning of the word "religion" rests on the meanings of the Latin term *ligare*, to bind. Even if we can be fairly certain that the word "religion" is rooted in this Latin verb—and that certainty is still up for grabs—we must ask: "What *kind* of binding are we talking about?" Some have suggested that "binding" refers particularly to the *Akedah*, the story in the Hebrew Bible of Abraham's binding of Issac to the sacrificial altar—the ultimate test of faith, and one that resonates with and in all traditions. Others suggest a broader set of meanings, focusing on the function of religion as one of *connectivity*, but also of *obligation*. To be bound to God (or, say, to the foundational Four Noble Truths of Buddhism) is, in a profound way, to be no longer alone in the world. At the same time, however, such commitments are also commitments to a certain set of *constraints*; for instance observing the Ten Commandments, carrying out the duty of all Muslims to make a pilgrimage to Mecca, or taking the Five Precepts which guide Buddhist lay people through the requirements of daily living. These are all practices that "constrain" religious practitioners, but such constraints are in the service of a larger freedom that comes with knowing who one is spiritually and what practices are demanded of one as a serious practitioner.

When we take such a broad view of religion, we cannot help but notice the many ways that "binding" comes to the fore in religious practice: animal sacrifice, covenantal circumcision, coming of age rituals partaking of the Eucharist, the list is endless. Sometimes this binding is tight, as we see in various forms of Orthodoxy. At other times, the "binding" is noticeably more elastic, expressive of another aspect of the term *ligare*, which is etymologically related to *ligaments*, the connective tissues in our bodies that keep our bones firmly aligned, but loose enough for freedom of movement. But whether we are speaking of strict Orthodox Jews or liberal, experimental Unitarian Universalists it is important to recognize that all religious institutions and movements contain both "strict" and "loose" approaches to religious practice and religious identity. Furthermore, to "bind" also means "to bind back" to one's truest, highest self, from which we all tend to stray.

Keeping these meditations on binding in mind, I want to offer a working *characterization* (as opposed to a static definition) of religion as (1) a culturally constructed conceptual framework (or "worldview") (2) for understanding and interpreting (not only in a scientific way) the most significant aspects of nature, life, and the human condition (3) that are expressed through a variety of sacred texts and/or practices, and (4) undertaken in community, whether physically present or not (as in rituals for/with the ancestors). Such a characterization is necessarily broad in order to make room for Lutherans, Zen Buddhists, Reconstructionist Jews, members of a Wiccan coven, and "spiritual, but not religious" people who look to nature as the primary source of meaning and authority.

To put this characterization in simpler terms, we might say that religion assumes and nurtures connections to "that which is larger than ourselves" and, in turn, the guiding concepts of a religion (e.g. salvation and resurrection, *moksha* [liberation], living by the Torah, the Holy Eight Fold Path) are expressed, preserved, and given form by sacred texts and practices that enable us to shape our lives around—as the old Protestant hymn goes—"the ties that bind." "That which is larger than ourselves" may be very precise or rather ineffable, but what is more important is that these "ties that bind" also include *ties to a community of people* (and sometimes other living beings) who share our conceptual framework and/or our practices.

Even *within* a particular religious tradition, I find myself increasingly encouraging my students to speak of *Buddhisms* and *Christianities* to account for the tremendous variety of religious expression even within a particular religious tradition. Our challenge, then, is to hold an elastic but not "anything goes" approach to religion, to consider the adjectival and adverbial dimensions of the term, rather than to pursue a categorical, nominative *definition*.

Mark and I agree that it is not that all of us *need* a religious tradition in order to lead a meaningful life, and that most religious people actually do not spend much time *defining* religion in their daily lives. Instead, most of us primarily pay attention to our personal psycho-spiritual experiences and what they might mean for our lives. It is no surprise then that when the psychologist William James sought to understand religion he approached it by studying individual narratives of religious life, which he presented and interpreted in his *Varieties of Religious Experience* (1902). Similarly, Paul Tillich's definition of religion as "ultimate concern," which Mark finds compelling, succeeds in pitching a "big tent" for religious life, especially in terms of avoiding the restriction of "religion" to a Christian deity or to "the supernatural," terms that we now see as quite limited when, say, Buddhism, Hinduism, aboriginal traditions, or various forms of "nature religion" are considered.

Of course, the danger of Tillich's approach is the flipside of his success, for upon reading Tillich many enthusiasts for his position are eager to label athletic exertion, landscape painting, or playing French horn concertos as "ultimate concerns." While there is some truth in interpreting Tillich this way—and the effects of athleticism, artistic expression, and performing great music often feel little different from religious experience—Tillich is careful to make distinctions. "Ultimate concerns" are only religious, he writes, if they are "ultimate concerns about ultimate things." In other words, Tillich wants to be clear that mastering Pilates or playing the French horn—while each may be significant and may even provide considerable insight beyond the details of the practice itself—is not what he is talking about *per se*. Rather, Tillich is suggesting that an ultimate concern is synonymous with religion when the *direction of that concern* is pointed to that which transcends human culture alone, or, as I put it earlier, "that which is larger" than human experience and the presumed centrality of the ego.

More recent theologians have expanded on James and Tillich, and for this part of our dialogue I will mention only two: the Christian theologian Sallie McFague and the writer and activist Rabbi Arthur Waskow. Over the course of her extensive theological thinking and writing, Sallie McFague has called on her readers to pay attention to the *metaphorical* dimensions of our language about God—language that is sometimes detrimental and sometimes rich with opportunities. To cite only one example, McFague argues that the metaphor of God as Lord, King, and Father is not as effective in our own time as it was in biblical times, when lords, kings, and fathers dominated social life. In our own democratic, post-feminist age, McFague writes, we need new metaphors to guide us to ethical, ecological, and social change-oriented ways of living. She proposes new metaphors—reminding us that these are *metaphors* and not literal *descriptions*—that include the idea of God as mother, lover (i.e. the Beloved), and friend, as well as the notion of the Earth as God's body. Over several publications McFague (1987, 1993, 1997) works through the significance of the metaphors she is proposing and demonstrates the ways in which particular visions of God—particularly in the Christian context—offer positive encouragement for ecological thinking and action.

Rabbi Arthur Waskow also urges his readers and students to understand the historically conditioned, and therefore limited, interpretations of the Divine that we have inherited. Waskow shows the ways in which the language of God as a revered and feared supreme-royalty emphasized but *one strand* of Judaism that saw nature as the mere stage for human–Divine activity. By contrast, Waskow uncovers the often hidden ecological history of the Jews' relationship to the land and to nature generally. Among his many contributions, Waskow re-reads the creation story with attention to the role of Adam as earth-keeper. "Adam"—stemming from the Hebrew word *Adamah* (soil)—is placed in the garden to "work" (*avod*, meaning both "to serve" and "to keep," not "to dominate," as so many have assumed). Rabbi Waskow also presents the ecological, agricultural origins of many Jewish holidays that were later constructed as celebrations of primarily historical occasions of God's actions on behalf of the Jews (e.g. the story of the Exodus from Egypt gets grafted on to the older spring barley harvest ritual and eventually the agricultural aspect of the celebration is almost forgotten). Waskow asks us to re-think what concepts of God will serve the challenges of our time while being true to our historical roots. For Waskow, the biggest challenges are promoting interfaith work, protesting war and injustice, and vigorously pursuing ecological health and the threat of global climate change, which he provocatively terms "global scorching."[1]

I am ending this first stage of our conversation with these reflections on Waskow's and McFague's theological and social/ecological justice work because they, in some sense, continue the contributions made by William James and Paul Tillich. In certain ways, all of these thinkers contribute to the organizing and stabilizing functions of religion. At the same time, all four of these writers recognize the volatility of religious experience (James), the necessity for a big conceptual tent under which all kinds of religious traditions and practices can be included (Tillich), and the necessary elasticity of "age old" religious histories, guiding concepts, and metaphors (McFague and Waskow). All of these thinkers offer contributions that mirror those of the other three, and in each case they speak to both the costs and the benefits of the "destabilizing" functions of religion which Mark Wallace so rightly urges that we recognize, confront, and interpret, lest our views of religion become all silver lining and no cloud.

Perhaps the ambiguity and potential instability of religion is why, when I look back to my childhood experiences in nature (and even my much more recent ones), I remember sometimes feeling powerfully comforted, inspired, and moved by the grandeur of God's creation and at other times feeling that the word "God"—whoever and whatever that meant—was not large enough to contain the enchanted mystery of the evolutionary process, not big enough to hold the vastness and beauty of the forest cathedral in which I found myself standing.

Wallace:

Rebecca, much of what you wrote resonated with me. In particular, I was struck by your personal comment about our like-minded religious identities. You recognize the common nature-based spirituality that grounds our different religious heritages, Judaism and Christianity, but also acknowledge their differences and the ways in which they have both been "nature denying."

To make this point let me begin with a brief aside. I don't know how to put this without sounding offensive to pious ears, but over the years, in many contexts, I have felt embarrassed about my Christian identity. I find the story of Jesus, church music and liturgy, spiritual and theological writings, and the general symbol system of Christian faith to be continually nurturing and life transforming. And I have many heroes of the faith—from Dorothy Day and Martin Luther King to Dietrich Bonhoeffer and, if I may be so bold, Barak Obama—who inspire and move me to reach toward the common good and try to live a life of integrity and charity towards others. But much of the time the public face of Christianity is troubled. Media preachers like Pat Robertson and James Dobson preach a gospel of division and judgment. Conservative Christian politicians such as James Inhofe and Sarah Palin employ a narrow interpretation of the Bible to rail against sex education in the schools, the separation of church and state, and climate change legislation. And the Catholic Church has been badly damaged by continual revelations of hundreds (or more) of clergy who have sexually abused male children over the course of many decades.

I have been able to reclaim my religious identity through ongoing conversations with friends and colleagues about how to articulate a progressive Christianity that functions as a counterweight to the preachers of exclusion. Some of this impetus comes from conversations with Jewish friends, especially Roger Gottlieb and David Abram, who have labored impressively to recover Judaism's nature-based identity. Years ago, when David wrote to me that he self-identifies as a "Jewish animist," I felt a light go off in my thinking because this turn of phrase captured exactly what I sensed about my own Christian love of Earth and its many inhabitants, sentient and non-sentient alike. Likewise, Rebecca, your forest ramblings and playtimes in sunflower fields in the Northern California of your youth evoke a similar sensibility of encountering something numinous and wonderful, perhaps even sacred, within the everyday world of your childhood.

Today, then, the basic orientation that drives my spiritual appreciation of nature is what I call "Christian animism"—the biblically inflected conviction that all creation is infused with or "animated" by God's presence. The term *animism* has its origins in the early academic studies of the vernacular belief systems of indigenous peoples in Africa and the Americas. It originated with the nineteenth-century British anthropologist E.B. Tylor, who used it to describe how primordial people attributed "life" or "soul" to all things, living and non-living. Sharing resonances with the Latin word *animus*, which means soul or spirit, among other definitions, animism came to stand for the orienting worldview of indigenous communities that nonhuman nature is "ensouled" or "inspirited" with sacred presence and power. As religions scholar Graham Harvey writes, animism is typically applied to religions that engage with a wide community of living beings with whom humans share this world or particular locations within it. It might be summed up by the phrase "all that exists lives" and, sometimes, the additional understanding that "all that lives is holy." As such the term animism is sometimes applied to particular indigenous religions in comparison to Christianity or Islam, for example.

(Harvey 2005: 81)

What intrigues me about Harvey's definition is his assumption that monotheistic traditions such as Christianity should be regarded as distinct from animism. Initially, this assertion makes sense in light of the historic Christian proclivity to cast aspersions on the material world and the flesh as inferior to the concerns of the soul. Pseudo-Titus, for example, an extra-canonical exhortation to Christian asceticism from late antiquity, urges its readers to cleanse themselves of worldly pollution by overcoming fleshly temptations: "Blessed are those who have not polluted their flesh by craving for this world, but are dead to the world that they may live for God!" (Ehrman 2003: 239). At first glance, Christianity's emphasis on making room for God by denying the world and the flesh is at odds with the classical animist belief in the living goodness of all inhabitants of sacred Earth.

In the main, however, Christian faith offers its practitioners a profound vision of God's this-worldly identity. Harvey's presumption that Christianity and animism are distinct from one another is at odds with the biblical worldview that all things are bearers of divinity—the whole biosphere is filled with God's animating power—insofar as God signaled God's love for creation by incarnating Godself in Jesus and giving the Holy Spirit to indwell everything that exists on the planet. The miracle of Jesus as the living enfleshment of God in our midst—a miracle that is alongside the gift of the Spirit to the world since time immemorial—signals the ongoing vitality of God's sustaining presence within the natural order. God is not a sky-God divorced from the material world. As once God became earthly at the beginning of creation, and as once God became human in the body of Jesus, so now God continually enfleshes Godself through the Spirit in the embodied reality of life on Earth.

Of the current models of the interconnected relation between God and Earth, *pan*-en-*theism* is closest to Christian animism. Panentheist theologian Sallie McFague, whom Rebecca highlights along with Arthur Waskow, is a foundational eco-theologian who argues for the mutual, internal relatedness of God and creation, but notes that God is not *fully* realized in the material world. God is *in* the world, indeed, but God is not "totally" embodied within everyday existence. McFague writes:

Pantheism says that God is embodied, necessarily and totally; traditional theism claims that God is disembodied, necessarily and totally;

panentheism suggests that God is embodied but not necessarily or totally. Rather, God is sacramentally embodied: God is mediated, expressed, in and through embodiment, but not necessarily or totally.

(McFague 1993: 149–50)

While my sensibility and McFague's are deeply aligned, my Christian animism pushes further by suggesting that God is *fully* and *completely* embodied within the natural world. Here the emphasis does not fall on the limited relatedness of God and world such that God, finally, can escape the world, but rather on the idea that the world *thoroughly embodies* God's presence. Unlike many Christian theologies which emphasize God's *transcendence*, my position, akin to McFague's, champions divine *subscendence*: God flowing out into the Earth; God becoming one of us in Jesus, to use Christian language; God gifting to all of creation the Spirit in order to infuse all things with divine energy and love. Now nothing is held back as God overflows Godself into the bounty of the natural world. Now all things are bearers of the sacred; everything that is, is holy; each and every creature is a portrait of God.

The biblical ideas of creation, incarnation, and Spirit are the fountainhead of the Christian animist vision of the sacred character of the natural order. From this living source, to paraphrase Harvey, all that exists is alive, all that exists is good, all that exists is holy. We will not save what we do not love, and unless, as a culture, we learn to love and care for the gift of the created order again, the prospects for saving the planet, and thereby ourselves as well, are terrifyingly bleak. But insofar as God is in everything and all things are inter-animated by divine power and concern, we can affirm that God is carnal, God is earthen, God is flesh. And with this animist affirmation the will is empowered, and the imagination ignited, to fight against the specters of global warming and the loss of biodiversity as the great threats of our time.

In every respect, therefore, the Earth crisis is a *spiritual* crisis because without a vital, fertile planet it will be difficult to find traces of divine wonder and providence in the everyday order of things. When the final arctic habitat of the polar bear melts into the sea due to human-induced climate change, I will lose something of God's beauty and power in my life. When the teeming swell of equatorial amphibians can no longer adapt to defor-estation and rising global temperatures, I fear something of God will dis-appear as well. I feel a deep sense of kinship with the first peoples of the Americas who experienced the sacred within the Black Hills of what is now South Dakota, or on top of Mount Graham in southern Arizona, and then found that when these places were degraded something of God was missing as well. Without these and other places charged with sacred power, I am lost on the Earth. Without still-preserved landed sites saturated with divine pre-sence, I am a wanderer with no direction, a person without hope, a believer experiencing the death of God on an erstwhile verdant planet now suffering daily from human greed.

Gould:

Mark, your final sentences evoke both the fear and the despair that come from experiencing what Carolyn Merchant has called "The Death of Nature" (1990), which, from a "Christian animist" point of view such as yours, must also mean the "Death of God."[2] The "Death of God" idea is not new, but in our own time, as Mark makes clear, God may be dying in a new way to the extent that the Divine is understood to be present in the natural world. I might add here that this notion of divine presence in nature is a longstanding one—certainly not something that Mark or I have made up! In the early Christian world—and later in Puritan culture—there persists an idea of the "Book of Nature" as a text of sorts to be read alongside the "Book of Scripture" to discern God's character and desires.[3] The act of "reading" Nature in order to discern spiritual messages can be traced from its Calvinist origins in early America (with preludes extending back to the first century of Christianity) to nineteenth-century liberal Christianity, to Thoreau's "post-Christian" reading of nature, and on into our own time when nature writing becomes an unofficial, spiritual genre akin to the literature of spiritual formation. We need look no further for an example than Mark's own *Finding God in the Singing River* (2005), which is a wonderful, provocative illustration of this kind of perspective.

Like Mark, I too have wrestled with what I have come to call "environmental despair," the powerlessness one feels lying awake at two in the morning, wondering if it is possible to have *any* effect on species loss and global warming. Over time, I have found it increasingly difficult to reconcile the central role of religion as a comfort in times of trial (consider, for instance, the crowds of people who flocked to their houses of worship in the wake of 9/11) and the historical complicity (in ecological degradation) of Christianity and Judaism, whose many leaders have portrayed God as being above and beyond nature and have insisted that religious history is strictly about the *history* of God and God's people, with nature serving merely as the stage for the drama. This perspective, to cite just one representative example, appears in Nahum Sarna's edited volume (on Genesis) of the widely respected Jewish Publication Society's commentary on the Torah. In his introduction, Sarna writes: "The God of Genesis is the wholly self-sufficient One, absolutely independent of nature" (1989: xiv). By contrast, one need only study Chapter Two of Genesis to discover a portrait of the human–nature relationship which emphasizes intimacy, kinship, and the mutual interdependence of humanity and the natural world. Or consider the Book of Job, where God asks rhetorically, "Do *you* know the time when the wild goats of the rock bring forth their young? ... Did *you* give the beautiful wings to the peacocks or wings and feathers to the ostrich?" These texts offer a sense of the complex, intimate interweave of nature, humanity, and the Divine that runs throughout both Jewish and Christian sacred texts (Genesis 2:15; Job 39:1 and 13).

But it is in the context of our shared experience of environmental despair that I would like to take Mark's arm, lead him to the quiet teahouse in Middlebury, Vermont, and sit him down for a psychological, spiritual, and theological pep talk. To Mark I would emphasize much of what he already knows, but may have lost track of in the midst of his despair. I would tell him: Judaism and Christianity definitely bear the problematic legacies of transcendence over immanence and we must face countless discussions *ad nauseum* of humanity's God-given "dominion" over the natural world. But these complicated concepts of "transcendence" and "dominion" pale by comparison with the abundant "non-dominion," "immanent in nature" themes and assertions that we find in our sacred texts. The ideas of the Divine in nature course through the Hebrew Bible like a river, appearing in Genesis, Proverbs, Psalms, Job, and beyond, not to mention in the spiritual/ agricultural principles that we find in Jewish commentary such as the Talmud (whose first book is entitled "Seeds" and provides instructions on prayer and agricultural practice in the same text!). And in the Christian context, as Mark has mentioned, there is perhaps no more dramatic example of the Divine in nature than the incarnation of God in Jesus. It is true that fears of paganism and pantheism are persistent in our texts, reflecting the cultural politics of the day, but the essential message is this: Our traditions are entirely too complex to be characterized as theologically "anti-nature."

Recently, religious organizations have begun to catch up with the ideas of their theological predecessors, such as Waskow and McFague. While late to join the environmental movement (because of misunderstanding and suspicions on both sides), religious organizations, from interfaith ecological action groups to denomination-based committees focused on policy, have emerged in force. Let me provide a few examples to make more visible this recent turn toward facing environmental problems from a spiritual/religious perspective.[4] A United Church of Christ (UCC) minister I know once provoked church members by coming before the congregation to deliver her sermon and then suddenly tipping garbage all over the altar. Such a dramatic display might have backfired, but because the congregation had a strong, positive relationship with their minister they interpreted her actions as urgent, prophetic ones and eventually began to invest more time, energy, and money in environmental causes.

Similarly, some Catholic priests have begun to link the offering of the Eucharist—the high point of the Mass—with the health of the planet. How can bread and wine be truly *sacred*, these priests have asked, if the grain comes from pesticide-soaked fields and the grapes are grown in a vineyard that has a large carbon footprint? For these religious leaders, *ritual sacrality is intimately connected to environmental health*; without this health, they argue, the sacred itself is diminished, as Mark has also pointed out. Progressive rabbis have taken a similar stance, persuading their congregants that the traditional *ner tamid* (eternal light) that shines over the Ark of the Torah should be exchanged in favor of a solar-powered one. How can eternal light be truly *holy*, they have asked, when electric "light" comes from impoverished coal fields and the correspondingly impoverished communities whose citizens are forced to be part of a business that is their only hope of a livelihood, but whose health effects threaten their lives? Far better, these rabbis and congregants argue, to derive "eternal light" from that original, holy renewable source—the sun.

In considering these exempla, some might protest that pouring garbage over the altar or installing a solar *ner tamid* is a "merely symbolic" action that does not have any real significant impact on environmental degradation and climate change. This is true to a certain extent, although less so if many more congregations throughout the land begin making serious, sustainable choices in their houses of worships and in their own daily lives. This is why a campaign such as the Evangelical Environmental Network's well-publicized challenge to families that asked, "What Would Jesus Drive?" had a noticeable effect on a community that does not historically embrace "liberal" environmental causes. More to the point, we do well to remember that *much* religious practice is *essentially symbolic* (such as wearing a Star of David around one's neck or kneeling at the Communion rail to express humility and gratitude). These actions convey various attitudes of heart, mind, and spirit, devotion, or exultation, or longing to be closer to God. As so many teachers, theologians, and clergy have pointed out—and Sallie McFague's work is a wonderful example of this—metaphors and symbols *matter*. In the Jewish world, for instance, we can see that the attempt to bring religion to ecology and vice versa has had the visible effect of actually bringing young people "back to Judaism," because they have come to see their home tradition as more relevant to their own lives and hopes for the world than they once had assumed.

Furthermore, as we have come to understand the "geography of impact" when it comes to pollution, toxics, and global warming we have become increasingly aware of the social justice dimensions of environmental problems. Environmental work, religious groups have helped us to see, is not simply the work of preserving pristine landscapes (a potentially elitist concern). Environmental work is also very much about preserving equally the health and well-being of *all* human communities. Needless to say, serving the poor, the oppressed, the sick, and the under-educated is the central responsibility of those Christians and Jews who take their spiritual lives seriously and *these social justice concerns are connected to, not separate from,* our environmental work.

As we wrote early on in this dialogue, Mark and I both often experience the sacred through our encounters with the natural world. Like Mark, I often fear that some of these encounters and, by extension, some aspects of God will disappear in the face of the forces of greed, consumption, and unchecked individualism that reign in our society. Like Mark, I know that if the river I sat by so often as a child—the pewter-hued river where I read poetry, thought about my future, delighted in the sprouting spring reeds, and also got engaged—were to die out because of apathy and disregard it would feel like a kind of Deicide, a mortal sin. As McFague has written, sin is living apart from the Source of life, refusing to take responsibility for natural and human communities. It is forgetting to play by the "house rules" of sustainable living on this planet. No doubt, if my dear Concord River—the same river that Thoreau often visited—were polluted beyond recovery I would feel like one of my limbs had been cut off, "the river limb" which in my eco-body is connected to the "mountain meadow limb," the "favorite old tree limb," and so on. A piece of myself and a piece of the Divine would have vanished.

And yet (here Mark, I am returning to the pep talk!) it is a central tenet of the Jewish tradition that we must *always affirm life*, even, or especially, in the midst of death, sadness, and loss. This persistent call to affirm life is why, even when sitting *shiva* (the traditional seven-day period of mourning) for a loved one, mourners are required by tradition to take a pause from grieving to celebrate Shabbat with whatever joy and gratefulness they can muster. And because *shiva* is always a seven-day ritual, there is never any escape, for *anyone*, from entering the sacred, joyous "Divine embrace ... of timeless time and placeless place"—the place of Shabbat.[5] In the midst of *shiva*, Shabbat is a central part of the Plan.

So when I am in the midst of environmental despair, I like to think of eco-religious institutions, thinkers, and practices as if they were so many organic grapes being gently crushed and fermented into a fine Shabbos wine. In such a context, I am fully aware of the extent to which our planet-home is sick and possibly dying. I mourn the death of sacred rivers and of the polar bears Mark mentioned, whose divine light—both fierce and playful—shines like a beacon on human folly. I do not pretend that these things are not happening. I grieve and I mourn. But then I bring the cup of all we have accomplished and of all that is still possible to my lips. I offer some to Mark. And we toast: L'chaim, to Life!

Notes

1 One iteration of these interpretations and arguments can be found in Waskow (2000). See also Rabbi Waskow's website for the Shalom Center (www. theshalomcenter.org), which reprints articles by Waskow and other scholars.
2 In the "Death of God" movement of the 1960s, God was said to be "dead" by various intellectuals and theologians who had essentially *thought their way out of* belief in God. The concept (and reality) of God seemed to them to be antithetical

to the central beliefs and values of modern, scientific life. The "Death of God" movement first appeared in the public eye when the April 1966 cover of *Time Magazine* famously asked, "Is God Dead?"

3 The idea of "two books," or the book of nature and book of scripture, goes back at least to St. Augustine in the Christian tradition. For instance, he writes, "It is the divine page that you must listen to; it is the book of the universe that you must observe. The pages of Scripture can only be read by those who know how to read and write, while everyone, even the illiterate, can read the book of the universe" (*Enarrationes in Psalmos*, XLV, 7 (PL 36,518)).

4 Some of these examples come from research I have conducted jointly with my friend and colleague Laurel Kearns, who wrote the Afterword to this volume.

5 The phrase beginning "Divine embrace ... " comes from music and lyrics composed for Shabbat by Rabbi Shefa Gold. See the website www.rabbishefa gold.com.

References

Ehrman, B.D. (2003) *Lost Christianities: Books that Did Not Make It into the New Testament*, Oxford: Oxford University Press.

Harvey, G. (2005) "Animism—A Contemporary Perspective," in B. Taylor (ed.) *The Encyclopedia of Religion and Nature*, New York: Continuum.

James, W. (1902) *Varieties of Religious Experience: A Study in Human Nature*, 1st edn, New York: Longmans and Green.

McFague, S. (1987) *Models of God*, Minneapolis: Fortress Press.

——(1993) *The Body of God*, Minneapolis: Fortress Press.

——(1997) *Super, Natural Christians*, Minneapolis: Fortress Press.

Merchant, C. (1990) *The Death of Nature*, New York: Harper One.

Sarna, N. (ed.) (1989) *Genesis, JPS Torah Commentary*, New York: Jewish Publication Society.

Tillich, P. (1957) *Dynamics of Faith*, New York: Harper and Row.

Waskow, A. (ed.) (2000) *Torah of the Earth: Exploring 4,000 Years of Ecology in Jewish Thought*, Woodstock, VT: Jewish Lights Publishing.

Further reading

Gould, R.K. (2005) *At Home in Nature: Modern Homesteading and Spiritual Practice in America*, Berkeley: University of California Press.

Tillich, P. (1951–63) *Systematic Theology*, Chicago: University of Chicago Press.

Van Berkel, K. and A. Vanderjag (2005) *The Book of Nature in Antiquity and the Middle Ages*, Leuven: Peeters Publishers.

——(2006) *The Book of Nature in Early Modern and Modern History*, Leuven: Peeters Publishers.

Wallace, M. (2005) *Finding God in the Singing River*, Minneapolis: Fortress Press.

Chapter 3

Case study

"Religion" in Appalachian environmental struggles

Joseph Witt

In the summer of 2009, I made my first research trip to Marsh Fork Elementary, a small public school in West Virginia that sits both at the base of a large coal slurry impoundment and at the center of many debates over the safety of mountaintop removal mining. I traveled there to observe a rally against mountaintop removal as part of my research on the place of religion in resistance to the practice. Though I had met with activists on previous occasions, this was to be my first experience at a protest in West Virginia. Driving to the rally that morning I noticed more and more "Friends of Coal" stickers on cars and other signs of pro-coal interests along the road. Finally, as I rounded the last corner toward the school, I was surprised to see not a group of protestors in opposition to the mine, but instead a large group of miners and their families organized in a counter-protest, clad in official blue and orange work clothes, brandishing signs reading "Outsiders: Go Home," and shouting menacingly toward every passing car.

I knew that the issue of mountaintop removal was contentious in coal country, but this was more than I had anticipated. Driving through the gauntlet of miners, I seriously considered giving in to the intimidation and just continuing on down the road, away from the heated protest. I *could* conduct my research through interviews in comfortable settings, after all, and never face the violence and intimidation that confronted the protestors themselves. Ultimately, though, I decided to continue with the plan and participate in the rally; and as a researcher, I gained extremely valuable insights on the issue of mountaintop removal that could have been lost had I chosen different research methods.

When researching issues of religions and ecology, the scholar is faced with numerous methodological choices such as those that presented themselves at Marsh Fork. How we approach the study of religions and ecology—whether through text-based research, ethnographic fieldwork, surveys, or any of a number of methodologies—impacts how we ultimately understand the connections between them. Additionally, what we mean by terms like "religion" directs our research in important ways. As I discovered that morning in West Virginia, researching these issues is not always comfortable or safe, but it is nevertheless vital for students and researchers to carefully consider both what we hope to understand about religions and ecology and what methodologies and theories best work toward that understanding.

In this case study, I briefly explain some of my own experiences researching religion and ecology on the ground, revealing how different perspectives on religion and approaches to research lead to differing results, or at least emphasize different elements of the wide nexus between religions of the world and the environment. Following a very brief explanation of mountaintop removal, I give examples of study from a more institutional perspective (focused on the religious organizations involved in the protest) and a more "ground level" perspective, drawing on expanded theories of religion and the experiences of individual activists. No single approach can provide a complete picture, and institutional and ground-level perspectives on religion and activism need not be mutually exclusive. Instead, the combination of approaches garners greater understanding and explanatory power.

Very simply, mountaintop removal entails moving the earth above underground coal seams with explosives and large machines and placing it in nearby valleys, gaining access to the exposed coal. Though strip mining is practiced around the world, mountaintop removal is particularly associated

Figure 3.1 A partially reclaimed section of mountaintop removal mine adjacent to Larry Gibson's ancestral land on Kayford Mountain, West Virginia.
Source: Photo by the author, July 4, 2009.

with the coal country of central Appalachia (mainly the states of Kentucky, West Virginia, Tennessee, and Virginia). Mountaintop removal differs dramatically from older forms of deep mining, where individual miners enter pits to remove the coal by hand. Instead, dynamite and large machines perform the digging, allowing the scale of mountaintop removal mines to far exceed even the largest deep mines.

While mountaintop removal is more economically efficient for mining companies, the negative environmental impacts of the practice are numerous. A 2005 United States Environmental Protection Agency (EPA) environmental impact statement noted that by 2001, 1,200 miles of streams had been buried or polluted by mountaintop removal (EPA 2005: 4). Along with watershed pollution, mountaintop removal dramatically alters the local ecology, removing mixed hardwood forests and replacing them with rocky fields often covered by non-native grasses. The waste from coal processing (called slurry) provides another area of concern for many Appalachians. Marsh Fork Elementary remains a focal point for anti-mountaintop removal protests largely because it sits at the base of a large slurry impoundment. The 2008 failure of a dam at a similar impoundment in Kingston, Tennessee, incited renewed interest in protecting the children of Marsh Fork.

In addition to these environmental damages, activists cite continued economic decline and social fragmentation as further results of mountaintop removal. While the mine industry argues that removal provides much-needed jobs, activists argue that the heavily mechanized practice actually forces skilled deep miners out of work and draws employees from outside of the region. Debates over mountaintop removal policies continue at local and national levels, but opponents remain certain that, while the land and communities of Appalachia bear the costs of the practice, they reap almost none of the benefits.

Mountaintop removal is an issue of great interest to scholars of religion and ecology precisely because it is so hotly debated. In the contemporary movement opposing this practice, we can find evidence of the power of faith to provide a language for resistance against ecological and social oppression, the importance of senses of place, and the complex interactions between religious values and broader social structures. There are multiple methods and scopes for examining religious resistance to mountaintop removal, but I briefly focus on two: institutional resistance from mainstream religious organizations (primarily the West Virginia Council of Churches, WVCC) and "ground-level" resistance from individuals who operate outside of the faith-based groups and articulate their own faith commitments and spiritual connections to the land (such as Larry Gibson).

Institutional religious opposition to mountaintop removal and strip mining has a lengthy history in Appalachia, dating back to a 1945 statement by the Annual Ohio Pastors Convention (Montrie 2003: 36). Today, numerous congregations, faith-based organizations, and religious governing bodies have joined in opposition to mountaintop removal. While Appalachia grows increasingly diverse and the contributions of Jewish, Baha'i, and other groups should not be minimized, most of the institutional religious opposition comes from Christian groups. These organizations are theologically diverse, but there remain some common features in their works. Generally, faith-based groups cite Biblical passages promoting a stewardship view of humans as responsible for taking care of God's creation. A quote from Psalm 24 is particularly popular: "The Earth is the Lord's, and everything in it." They also frequently present mountaintop removal as a social justice issue, and they almost always call for compassion toward miners, who are portrayed as operating out of material need, not greed.

One of the clearest expressions of these themes emerged in 2007. That year, the WVCC, an ecclesiastical body representing the interests of fourteen Christian denominations throughout West Virginia, released an official statement in opposition to the destructive mining practice. The statement articulated a clear Biblical mandate for conservation, arguing that "Creation is a revelation of God, brought forth by God's word." Speaking specifically about mining in Appalachia, the Council continued, "Our West Virginia mountains are a wonderful example of the beauty of Creation ... The mountains are full of blessings for which to thank and praise our God." It concluded with a call for continued work, saying, "In obedience, we are obligated to care for God's wondrous Creation that we may one day walk with God in the garden without shame" (WVCC 2007). Significantly, the statement did not call for the complete cessation of mining or even mountaintop removal, but instead proposed that the proper government agencies more strictly enforce national strip mining regulations. Partly for political reasons, a major association like the WVCC cannot oppose the mining industry, which most Appalachian politicians and many of the churches' congregants support.

For the student or researcher, statements from faith-based groups like the WVCC are easily accessible. They are often clearly articulated and available online or in archives. To understand the institutional faith-based opposition to mountaintop removal, textual and primary source research remains the best method. Furthermore, religious institutions aid the opposition movement against mountaintop removal through their contact with policy makers and their outreach abilities. In addition to these groups, however, the movement is also peopled by a number of individuals with diverse faith commitments. Some individuals, like activists Judy Bonds, Maria Gunnoe, and Allen Johnson, serve as figureheads for the movement and articulate their values clearly in the media. Bonds, for example, was featured prominently in Bill Moyers's PBS documentary "Is God Green?" (2006) as one of a growing number of evangelical Christian environmentalists. There are numerous others variously engaged in the opposition movement, though, who do not receive the same level of media attention. Understanding the diverse religious values held by these individuals requires different methods, and possibly even different conceptions of "religion."

For example, Larry Gibson, the owner of a small island of private land surrounded by a mountaintop removal site on Kayford Mountain, West Virginia, is not considered a particularly religious man by those who know him. However, Gibson maintains a deep and inspiring connection to his land and his family's history there. His family has owned the land around Kayford Mountain since the late 1700s, but in 1906, like many others in the region, his ancestors sold the mineral rights to coal company investors (interview with author, Kayford Mountain, West Virginia, July 5, 2009). Strip mining started on Kayford Mountain in the late 1980s, and today it covers hundreds of acres and threatens two of Gibson's family cemeteries. Since mountaintop removal began at Kayford, Gibson has devoted almost all of his energy to raising awareness about mountaintop removal and preventing further destruction to his ancestral land. For Gibson, the land itself and the implicit responsibility he feels to preserve it for future generations establish a central set of values. As he is fond of saying, "My mother gave me birth, but the land gave me life." In an interview he further revealed his profound connection to the land: "Appalachia is a rare, special place. It embraces you no matter what part of Appalachia you're in" (interview with author, July 5, 2009). Such commitment to land and family can certainly be called religious insofar as it reveals something about the community that shaped Larry Gibson, the way he views the world, and what he considers most important. While Gibson does not present his beliefs in a formal statement, methods like participant observation and interviewing can help to reveal the complex religious and environmental values that motivate him and others like him.

In Appalachia, mainstream faith-based groups and religious individuals cooperate in opposition to mountaintop removal. Depending upon how one focuses on the interconnections between religions and ecology, whether through the statements of official faith-based groups or in the practices of individuals, one finds differing shapes and textures of religious concern. A wide angle that incorporates both is necessary to produce a complete picture. The field of religion and ecology by its very nature promotes interdisciplinary work and scholarly creativity, and in the case of mountaintop removal, a full quiver of approaches to "religion" is needed to fully understand the experiences of those involved.

Discussion questions

1 Are you convinced that mountaintop removal mining is an issue of *religious* concern? How might the participation of religious institutions and religious people change the debate on this subject?

2 Based on the primary information presented here, what contrasts do you see between the perspectives of the West Virginia Council of Churches

and Larry Gibson? How should researchers properly account for those differences?

3   Which definitions of religion discussed in Chapter 1 seem most compatible with a study of religious institutions like the West Virginia Council of Churches? Which definitions seem most compatible with a "ground-level" study of individuals like Larry Gibson?

4   What do you think might be learned from studying religion among those who support mountaintop removal mining? What methods would be most appropriate for such a study?

References

Montrie, C. (2003) *To Save the Land and People: A History of Opposition to Surface Coal Mining in Appalachia*, Chapel Hill: University of North Carolina Press.

United States Environmental Protection Agency (EPA) (2005) *Mountaintop Mining/ Valley Fills in Appalachia: Final Programmatic Environmental Impact Statement*, EPA 9–03-R-05002, available at http://www.epa.gov/region03/mtntop/pdf/mtm-vf_fpeis_full-document.pdf (accessed September 8, 2009).

West Virginia Council of Churches (WVCC) (2007) "Statement on Mountaintop Removal," available at http://www.wvcc.org/docs/MountainTopRemovalResolution2007.pdf (accessed September 30, 2009).

Further reading

End Mountaintop Removal Action and Resource Center (2010) http://www.ilove-mountains.org (accessed January 23, 2010).

Part II

Ecology

Chapter 4

Ecology
What is it, who gets to decide, and why does it matter?

Whitney A. Bauman, Richard R. Bohannon II, and Kevin J. O'Brien

In recent years, books about "ecology" have included scientific discussions of wetland ecosystem restoration, European political theory, congregational studies in suburbia, and a memoir of growing up poor in South Georgia. All of these books are, indeed, about ecology; however, the authors mean very different things by the term.

This book is about ecology because it concerns what happens when the study of religion is shaped by the natural world and how that natural world forms a context for religious beliefs and practices. Our attention to religion is grounded in ecology. This is not always a straightforward project, however, precisely because there are so many definitions and dimensions to any discussion of ecology.

Like religion, ecology is best understood as a broad idea that covers a lot of territory and can be bent and shaped in various ways. This is evident in the foundations of the word, because it was introduced to represent both a specific science and a broad theological project. Ernst Haeckel (1834–1919), a German biologist and public intellectual, coined the word "ecology" as a call for a new science based on the Darwinian idea of natural selection, a science to study organisms in relationship with their living and nonliving environments. However, Haeckel believed that such study of nature would not only produce data and analysis, but also reveal the "order of nature" and the "virtues" by which human beings could live harmoniously with it. He wrote: "the orderly course of evolution, according to fixed laws, now leads the human spirit through long eons from a primeval chaos to the present 'order of the cosmos'" (Haeckel 1895: 32–33). Haeckel believed that his study of organisms in their contexts would lead to cosmic truth. So, ecology as Haeckel understood it is both a natural science and a worldview.[1]

Haeckel derived the name for his science from *oikos*, the Greek word for household, so ecology is most literally the study of how organisms function in their metaphorical "houses," the natural environments upon which they depend. As scholars of religion and ecology frequently note, this links ecology to two other words also derived from *oikos*: economics, the study of how humans manage households and systems, and ecumenism, the effort to foster

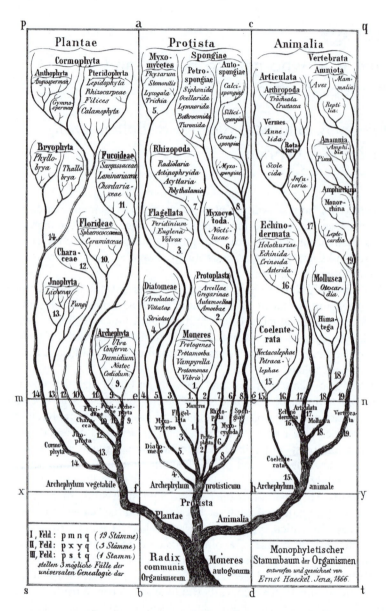

Figure 4.1 Ernst Haeckel, who coined the word "ecology," is also credited as the first thinker to envision the evolution of species as a "tree of life," which he depicted in this drawing from *The General Morphology of Organisms* (1866). Haeckel's emphasis on the interconnection of species, and to some extent his spiritual beliefs, is reflected in his labeling the trunk of this tree as "*radix communis organismorum,*" or "the common root of all life."

understanding and unity between different faith traditions. Ecology is and always has been both a project of scientific research and a broader pursuit with social and religious implications. Partly because of this origin, scholars continue to argue about what ecology means and how it can best be used. These arguments matter because they change the ways we understand, relate to, and care about the world around us.

This chapter will explore three such arguments. First is an argument about who has the authority to do ecology. For some, ecology refers to a science that uses experiments and careful fieldwork to understand organisms in their contexts; for others, ecology references a broad worldview emphasizing the moral interconnectedness of all things. Should ecology emphasize the authority of experts to understand the world, or the common task all peoples have in accepting our place in nature?

A second argument questions what ecology can tell us about "nature" itself. Sometimes the term emphasizes the singular natural world that all people and all creatures have in common, while at other times it denotes the different lenses and social constructions every person and culture uses to interpret the world. Should ecology remind us of the reality of nature beyond human culture, or should it help us see the limitations of any distinction between "nature" and "culture"?

A third argument focuses on how ecology influences religion. In some scholarship, ecology is seen as an inherent component to be identified within existing religious traditions, while others see it as a challenge that will reshape or replace those traditions. Is the contemporary reality of environmental degradation an unprecedented challenge calling for transformation, or is it a continuation of longstanding trends that call believers back to the spiritual roots of their traditions?

Of course, these arguments are too important and too complex to think that we can easily choose one side or the other in each. In all cases, the best answer is probably some version of both perspectives. But there are nevertheless choices to be made in how we think about ecology and how that shapes the ways we understand religion, the natural world, and the threat environmental degradation poses to both.

Science and morality

To understand ecology, one must first recognize it as a subdiscipline of biology, a field of scientific study based on careful observation and repeatable research. Most broadly, ecology in this sense is the study of organisms in their living and nonliving contexts. The science of ecology is based on the idea that every part of the natural world is connected to other parts. So, we cannot understand plants or animals in isolation, but must instead pay careful attention to their interactions with one another and with the world surrounding them.

Because scientists seek to be as precise and careful as possible in the questions they pursue, very few would claim to be experts in "ecology" as a whole. Instead, ecology is divided among a wide variety of questions and perspectives of specialization. Some ecologists articulate their focus by naming the object or region of their studies, such as disease ecologists, marine ecologists, animal ecologists, or arctic ecologists. Another approach to classifying ecology focuses on the methods and scales of attention used: At the smallest scales, physiological ecologists examine the chemical and biological factors shaping interactions between individual organisms and their environments, and behavioral ecologists examine the adaptations of organisms to their surroundings. Population ecologists study the changes and adaptations within a collection of organisms from the same species in a particular area, and community ecologists study patterns and processes among groups of organisms from different species. Ecosystem ecologists study the flows of energy and matter within a spatially explicit unit of organisms and abiotic material, and landscape ecologists study the broader-scale patterns of environmental change across multiple ecosystems.[2] In each case, ecology is about the organism-in-relation, but ecologists are always working to isolate a specific subset of these relations rather than deal with every possible connection in every possible system.

The varied approaches to the science of ecology are important because they emphasize the complexity of this academic discipline. Ecologists have developed a broad set of tools with which to understand the organisms, systems, landscapes, and processes that make up nature, and these tools require extensive expertise and scientific rigor. An ecological study in this sense would not attempt to understand climate change as a whole, but rather the impact of climate change on a particular species of tree in a particular forest. An ecological scientist would not aspire to become an authority on extinction and biodiversity loss in their entirety, but rather on the environmental threats facing one species or one ecosystem. Ecology as a science is therefore a broad and diverse pursuit that requires the focused work of many well-trained researchers.

However, the complexity of ecological science is just one dimension of the complexity of ecology, because the term is also used in religious and philosophical settings to make much broader and more sweeping claims about reality. Inspired by the assumptions and findings of scientific ecologists, theologians and activists derive from "ecology" a broad lesson about the interconnectedness of all things and so use the term to call for a vision of human life and the natural world as radically communal. In other words, ecology is used as an alternative to the dominant worldview prevalent in the West, which understands humans as isolated individuals and distinguishes our species from others. Given ecology's basic claim of interconnectedness, the argument goes, all people are related to and dependent on one another and natural systems. This claim builds on the science of ecology, but represents a far more sweeping and generalized use of its findings than most scientific researchers would advocate.

For example, the Confucian scholar Young-chan Ro argues that ecology is primarily an attitude human beings should adopt toward the world around us:

> Ecology, thus, must be based on a reciprocal receptivity with nature and the universe, by "seeing" and "listening" to the wonder, mystery, and pain of the universe ... [H]uman beings must be understood in light of the universe rather than the human rationality or *logos* being imposed on the universe.
>
> (Ro 1998: 184)

Here, ecology is about learning from and being open to "the universe" and its "wonder." This is connected in some ways to the scientific attempt to understand the natural world, but it paints in much broader strokes, and assumes that the universe is sharing a message that all human beings can hear.

In this sense, ecology is the observation that everything is connected to everything else and that there is no organism on earth that is not part of a web of connections and relationships; every particle in space emerged from the same cosmic birth, and every object in existence is linked by gravitational and physical forces. Nothing is separate, nothing is alone. For many activists, this is a vital and transformative truth; the more we can accept our inter-connections with all other things, the more we will respect and conserve the world around us rather than dismissing and consuming it. Ecology in this sense calls for holistic and sweeping action. It is not enough to preserve the "environment" that surrounds us and provides us with resources; we must instead recognize that we are *part* of the systems around us, that we exist in an exchange of matter and energy. This implies an ethical lesson: Because all things are interconnected, we should strive to nurture and support connections, to coexist with all that is.

A key example of this kind of thinking can be found in the work of the Catholic priest and environmental theologian Thomas Berry, who developed a sweeping argument about humanity's future on Earth in his book *The Great Work*. Berry's hope is crystallized in what he calls "the ecological movement, which seeks to create a more viable context for human develop-ment within the planetary process" (1999: 58). For Berry, anyone who has grasped the reality of cosmic interrelatedness and planetary interdependence is "an ecologist."

Berry and many thinkers inspired by him write about an "ecological crisis" facing contemporary humanity, a crisis that includes environmental degradation—climate change, species destruction, toxic pollution, and environmental injustices—but also implies an explanation for these problems: wrong relationships within humanity and between our species and the rest of the world. This is a significant departure from ecological science, from the narrow and defensible claims that researchers are willing to make about the character of organisms and their contexts.

Indeed, many scientific ecologists go out of their way to distinguish their work from the "ecology" of activists and religious believers. Along these lines, the scientific theorists Timothy Allen and Thomas Hoekstra carefully distance their research from the moral claim of holistic interconnectedness:

> The folk wisdom of ecology that says everything is connected to everything else is only true in an uninteresting way, for the whole reason for doing ecological research is to find which connections are stronger and more significant than others. We do not wish to show that everything is connected, but rather to show which minimal number of connections that we can measure may be used as a surrogate for the whole system in a predictive model.
>
> (Allen and Hoekstra 1992: 284)

Science, from Allen and Hoekstra's perspective, is not about the assertion of fundamental truths or morals, but rather about modeling and measuring systems as well as possible. Ecological science assumes a basic level of interconnection, but it works to model these connections as a path to partially understand particular systems, not to make universal ethical claims. Scientists primarily ask questions about how things work and what is real rather than about how human beings should live and what is right.

The two approaches to ecology are, of course, related, and they are certainly not mutually exclusive. Many scientists are committed to activist causes and would appreciate that their findings have moral implications, while many activists respect the distinct role that scientific ecology should and does play in modeling reality rather than making moral arguments. However, the difference remains important. Ecology as the complicated pursuit of truth about the ways organisms and ecosystems are organized is the realm of scientific experts, and while it may have much to teach everyone about the world we share, it is not a project to which everyone can contribute.

Ecology as a moral argument about interconnectedness, on the other hand, is broadly democratic: It teaches a lesson that affects everyone equally. If everything is interconnected and everyone is called to embrace and act on this truth, then ecology belongs to all people. However, this is a much less specific and detailed claim than the findings of scientific ecology, and it is much more difficult to capture the complexity and richness of the world simply by emphasizing the world's interconnectedness.

For instance, many religious interpreters of "ecology" emphasize holism and interconnectedness by suggesting that ecosystems make up a harmonious system in which everything has a "natural" or "proper" place. This sort of claim simply cannot be corroborated by the science of ecology, which emphasizes that the Earth is characterized by open, evolving systems made up of a nuanced interplay of competition, struggle, and cooperation. Along similar lines, many scientific ecologists critique religious interpretations that assume ecological systems are static, that there is a true and absolute "equilibrium" to which nature can be restored. Most contemporary ecology refutes this claim, describing ecosystems as inevitably and always in flux, constantly changing. Ecosystems change and evolve because they are formed by the steady exchange of energies and materials through time.[3]

In the field of religion and ecology, ecology is both a subdiscipline of scientific expertise and a broad claim about the nature of reality. In different texts and different traditions, these ecologies will have different priorities, and it is vital to mark the difference and make decisions about which approach to ecology will be given the most attention and emphasis.

4A

What is the relationship between the science of ecology (an attempt to understand the world pursued by scientific experts) and the metaphysical claim of ecology (a universal lesson based on the interconnectedness of all things)?

Nature as common and contested ground

As both a branch of natural science and a moral claim about the interconnectedness of reality, ecology is based on assertions about what is *real*. When researchers observe the behavior of ants or antelopes, they are working to explain the world we all share, to make models that describe reality in useful ways. When religious leaders and activists preach that interconnectedness can transform human behavior, they are grounding their arguments in an understanding of earth's ecosystems and the cosmos as a whole. Both of these approaches to ecology make claims about nature.

However, "nature" is yet another complicated and contested word that raises a number of questions and arguments. A key question is: Are human beings and our behaviors natural? On one hand, it seems not, as there are important differences between our species and all others. We have taken a dominant role on the planet in a way no other creature has managed. Human beings create technologies that profoundly transform the world and its materials in unprecedented ways. Furthermore, we are capable of self-reflection and make conscious decisions about our actions in a way that may be unique. For these reasons, many people think of human beings as separate from the rest of the world, and think of "nature" as the reality beyond us, the world of forests, animals, and atmospheres unaffected by human beings and human culture. From this perspective, nature is that which is outside human control and influence.

On the other hand, it is beyond doubt or debate in scientific circles that human beings evolved from other creatures: We are a species like all others, and while our reach and influence may be dominant, this can be understood as part of an ongoing cycle of competition and relationship that occurs in all ecological systems. While it is true that our technology changes our environments in profound ways, we are not the only species that has an impact: beaver dams interrupt the flow of rivers, algae can profoundly change the chemical and biological character of rivers and bodies of water, and bee pollination drastically shapes the distribution of plants in many ecosystems. While human beings seem more self-conscious and intelligent than the other animals we encounter, work on primates, whales, dolphins, and elephants suggests sophisticated forms of communication, play, grief, and many characteristics that hint at something like thought and language. Furthermore, many human actions can still be understood as heavily influenced by instinct, impulse, and chemistry rather than by intention and reason. Thus, there are grounds to argue that human beings are a part of nature, that we are ourselves natural.

Whether nature is understood as distinct from or related to human cultures, the *idea* of nature is indisputably a product of human culture. When we talk about the natural world, we reflect the values and assumptions of our societies. This means that nature has social implications, and that discussions of nature reveal much about the ways we justify and understand cultural systems and human actions. "Nature" is a word invented and used by human beings, a word which has been frequently misused by those with power against those without it. It is a word that has historically contained a lot of power. For example, ecofeminists have pointed out that patriarchal societies tend to think of women as intricately connected to nature, and that justifications for subjecting the land to human will are often linked to justifications for subjecting women to men's will. Nature is also used in patriarchal contexts to argue that the "natural" place for women is in the home. When women are considered natural, nature tends to suggest inferiority.

Along similar lines, Native American and other postcolonial activists have noted that European settlers dismissed the original inhabitants of other continents as "uncivilized" and therefore "natural." This attitude justified denying these peoples basic property and human rights: Because indigenous peoples were seen as less civilized, they were treated like animals. A similar impulse can be found when sympathetic colonizers sought out "noble savages" who could teach civilized whites how better to live as "nature" intended. Contemporary indigenous peoples face the same stereotype with a different impact, as they are often assumed to be "closer to nature" and therefore uninterested in or unqualified for the trappings of technological culture.

So, nature is not just about reality beyond human beings, it is also about how that reality has been used to shape, justify, and disguise cultural choices about how human beings treat and relate to one another.

These complications and challenges have led many scholars to turn away from "nature." The word is fairly rare in the work of most ecological scientists because it is so broad and imprecise, because it is politically controversial, and because it is increasingly difficult to find any place or creature on earth that is natural in the sense of not being influenced and shaped in some way by human activity. In a 1997 article that chronicles "The Human Domination of Earth's Ecosystems," for instance, four scientists observed that "no ecosystem on Earth's surface is free of pervasive human influence," noting that human actions have changed the air, water, and land of the entire planet, and so all systems and all creatures are shaped by human culture (Vitousek *et al.* 1997: 494). If nature is that which is beyond human influence, there is no nature left on our planet.

This was the argument behind one of the first popular books written about global climate change, Bill McKibben's *The End of Nature* (1989). Most of McKibben's book is taken up by reporting the facts about climate change: Human industrial activity releases enormous amounts of climate-changing gases, which trap heat energy and thereby change the earth's atmosphere in fundamental and unpredictable ways. While reporting these facts, however, McKibben also notes that climate change marks a broad shift in our relationship with the Earth: "We have changed the atmosphere, and that will change the weather. The temperature and rainfall are no longer to be entirely the work of some separate, uncivilizable force, but instead in part a product of our habits, our economies, our ways of life" (1989:47). McKibben suggests that it is no longer possible to think of the world as bigger than or beyond us, and so that idea of nature is no longer relevant.

Historian William Cronon responds to McKibben's argument by suggesting that nature has not ended because in fact it never really existed. Cronon argues that there is no sense romanticizing pristine and untouched wilderness, because humans have never lived in or with such a place: "everything we know about environmental history suggests that people have been manipulating the natural world on various scales for as long as we have a record of their passing" (1996: 83). There is no wilderness in recorded history that was not influenced by humanity.

Of course, Cronon does not mean to suggest that there is nothing outside of our species. He is aware that Earth existed and thrived for countless millennia before humans evolved; forests flourished, trees fell and made sounds long before humans appeared. Still, Cronon points out, "wilderness" and "nature" are human constructs, ideas in our minds. Such ideas could not exist until human beings developed them. If nature is something that people attempt to observe and understand it cannot be something entirely separate from people. Indeed, Cronon argues, to celebrate nature as a world without us is to set ourselves up for disappointment, because human beings will never experience a world that does not contain human beings.

While they disagree on exact definitions, McKibben and Cronon agree that we can no longer talk about nature as distinct from human intervention. However, there remains an argument for such talk, because many people have long celebrated the ideal of a pristine, wild natural world. Indeed, in one of the pioneering works in religion and ecology, Catherine Albanese teases out a theme of "nature religion" in American history, looking at figures and movements as diverse as Thomas Jefferson, Henry David Thoreau, Christian Scientists, and ecofeminist paganism. Albanese does not argue that these figures were all members of the same religious tradition, but rather identifies a trend in American history, a "symbolic center and the cluster of beliefs, behaviors and values that encircles it," which she names "nature religion" (1990: 7). Nature, she finds, provides a theme in the religiosity of the peoples of North America. This raises questions about whether such a pervasive and powerful idea is as mortal or as meaningless as McKibben and Cronon suggest.

Another defense of nature comes from a certain kind of environmentalism, that which seeks to protect the natural world as a separate and distinct reality. When the Sierra Club prints calendars to inspire and mobilize membership, it chooses pictures of mighty sequoias, panda bears, and tropical rainforests, precisely because these images feel "natural." When people advocate for parks in cities, they are creating a managed system of trees and grass, but they frequently appreciate these regions precisely because they feel more "natural," because they seem to be an escape from the rest of urban life. It may be that there is no ecosystem free from human influence, but the idea of nature still seems real and relevant to many people. Those who organize fights against climate change know this, and so many continue to appeal to "nature" and "wilderness" as what must be saved. McKibben and Cronon's arguments against "nature" need to be weighed against the rhetorical power of the idea.

When scholars of religion and ecology talk about "ecology," we refer to the real world around us. But careful thought about that world, about nature, reveals that it is complicated and difficult to understand, and that our relationships to the world around us must be thoughtfully studied and re-examined. Taking ecology seriously means taking nothing for granted.

4B

Does the word "nature" have a useful meaning? Is it helpful to talk about the world beyond humanity and human culture? Did such a world ever exist? Do you think it exists today?

Ecologies and religions

Despite the many different uses of the terms, most people who are concerned with ecology and nature agree that there is an urgent and immediate reason to study both today: the rampant and drastic degradation of the environments upon which all life depends. Complexities and disagreements about ecology are important primarily because they mark out different responses to such degradation. Those who stress ecology as a science tend to emphasize the importance of expertise and technical knowledge in diagnosing and solving environmental problems, while those who think of ecology as a broad interconnectedness are more interested in changing the ways all people think about the world around them. Those who believe ecology can refer to a natural world beyond humanity frequently do so out of a desire to preserve that world, while those who critique the idea of nature often do so in order to inspire more responsible management of and interaction with the nonhuman world, or to defend people and places that have been ignored or harmed in previous attempts to save nature.

One more debate about how ecology influences responses to environmental degradation is specific to religious communities: Is environmental degradation a problem to which religions are prepared to respond constructively? If religious people seek to do something about this problem, are they best served by *recovering* wisdom in the traditions they have inherited, by *reforming* those traditions in light of the new situation, or by *replacing* traditional religion in favor of something new and more suited to the current crisis? This question has been asked in different ways of virtually every religious tradition currently practiced, but for sake of clarity it is worth taking just one example: Christianity. Of course, many other traditions are certainly worthy of focus, but scholarship on religion and ecology began in large part because of an influential essay in 1967 that blamed the environmental crisis on Christianity (White 1967); since then, scholars and practitioners have produced a large array of literature attempting to recover, reform, and replace Christianity in light of ecological crisis.

Zoologist and evangelical theologian Calvin DeWitt, for instance, writes extensively about the validity of core Christian ideas as a response to environmental degradation, and clearly believes that his faith tradition has the resources necessary to constructively respond to the carelessness and inattention that have led to ecological devastation. In an essay included in the volume *Christianity and Ecology*, DeWitt argues that the Bible contains divinely inspired wisdom about creation, and that if we pay attention to this text we can learn to relate to other creatures as God intends. A careful reading of the Bible, DeWitt argues, reveals "that authority over things belongs to the Author of those things: we have no authority to destroy what we ourselves did not create; destruction of a grand master's work by its onlooker, beholder, or curator may be a disgrace to their Creator"

(2000: 297). For DeWitt, a traditional belief in the sovereignty of God as creator leads clearly to an awareness that contemporary environmental degradation is blasphemous.

DeWitt also finds in the Bible clear instructions for how to move toward a better relationship between human beings and other creatures. Citing the second chapter of the Book of Genesis, he notes that human beings are expected to "keep" God's garden, which means that human beings have been placed by God into relationship with all other creatures, called to mutually serve one another and the world as a whole. The job of human beings, DeWitt argues, is to ensure that all creatures can "maintain their proper connections—with members of their own kind, with the many other kinds with which they interact, with the soil, air, and water upon which they depend for their life and fruitfulness" (2000: 303). In other words, DeWitt finds the ecological lesson of interconnectedness in the Bible. For him, the resources to respond to environmental degradation already exist within the tradition; they must simply be heard. DeWitt seems to believe that the response of Christians to ecology should be a recovery of the ecological wisdom waiting to be found in their scriptures.

A markedly different approach can be found in the introduction to the same volume, which notes that Christianity has not always lived up to such high principles and may benefit from insight and adaptation from outside. The editors, Dieter Hessel and Rosemary Radford Ruether, call for an "ecological reformation" of Christianity, which begins with an admission of the "fundamental failures" of Christian traditions, particularly the failure "to recognize intricate and interdependent relationships involving humankind with the rest of nature." In order to overcome this historical failure, they argue that Christianity must be rethought, that people of faith must "utilize knowledge gained from contemporary biophysical sciences" in order to respond realistically to environmental degradation (2000: xxxvii). Unlike DeWitt, Hessel and Ruether do not assume that their tradition provides clear access to the will of God, and so they do not assume that the tradition will provide the necessary answers to the challenge of environmental degradation. Instead, Christianity should adapt to contemporary challenges; it is a living, developing, and flexible tradition.

The goal of reformation strikes a middle path between assuming that the tradition has all the answers and that it has none: It assumes that there is validity in what is inherited but also that some dimensions of this will need to be rethought or reanalyzed in light of contemporary reality. Thus, a call for an "ecological reformation" is an attempt to emphasize the validity of the tradition while also leaving room for significant change in light of ecological insights and environmental degradation. For authors like Hessel and Ruether, Christianity is a vital and relevant tradition, but it must change and develop if it is to remain so,

A third approach does not seek to recover or reform Christian traditions, but instead moves away from them in favor of something more suited to contemporary problems. One example of this approach comes in the work of Bron Taylor, who focuses his attention on "dark green religions," which he defines as those that develop "from a deep sense of belonging to and connectedness in nature, while perceiving the earth and its living systems to be sacred and interconnected" (2009a: 13). He writes that religions like Christianity might become "green," but they will "view their environmental responsibilities as, at most, one of a variety of ethical responsibilities," and so will not prioritize the natural world as much as *dark* green religions (Taylor 2009b: 90). Taylor worries that this will not be a sufficient response to contemporary environmental degradation, that "most of the world's major religions have worldviews that are antithetical to and compete with the worldviews and ethics found in dark green religion" (2009a: 178). He therefore catalogues and advocates religious perspectives that are based in and fundamentally aligned to the natural world rather than traditional religion.

Taylor does not spend much time analyzing Christianity or any other major religion, but instead focuses on a move toward the "dark green religions" which place sacred value in the world of nature. Such religions are rooted in ancient traditions of animism and nature spirituality, but Taylor is primarily interested in their expression among contemporary environmentalists, who have combined these traditions with the insights of contemporary scientific ecology. "Dark green religion" represents for him a willingness to develop a new spirituality for a new reality, drawing on the old only insofar as it serves the cause of environmental conservation.

Like the advocates of an "ecological reformation," Bron Taylor values flexibility and responsiveness, but unlike them he does not seem to believe that a tradition like Christianity will be as flexible as is required by contemporary challenges. Unlike DeWitt, he does not believe that there are inviolable revelations or sacred texts that will provide clear and final answers. Thus, he replaces traditions like Christianity with a call for a different and—from his perspective—far more ecological religion.

These examples represent three distinct ways of relating ecology to a traditional religion like Christianity. DeWitt recovers the ecological themes that he believes have always existed in his religion. Hessel and Ruether call for a reformation of their tradition, which preserves its key elements but adapts others in light of contemporary realities. Taylor replaces mainstream religions like Christianity with a different kind of religion grounded much more firmly in the natural world understood according to contemporary ecology. The same sorts of debates—between recovery, reformation, and replacement—go on among Hindus, Buddhists, Muslims, Jews, Taoists, Indigenous traditionalists, and among many other religious and spiritual groups.

4C

Religious people are being called to take ecology seriously in light of environmental degradation, but does this mean a recovery of the wisdom inherent in religious traditions, a reformation of those traditions, or an effort to replace them with more suitable and relevant traditions?

Complexities in religion and ecology

These debates—about how equipped traditional religions are to respond to environmental degradation, about whether "nature" is something separate from or part of human cultures, and about whether ecology is primarily the purview of scientists or all people—reflect live questions in religion and ecology. The three authors of this chapter vary as to where we fall on these issues, and we value the conversations that emerge out of our disagreements. As you continue to examine this field of religion and ecology, perhaps you will develop clear preferences on how you use the term ecology, how you think about the relationship between humans and nature, and about how you can imagine religious traditions responding to environmental degradation. Alternatively, you might find that a pluralistic approach that adaptively shifts between multiple answers will better suit you.

However, in understanding this scholarly field, your first response to these options should not be to decide which one is right, but rather to recognize the strength of each position and therefore the complexity of thinking about how diverse groups of believers and scholars are responding to ecological realities. Recognizing and appreciating the diversity of responses available to ecology, the natural world, and environmental degradation is a vitally important part of understanding both religion and ecology.

Notes

1 We thank our friend and colleague Evan Berry for sharing his research on Haeckel's scientific and spiritual goals.
2 For a clear, introductory discussion of the science that emphasizes this categorization, see Dodson *et al.* (1998).
3 For a discussion of this "new paradigm" in ecology and its implications for theology and religious studies, see Lodge and Hamlin (2006).

References

Albanese, C. (1990) *Nature Religion in America: From the Algonkian Indians to the New Age*, Chicago: University of Chicago Press.
Allen, T.F.H. and T.W. Hoekstra (1992) *Toward a Unified Ecology*, New York: Columbia University Press.

Berry, T. (1999) *The Great Work: Our Way into the Future*, New York: Bell Tower.

Cronon, W. (ed.) (1996) *Uncommon Ground: Toward Reinventing Nature*, New York: W.W. Norton & Co.

DeWitt, C. (2000) "Behemoth and Batrachians in the Eye of God: Responsibility to Other Kinds in Biblical Perspective," in D. Hessel and R. Ruether (eds) *Christianity and Ecology: Seeking the Well-Being of Earth and Humans*, Cambridge, MA: Harvard University Press.

Dodson, S.I., T.F.H. Allen, S.R. Carpenter, A.R. Ives, R.L. Jeanne, J.F. Kitchell, N.E. Langston, and M.G. Turner (1998) *Ecology*, New York: Oxford University Press.

Haeckel, E. (1866) *Generelle Morphologie der Organismen*, Berlin: Reimer.

——(1895) *Monism as Connecting Religion and Science: The Confession of Faith of a Man of Science*, trans. J. Gilchrist, London: Adam and Charles Black.

Hessel, D.T. and R.R. Ruether (eds) (2000) *Christianity and Ecology: Seeking the Well-being of Earth and humans*, Cambridge, MA: Harvard University Press.

Lodge, D.M. and C. Hamlin (2006) *Religion and the New Ecology: Environmental Responsibility in a World in Flux*, Notre Dame, IN: University of Notre Dame Press.

McKibben, B. (1989) *The End of Nature*, New York: Random House.

Ro, Y. (1998) "Ecological Implications of Yi Yulgok's Cosmology," in Mary Evelyn Tucker and John Berthrong (eds) *Confucianism and Ecology: The Interrelation of Heaven, Earth, and Humans*, Cambridge, MA: Harvard University Press.

Taylor, B. (2009a) *Dark Green Religion: Nature Spirituality and the Planetary Future*, Berkeley: University of California Press.

——(2009b) "From the Ground Up: Dark Green Religion and the Environmental Future," in D.K. Swearer (ed.) *Ecology and the Environment: Perspectives from the Humanities*, Cambridge, MA: Harvard University Press.

Vitousek, P.M., H.A. Mooney, J. Lubchenco, and J.M. Melillo (1997) "Human Domination of Earth's Ecosystems," *Science* 277: 494–99.

White Jr., L. (1967) "The Historical Roots of Our Ecologic Crisis," *Science* 155 (3767): 1203–07.

Further reading

Adams, C.J. (ed.) (1993) *Ecofeminism and the Sacred*, New York: Continuum.

Lodge, D.M. and C. Hamlin (2006) *Religion and the New Ecology: Environmental Responsibility in a World in Flux*, Notre Dame, IN: University of Notre Dame Press.

Latour, B. (2004) *The Politics of Nature: How to Bring the Sciences into Democracy*, Cambridge, MA: Harvard University Press.

Soper, K. (1995) *What Is Nature? Culture, Politics, and the Nonhuman*, Malden, MA: Blackwell.

Weaver, J. (ed.) (1996) *Defending Mother Earth: Native American Perspectives on Environmental Justice*, Maryknoll, NY: Orbis Books.

Worster, D. (1994) *Nature's Economy: A History of Ecological Ideas*, New York: Cambridge University Press.

Chapter 5

Ecology

A dialogue

Celia Deane-Drummond and Lisa Sideris

Celia Deane-Drummond:

Ernst Haeckel's thought on what ecology might mean is a useful starting point to any discussion about ecology, nature and environment. His idea that ecology said something about the "order of nature" as well as something about the virtues through which humanity might live in relationship with it still has resonance today. The temptation, it seems to me, is that scientists, *qua* scientists, may be reluctant to make any claims about the moral implications of their science. This is sometimes confusing for an audience, who, on the one hand, want to know what the science might say because of its perceived objective authority and, on the other, want to know the implications of those findings in practical terms.

Also important is the shift from an understanding of ecology as a balanced network of relationships, in the way Haeckel imagined, to something far more fluid and in flux. If we ignore this shift entirely, philosophers and theologians will go on thinking of ecology in terms of this balance, or "order of nature," and find ways of promoting it. However, in my view, a theologian has to take account of what that science might say, even if, when it comes to ethical implications, theology is ready to say something on a more secure footing compared with scientists.

Haeckel's discussion of human virtues is a great way into this ethical discussion, because a discussion of virtue unites diverse religious perspectives. Diversity between these perspectives is important, of course, and if we are sensitive to different cultural contexts for religious traditions, then something of that diversity has to stand. At the same time, in view of the enormity of the practical problems facing humanity, the solution is not simply to go "deep green" in a deliberate turning away from different traditions of faith, intoxicated by novelty. Instead, we must find ways in which common ground might be sought through an appreciation of traditions. One such thread of common ground is recognition of the importance of the virtues of wisdom, compassion, and respect, alongside justice, temperance, fortitude and hope.

There are no doubt many other virtues as well, but perhaps it's worth focusing on just one, wisdom. We can find this virtue, and its emphasis on deliberation, judgment, and action, in many religious traditions. Where there are difficult or complex decisions to be made about environmental responsibility, I believe that wisdom may have something to offer. In the classic Christian tradition, wisdom meant taking account of the relationship with God, as well as other relationships.

One reason I support appreciation and recovery of classic traditions is that I do not think any tradition is static or constant. To study a tradition is to revisit it. This means, in part, to recognize what might have gone wrong within it, and to call people to change. This is a challenge not so much to the tradition itself, but to the ways in which it has been appropriated.

A tendency towards anthropocentrism in Christian theology is a good example of what I mean by this revisiting of tradition. Many of the strongest critiques of traditional theology have been against anthropocentric readings, that is, readings that seem to give human beings a higher status compared with other creatures. Often, the argument goes, this is linked to patriarchy, such that both women and nature are oppressed or excluded from the public domain. Some seek to solve this problem by divinizing the natural world, but I worry that this goes too far from the tradition, and so creates a further gulf between traditional religious believers and ecological responsibility. Instead, I would press for an understanding of humanity as creatures alongside other creatures, but also realize that humanity has particular powers and thus responsibilities. One of these responsibilities is an exercise of virtues not just for human flourishing, but also for the flourishing of all creatures.

Lisa Sideris:

In a discussion of nature, ecology, and the environment, nature is the term of greatest importance. In my view, the most significant fact about nature, whether one is religious or not, is that humans did not create it. Darwin's theory of natural selection tell us how it works, for example, but, as Darwin himself realized and as many readers of his book have noted, the *Origin of Species* was not really about the origin of species, in terms of specifying how the first life-forms arose; rather, it was about how they had evolved. Scientists are still working on the questions of how life first arose, but we know that it arose independently of us.

Nature, as I understand it, is an autonomous entity, something that has a distinct identity apart from human culture and creations, human desires, human expectations. It is precisely because nature is in some sense separate from us that we can marvel at it and see it as a source of wonder and awe, an order that, as theologian James Gustafson says, may either sustain or threaten us, and has been known to do both. Nature's value is clearly non-anthropocentric—that is, it is valuable in and of itself, not in relation to us. But, in my view, whether or not one construes nature's value as theo-centric (that is, valuable insofar as God values it) or ecocentric is irrelevant, so long as the center of value lies outside of us. Either way, the important fact is that humans didn't create it. Nature was not made for us or by us. That is precisely why nature, as "not-us," has meaning for us.

Deane-Drummond:

I agree with you, Lisa, that Darwin's theory by natural selection shows us something of the value of "nature" quite apart from human beings, if by "nature" you mean something other than humanity. But defining nature in this way presupposes a certain objectivity that is most characteristic of sci-ence and scientific method. It also presupposes a historical view of nature; that is, nature is valued because it evolves prior to human beings. Yet, and I am sure you agree as well, Darwin's theory also emphasizes particularly the importance of viewing different species as in continuum with each other. This is why ecology is related to evolutionary theory, since ecology is about the interrelationships in space, whereas Darwin's theory is about inter-relationships in time. Both challenge in some sense a clear demarcation of humans from other creatures, while, at the same time, challenging, as you suggest, any thought that other creatures are simply there for human use or as a resource. One of the characteristics of humans is an ability to think about and reflect on such things as universals, in a way that marks us out from other species.

Human religious instinct is also different from other creatures' instinct, in that the evolution of religious tendencies in humans came about relatively late in the cultural explosion of our early hominid ancestors. However, I think it is also very important to stress the social nature of animals, that cooperation evolves early on, and that basic rules for justice-making and moral order can also be found in other social species. This means that our distinctiveness as moral creatures is not as unique as we might suppose.

Sideris:

I worry that the more humans turn nature into just an extension of our culture—which is one way of describing what the environmental crisis entails—the less meaning it has. The less meaning it has, the less we will be attached to it. Certainly, there is a kernel of anthropocentrism in this state-ment, but I would still maintain that what allows us to be captivated and enchanted with nature is its otherness and separateness from us. In this sense, I follow thinkers such as Rachel Carson and Bill McKibben who understand a sense of wonder with nature as prior to what we call environmental con-cern. Nature confronts us as mystery. By this I mean not that we cannot ever understand it but that scientific understanding of nature does not exhaust its meaning and cannot dispel its wonder. Environmentalism alone, in the absence of wonder (whether wonder is religiously grounded or not), can lead us to view nature primarily as a problem.

As Gabriel Marcel (1976) notes, *mystery* and *problem* are not the same thing. Without the sense of wonder at what nature is, we are in danger of seeing nature primarily as a problem to be solved, either in terms of solving environmental problems, or more broadly in the sense of believing that science progressively solves nature's mysteries, as a scientist like Richard Dawkins would have us believe. The Dawkinsian view of science and nature is one that Rachel Carson explicitly rejected half a century ago. In my opinion, she was exactly right. Science can to some extent help us understand nature as a problem, as with helping us understand environmental problems or, more generally, in helping us understand how nature works. When understood appropriately, science can even increase our already existing sense of wonder at nature.

But wonder at nature must be the foundation for appropriate ethical engagement with it. It is nature that sets limits (and creates possibilities) for human life. By respecting those limits, we reconnect with something meaningful. Depending on its objects, wonder may thus be virtuous or not. Wonder at science itself, for example, over and above nature, strikes me as problematic because it may simply flatter us. As Carson would put it, it can easily foster a kind of idolatry, an intoxication with our own powers.

Deane-Drummond:

I agree that a focus on wonder is crucial. Religious ethics is not simply about an encouragement in the exercise of the virtues; it is also about trying to create a different ethos, or space, where it is easier to make responsible decisions. Wonder is relevant here because it motivates people to pay attention, to rethink their view of the world, and to take the time to make responsible decisions.

It is also important to mention that we should not rule out the possibility that other creatures may experience some sort of wonder as well. Often, in primates at least, this seems to be in response to the very kind of aesthetic experiences that humans respond to, such as beauty in the rest of the natural world. Although, as far as I know, much of this is anecdotal, it challenges humanity to think about other creatures in a more sympathetic way. Of course such experiences are not going to be the same for other animals, but the possibility of some shared experience perhaps makes empathetic relations more likely. I have been influenced here by the work of Marc Bekoff and other animal ethologists.

As you note, we see a type of wonder in the practice of science. Many scientists—certainly including ecologists—are first motivated to begin an investigation by wonder. The early scientist Francis Bacon made this point when he married wonder to curiosity. I discuss this and other aspects of wonder, including that experienced by ecologists like E.O. Wilson, in my book *Wonder and Wisdom* (2006).

So, I agree with you that if we do not learn to love the natural world we will not really care about it beyond the bare needs of our own survival. Perhaps some discussions about climate change can begin from basic survival, but an appeal to nobler emotions of wonder and respect for the natural world provides a more enduring motivation. Wonder is also found across different religious traditions, as well as outside these traditions. In Christianity, this means that theologians should work to connect human wonder with insights about God, particularly through liturgy, because this can begin to build a way of seeing the world that fosters interrelation.

Wonder is also important because it creates the aesthetic space in which we might think about other possible worlds, freed in some sense from the relentless desire for consumer goods that pervades the modern mind-set. This is why many religious commentators think that the current crisis expressed as climate change is a moral and spiritual crisis, for it expresses what Alastair McIntosh (2008) calls a pathological, addictive tendency to ecocide—human beings go on behaving in the same way, even though they know full well that it is damaging them and all around them.

I think this indirect, theological approach to ecology will have a more lasting impact on environmental ethics than just telling people that they are not doing enough to reduce their carbon footprint. Making people feel guilty or fearful is never a good enough motivation for change. Instead, a practical journey into contact with the natural world, however minimal this might be, can reignite a passion for an alternative.

However, I would also argue that wonder on its own is too free floating to be helpful if it does not combine with wisdom. Wisdom in this sense is an awareness of the respect owed to the natural world and its creatures, which leads us to ask, "What decisions need to be taken, and when?" Wisdom moves beyond simply affirming nature, encouraging people to act responsibly and appropriately. Wisdom is practical.

Practical wisdom also points ahead to the more political aspects of ecology that so often come to the surface in religious discussion. For practical wisdom, according to the classic tradition of Aquinas, gives a shape to what it might mean to exercise compassion or justice. It is no good just thinking we need to exercise compassion toward every living creature; practical wisdom suggests the manner in which we can *act* compassionately and appropriately in real-life situations.

As a minimum, all creatures need to be recipients of what I would term eco-justice. Environmental injustice—the disproportionate suffering of those people who are the most marginalized and impoverished—must be considered as part of any discussion of ecology. It is not enough, in other words, just to concentrate on the protection of biodiversity if this means that human beings are ignored. By the same measure, though, so called development programs that seek to improve human lives but do not take biodiversity into account are missing a holistic appreciation of what human flourishing might mean.

These matters are vital in political and economic negotiations about environmental issues, and so someone must speak for those nations and peoples who lack the political or economic authority to speak for themselves. This is a matter for justice-making, a moral issue, and an opportunity for religions to make a contribution to public debate by advocating for those who have too often been ignored. Ecotheology is therefore not just a concern for its own communities and practices; it also seeks a place at the negotiating table of international relations.

Sideris:

Another dimension of wonder is an appreciation for those aspects of the natural world that do not conform to our expectations and do not strike us as "perfect" or beneficent arrangements. That sense of wonder is sustained by human interactions with nature as an autonomous and mysterious entity that underscores our relative insignificance, and thus can instill in us a sense of humility.

So, what we stand to lose by despoiling the natural environment is, as Bill McKibben would argue, perhaps not the end of nature *per se*—something will persist without us—but the end of the idea of nature or the end of a certain perspective on ourselves. So, while I recognize that nature is in part an idea, that idea is critically important to discerning who humans are *vis-à-vis* nature and what is valuable in nature. Rain that falls more heavily or in new places as a result of climate change is still rain; it may still nourish our crops and children may still splash it the mud-puddles it makes. It may even be beautiful. But its meaning has changed. It is now rain that, in McKibben's words, has "become a subset of human activity" (1989: 76). A natural world dominated by humans and human creations is a world in which humans are all alone. That's what the end of nature means.

Yet, to talk about "the end" of nature leaves us with a feeling of immense hopelessness. We should not end there, because I agree with Celia that fear-based approaches, or appeals to our feelings of guilt, will not be successful without a strong, cultivated sense of wonder. Ideally, this cultivation should begin with childhood, though too much of our environmental education of children today begins simply with an education in fear and loss—loss of the rainforest, of polar bears, of a comfortable climate for humans.

Efforts to halt climate change, in particular, too often take the tack of fear and despair. Among those who accept the evidence for climate change and want to do their part to help, fear induces feelings of helplessness and anxiety; among those who deny that climate change is real, fear-based approaches allow them to dismiss the issue as just so much more "apocalyptic," gloom and doom rhetoric.

As you suggest, environmental problems stem in part from a fundamental crisis of character. But changes of character have to come from within individuals, and for that to happen we have to comprehend all that we stand to *gain*—not just what we have to give up—by living differently. One thing we may gain is a life that is actually well lived—a good life, understood in the terms of the virtue tradition that you are drawing upon, Celia.

The alternative vision—and alternative lifestyle—that we need in order to address environmental problems must be couched in terms other than mere sacrifice. Learning to live within natural limits ought to be seen as something joyful. Instead of focusing on what we have to give up (our cars, the global availability of goods, our superstores, etc.) we should consider the gains: reconnection to local communities and bioregions; the joy of producing at least a part of one's own food or fuel, rather than passively consuming; the simple satisfaction of physical labor. Wonder gives us the energy, the moral motivation to do this work. Perhaps this is what Celia means, in part, by connecting "wisdom" to wonder. Wonder at nature can help to engender a host of related "environmental" virtues—generosity, humility, simplicity, farsightedness—that enable us to flourish and allow future generations a chance of flourishing as well. Those virtues, when cultivated, can indeed be their own reward. They enable us to live within natural limits, to develop daily rituals that tap into what is wondrous about nature, without destroying it.

Like you, Celia, though perhaps for different reasons, I would not call for "divinizing" nature. In my view, the danger is not that such a move might alienate traditional believers (however true that might be), but that our wonder at nature turns out to be ultimately or primarily wonder at God. Such wonder is only secondarily wonder at nature, as a mere stepping stone or signpost to God, or to some more perfect world to come.

This is a point at which I think we disagree: I am increasingly persuaded by the argument that nontheistic forms of wonder are more potent. Wonder ultimately directed at God is a kind of conversation stopper: Wonder "ends" in and with God in more than one sense. I worry that theistic wonder answers too many questions about the objects of wonder. In this sense, it becomes something like wonder at science, where one's wonder is directed at the explanation of the mystery that science provides, and not at nature. I worry that this is similar to the Dawkinsian approach to science discussed above.

"Theism sees God as the maximally wonder-evoking being," R.W. Hepburn (1984: 142) writes. "High though the claims of theism can legitimately be pitched in relation to wonder, they can be pitched excessively high" (1984: 143)—so high that they tend to miss nature itself. I essentially agree with Hepburn's argument that "existential wonder can be evoked by the pure thought of the world's existence as contingent and inexplicable: hence in the absence of any theistic surmise" (1984: 143). In other words, wonder at nature itself is possible—and perhaps preferable—to wonder at nature as God's work.

I do not mean to say that nature is inexplicable in the sense that we are in a state of complete ignorance and mystification. Rather, nature remains inexplicable in that we have no answer to the basic wonder-generating question of why there is something rather than nothing. Theism, I fear, tends to answer that question with too great finality and too much assurance.

Deane-Drummond:

I do defend the idea of wonder as opening up the possibility of religious experience, and I would argue that there is no need to consider theism as promoting any sort of separation from "nature" in the way you seem to suggest. The kind of theism I would want to defend is not Gnostic, pre-supposing separation of spirit from matter, but fully, deeply incarnational. This is, of course, a Christian position, namely that God became deeply incarnate in the material world—but it is also a very ancient tradition, going back to the first centuries of the early Church. This means that in experiencing wonder in the natural world, those with faith also experience it as religious awe.

The linking of awe with wonder goes back to Augustine, but it is also common in many of the nature mystics, and in the poetry of the Jesuit priest Gerard Manley Hopkins. For him, and others like him, wonder was about finding God in all things. This reinforced a commitment to pay attention to the natural world, a commitment that is the basis of all true science, and, I would argue, the ground for environmental responsibility. So it seems to me that wonder and religion work together, rather than apart from each other. The experience of such wonder in engagement with other creatures reinforces respect for their uniqueness as creatures, rather than acting as a distraction from that uniqueness. Wonder apart from knowledge of God is, of course, still quite possible, but it points to forms of natural theology, that is, it has resonance with religious experience, whether it is acknowledged or not. Further, I would suggest that a uniquely human way of wondering has the possibility of a more self-conscious experience of religious awe that can serve to intensify love and commitment to the natural world. While I do not deny that the possibility of a detached form of mysticism is present, this remains a temptation rather than a necessity.

The danger of a separation of wonder from theism (though certainly not inevitable) is that human beings will not find in such absorption with nature the means through which to hope; the natural world may even replace God as the fundamental commitment of humanity. As such it becomes another idol, perhaps rather more desirable than a consumer culture, but an idol nonetheless.

References

Hepburn, R.W. (1984) *"Wonder" and Other Essays: Eight Studies in Aesthetics and Neighbouring Fields*, Edinburgh: Edinburgh University Press.

McIntosh, A. (2008) *Hell and High Water: Climate Change, Hope, and the Human Condition*, Edinburgh: Birlinn.

McKibben, Bill (1989) *The End of Nature*, New York: Random House.

Marcel, Gabriel (1976) *Being and Having: An Existentialist Diary*, Gloucester, MA: Peter Smith.

Further reading

Bekoff, Marc (2002) *Minding Animals: Awareness, Emotions, and Heart*, Oxford and New York: Oxford University Press.

Deane-Drummond, C. (2006) *Wonder and Wisdom: Conversations in Science, Spirituality and Theology*, West Conshohocken, PA: Templeton.

—(2008) *Ecotheology*, London: Darton, Longman and Todd Ltd.

Sideris, L. (2003) *Environmental Ethics, Ecological Theology, and Natural Selection*, New York: Columbia.

—(2006) "Religion and the Meaning of Ecology," in Roger Gottlieb (ed.) *The Oxford Handbook of Religion and Ecology*, Oxford: Oxford University Press.

Sideris, L. and K.D. Moore (eds) (2008) *Rachel Carson: Legacy and Challenge*, Albany, NY: SUNY.

Chapter 6

Case study

Images of "land" among Muslim farmers in the US

Eleanor Finnegan

Images of land among Muslims are as diverse as the groups that have held them. The Islamic textual tradition concerning land is built upon the idea that land is owned by God and given as a gift to God's creatures. Therefore, people can use land for their benefit if it does not cause excessive harm. For several groups of American Muslims, such as various communities of immigrant and convert Sunni Muslims (including several groups of Sufi Muslims) and the Nation of Islam, farms play an important role in the religious community. For these Muslims, Islamic ideas and practices, as well as the experience of farming, have influenced ideas about land. Among these groups, land has often been a place where Muslims can embody their religious and environmental values and are free to create religious communities, institutions, and identities. It has also helped shape environmental and religious ideas and practices.

The following are excerpts from interviews held at the Dayempur Farm during the summer of 2009. The Dayempur Farm is one of the community institutions of the Sufi group the Dayemi Tariqat. Members follow the teachings of Sheikh Din Muhammad Abdullah Al-Dayemi, an American who was trained by sheikhs in Bangladesh to bring their lineage to the United States. Most members and the sheikh live in Carbondale, Illinois, where the community owns and runs a restaurant, general store, schools, alternative medicine clinic, park, and community house. The community remains connected to Bangladesh and has branches in South Carolina, Colorado, Texas, and Germany.

The farm, which was started when the sheikh moved the community to Illinois in 1995, is located thirty minutes south of Carbondale in Anna. They now own 60 acres, but only cultivate 2.5. There are four full-time employees, every member of the community has to volunteer on the farm at least one day a month, and students in the community's school have lessons on farming once a week. The farm grows herbs, vegetables, fruits, and nuts that are used for communal meals and medicines and in some of the community's businesses. Extras are given to community members or handed out at the store. Between May 2008 and May 2009, the community harvested 1,000 pounds of produce.

The first interview was with Jamal, the staff member responsible for maintaining the buildings and equipment. Trained as an educator, he began working in the community's office when he moved to Carbondale. After becoming more involved with the farm by volunteering for a building project, he was offered a full-time job. In his answers to the following questions, he demonstrates how the land of the farm has many different meanings. As a place to live out one's values, the farm can exemplify the qualities of God, distract from one's spiritual quest, and allow for many kinds of learning.

ELEANOR: Why did you become involved with the farm or with the community in general?

JAMAL: Yeah, those are two different questions. Well, yes and no, they're two different questions. I mean, I would be involved in the community if I weren't involved in the farm. And what drew me here, the simple answer is love …

A deeper thing that keeps me interested or engaged in it [the farm] is because this is a very concrete expression of that core value of how to live or of how to spend energy and feel like it's working and relevant. And for me that's helpful. I had at one point … was considering going down more academic routes and things like that, and it fits for me to have actual physical work as an expression of interests and values and beliefs.

ELEANOR: Have you faced any difficulties since becoming involved with this community?

JAMAL: … Yeah sure. Islam is a path of surrender. That's the kind of whole shtick; that's the whole deal. So if you talk about what surrender means, at its core it's giving up all of your attachments, and our attachments are very tenacious, because they're attachments. I'm attached to thinking I'm a certain this or that. Or, we talk about these five modes of attachment, of being the controller or being the doer or being the owner, being the recipient of the fruits of my actions, um, or, ah, what is my fifth. I'm spacing out. Um, yeah, control, owning, doing, yeah. You get the idea. You know, if the aspiration is to basically let go of those, there's nothing but struggle in that.

I think difficulties, in terms of this work and this project, ignorance is a big one. We've come out of it with really good intentions, but without knowing much of anything and finding it hard, to, ah … I mean we're struggling with this right now. Having our organizational skills, our communication, our prioritizing, our basic material management, all of those things keep pace with our ambition and visions, because we have been good at starting a lot of new things, but it's been hard to have the systems in place and the people in place to maintain them and keep them healthy. You know, we can start an orchard and put trees in the ground, but we didn't really know ahead of time which varieties to pick and how to manage them once they were in the ground. And that kind of thing has come up over and over again, where we'll start a project with the best intentions where we really haven't figured out [chuckles] how to sustain it or how to design it in the best way. So we're becoming better at it …

And there's, you know, simple things of doing. If not everybody's doing it around it, it makes it a little harder to find support or find materials that are appropriate, or find the wisdom or experience around us. Like trying to grow grapes or peaches organically around here, there's nobody who's doing it. So it's really hard.

(Jamal, interview with the author,
August 3, 2009, Anna, IL)

The following excerpts are from an interview with Ra'fi. As soon as he graduated college in 1999, he moved to Carbondale and immediately became involved with the farm. He works at the farm full time and is involved in land management. Having grown up in Puerto Rico before moving to New York in his teens, he is the only staff member who had a background in farming. Like Jamal, he sees the land of the farm as a place to live his ideas and to learn spiritual truths. However, he also reflects on the role of the farm in community building, inspiring others, and shaping his understanding of religious practices.

ELEANOR: How do you understand the project here? Do you see this farm as something that's an environmental project, that's a social project, spiritual project, all of those things?

RA'FI: I see this as something that includes all those things you said, but it's really more for me. It's a way of life. It's a way of building relationships. It's a way of providing for our basic necessities. It's a place for the community aspect to fill its vision in terms of what it means to be sustainable through our food, through our water, through our kind of knowledge of building a land-based project. So it's a place for the community to fulfill its vision and at the same time it's also a place that allows for the exchange of ideas with other people and for the providing [of] some sort of perhaps inspiration, perhaps a modeling, an example that, that the ideas that we try to build out here are not just on to this place as some, some kind of isolated unit, but that can be replicated and implemented into one's own personal life or personal home regardless of where you're at, whether it's the city or the country, so that at least you could draw from something, some aspect of this to make perhaps changes that could be impactful to the environment or to the [mumbles a word] as well. So it carries a lot, the place carries a lot of, it is very multifaceted, but in the most general scope it's really just kind of the whole way of life, that this isn't like you go into your work, this is you're just participating into something that is an extension of your own self.

ELEANOR: Has being involved in the farm influenced your religious ideas or practices at all?

RA'FI: Yes, um [long pause], when we study the history of the path, of course we need to study the history of the Prophet, peace be upon him, what he built in the Medina period of his work. And, when we study that, what we find is this person through his wisdom was able to create, was able to change the course of history, and create an amazing society structure that was never really seen before, definitely not in that part of the world. So I feel like we have … a very rich example to learn from, so the more I study the life of the Prophet Muhammad, peace be upon him, and the more I'm able to see the wisdom of what he was able to create, the more he inspires this work for me. And, by doing that, what ends up happening is that [I] begin to see the work of the farm or creating a land-based [project] as something that is not separate from your daily life. Like, this is a spiritual practice. A spiritual practice doesn't mean that it isn't necessarily exclusive to prayer or meditation but that you can be in communion with God or the spirit, whatever you want to call it, through your very action that you take, and having, making the conscious to keep that in mind and remembering that it's in every aspect of our work. It's a shift in the spiritual view, because so often what we assign as spirituality are those things that fall under, you know, let's say prayer or mediation or reading of scripture. But, I mean that's one expression, and we have that and we do that, but to have the expression of your whole every single thought, every single word, every single action be your prayer, your meditation then, it sets up a different relationship. So, in that sense, it's drastically changed my view of what it means to have spiritual practice, or spiritual ideology, or spiritual life.

Another thing is that, within the same tradition, as we look to the Prophet Muhammad, all of our ancestors have said that in order to have a community that is impactful, you need a land base. Without a land base it's, ah, there's so much you can do and if you go through the history of any revolutionary movement that has had success or has been impactful, you need to look into the land base and what they were able to create on a very grassroots level.

(Ra'fi, interview with the author,
August 3, 2009, Anna, IL)

Discussion questions

1   Based on what you read above, how would you characterize the relationship between land and religion for these two people?

2 What is the intrinsic significance of land (beyond the religious significance) for them?
3 What, specifically, seems to be influencing the ideas about land in these interviews?
4 How does the material world of the farm relate to the spiritual aspects of life? In what way might the particular case of this farm in Anna, IL, teach us something about the relationship of land and spiritual life more generally?
5 Are the concepts of "nature" and "ecology" discussed in previous chapters at all relevant to the ideas raised in these interviews? Why or why not?

Further reading

Dannin, R. (2002) "West Valley," in *Black Pilgrimage to Islam*, New York: Oxford University Press.

Izzi Dien, M. (2000) *The Environmental Dimension of Islam*, Cambridge: The Lutterworth Press. (See especially the section "The Earth," pp. 37–45.)

Ruperto, Abdur Ra'fi-Raphael (2009) "Dayempur," in *Divine Remembrance: The Journal of the Dayemi Tariqat* XIV(2): 32–33.

Westcoat, J.L. Jr. (2003) "From the Gardens of the Qur'an to the 'Gardens' of Lahore'," in R.C. Foltz, F.M. Denny, and A. Baharuddin (eds) *Islam and Ecology: A Bestowed Trust*, Cambridge, MA: Harvard University Press.

Part III

Key issues

Chapter 7

Intellectual and organizational foundations of religion and ecology

John Grim and Mary Evelyn Tucker

Religious responses to environmental crises

The work of the scientific community has made us aware of the inter-connected character of our planetary environment. What is coming into human consciousness is both a sense of awe and wonder after seeing Earth from the moon—that blue ball in black space—as well as a sense of the manipulative grasp that we have on our planet. Rather than finding a single and final perspective, we are beginning to acknowledge our limitations for understanding a dazzling array of ecosystems. Yet, we sense the complex movements of air, water, soils, and peoples throughout this vast living Earth.

While these new images of interconnection are born of science, they are also related to older realizations embedded in the vast array of religious traditions in the human family. Just as religions have been vehicles for meaning-making, for the aesthetic play of knowing relationships with nature, we know they have also been major political players throughout history. Our contemporary quest for a sustainable future moves along this interplay of meaning and politics. In the contemporary period, the world's religions have often been positioned at the margins of these interplaying forces. However, the field of religion and ecology has emerged as an effort to understand the roles of the human both in the despoliation of Earth and in nurturing life. For interactive life is the foundation of the Earth community and its dimin-ishment in current industrial civilization is contributing to the extinction of some 20,000 species a year. We can call this biocide. While the religions have formulated ethics for suicide, homocide, and now even genocide, many reli-gions seem unable to fathom the import of this dying of life. In addition, climate change and the pollution of water, air, and soil have reached a cri-tical threshold threatening the sustainability of civilization itself. In short, the environmental crisis, with its many aspects, may be the largest challenge humans have ever faced.

Our concern, then, is to identify and encourage the ways in which various religious expressions respond to this crisis that clearly has moral and spiri-tual dimensions. In response to this crisis and in collaboration with hundreds of colleagues, we have organized some 25 conferences, edited two series of books, and helped to establish a new field of study with implications for transformative change. In the midst of this collaborative work we recognize both the problems and the promise of religions in contributing to a sustainable future. Religious fundamentalism and intolerance continue to cause divisions and even at times violence. Yet important endeavors promoting interreligious dialogue and conflict resolution are being made around the planet. Many of us in religion and ecology argue that religions may discover their common ground in care for Earth and for those suffering from environmental degradation and injustice. It is now clear that this will require major effort from both the academic and engaged religious communities. As Laurel Kearns argues in the Afterword of this book, theory and practice, ideas and action require one another for lasting change.

To serve these ends, in addition to publications and conferences, we have created a major international website related to cultural and religious understanding of environmental issues. All of this work is intended to support both the academic field and the emerging social force of religious environmentalism. It comes together under the organizational umbrella of the Forum on Religion and Ecology at Yale (http://fore.research.yale.edu/). In what follows we want to highlight some of the intellectual, institutional, and ethical roots that have come together to support this field of religion and ecology. Though not exhaustive, the following are some of the necessary events and actors without which this field would not exist as it is today.

Intellectual roots of the field

Our work with the Forum arises from our academic training as historians of religions.[1] We studied with Thomas Berry (1914–2009), who established a comprehensive History of Religions program at Fordham University. For some 25 years while Thomas directed the Riverdale Center of Religious Research along the Hudson River just north of New York City we met there for meals and conversation. Each summer, he would hold a conference where he would present his latest thoughts on topics ranging from ecological spirituality, to ecological economics, to the conditions for viable human–Earth relations. Even after he retired to his home in Greensboro, North Carolina, in 1995 we kept in close touch and he participated in many of the conferences we organized at Harvard.

Poetic, insightful, and original in his thought, Thomas Berry introduced students to the diverse religious traditions with a profound empathetic feel for the pulse of their spiritual dynamics.[2] Thomas especially oriented us towards exploring the cosmology of religions, namely the ways in which the power and beauty of the surrounding universe evoked in peoples a response in story, symbol, and ritual. Under his guidance we reflected on the correlations between rituals, texts, commentarial teachings, and stories of creation.

All traditions were understood as constantly challenged by their concern for continuity in the midst of historical change. In this sense the world's religions were not limited simply to their institutional expressions but were seen to be creating broad cultural norms and values. Thomas forged ahead, articulating "cultural codings" that related to our hidden, unconscious, embodied "genetic codings." All civilizations, he conjectured, responded to these configurations with cultural practices integrally woven into such basic human mammalian urges as to mate, to eat, and to breathe. Successful cultures established profound linkages, he believed, between these basic genetic drives and cultural practices expressing those drives. Increasingly, Thomas came to see the inherent flow of human cultural embodiment in relation to Earth processes and the importance of narrative. "With a story," he would say, "people can suffer catastrophe and survive. With a story, they gather the energies to change their lot." He mused that the West was between stories (scientific and religious) and he cited Oswald Spengler (1923), Arnold Toynbee (1949), Christopher Dawson (1929), and Eric Voegelin (1952) to give nuance to his historian's view. Stitching his arguments together with a sense of the ages of the human, he drew from Giambattisto Vico (1999) for perspectives on our age and its transformations.

In the midst of these studies, Thomas was always connecting the worldviews of these traditions to the challenges of our modern circumstances. He encouraged engaged scholarship and was himself a public intellectual continually reaching out beyond the walls of academia.

Thomas's interest in cosmology and the role of the human led him to the thought of the French Jesuit paleontologist Teilhard de Chardin (1881–1955). Teilhard had first articulated his intuition regarding the unfolding universe while serving as a chaplain on the battlefields of World War I. Teilhard came to his vision of a dynamic, evolving universe by studying the fossil record, especially the development of humans. His major work, *The Human Phenomenon*, describes the emergence of the human as continuous with the evolutionary process and the work of the human as indispensable to the continuity of the process (Teilhard de Chardin 2003). For Teilhard the universe is the "divine milieu" at one with the evolutionary process.

This immense evolutionary perspective provided Thomas with a radical new story for our times. Thomas appreciated Teilhard's capacity for understanding the emerging universe as a coherent narrative. Yet Thomas also pushed beyond Teilhard by reading widely in the contemporary scientific literature to focus on the growing environmental crisis. His unique contribution was to articulate the conjunction of cosmology and ecology, namely the story of evolution and our interdependence within Earth's systems in a "new story" or a new religious narrative (Berry 1988).

For Thomas, the world presents itself not simply as a collection of objects but as a communion of subjects. In addition, Thomas's years of reading the sacred texts and studying the world's religions brought him to a sense of the felt depths of this new story in the diverse intuitions of religious traditions. For Thomas this affective sense of cosmology was never about foregrounding scientific data as the exclusive story. Rather, the world revealed itself for cultural tellings and our historical context gave expression to evolutionary unfolding in new and creative ways. At one point, while flying back from the Seychelle Islands looking down over the great expanse of the Nile River, he came to the realization that he was a "geologian." That is, he was a person who arises from the great ages of Earth's history to be a self-reflective part of this process. This is a crucial dimension of what he would call the "new story."

Inspired by Thomas, we asked ourselves what contribution we could make as historians of religions that might help stem the tide of environmental degradation. From Mary Evelyn's perspective, a burning question focuses on the rapid economic and industrial modernization of China and India and how their traditional values might contribute to an Asian environmental ethics. From John's view, the diverse and recurring insights of indigenous knowledge continue to raise questions regarding human communities' knowledge of, interaction with, and use of the world in sustainable, intimate, and affective ways.

Though it is hard to imagine our work or the field of "religion and ecology" without Thomas Berry, it would also be impossible without the collaboration and influence of many other scholars. The academic study of religion and ecology draws on many disciplines and thinkers to develop theoretical, historical, ethical, cultural, and engaged dimensions. Some of the theoretical and historical foundations of religion and ecology have been laid by key philosophers and historians of ideas. These include Clarence Glacken (1967), who developed a study of nature in western culture, and Arne Naess (2008), who drew on the thought of Baruch Spinoza and also on South Asian meditation texts to elaborate a theory of deep ecology emphasizing the primacy of the natural world over human prerogatives. Other philosophers and ethicists, such as Baird Callicott and Holmes Rolston III (1989), have helped to develop the field of environmental ethics. Baird Callicott and Roger Ames published one of the first volumes exploring Asian traditions and ecology (Callicott and Ames 1989). Cultural dimensions of environmental realities have been studied by anthropologists, for example Julian Steward, who coined the term "cultural ecology" to describe the relations between the environment and the economic and technological aspects of society (Steward 1972). Furthermore, anthropologist Roy Rappaport (1979) extended cultural understanding of the ways in which ritual sustains social life in specific bioregions. Geographers such as Yi Fu Tuan have investigated the spatial and ecological characteristics of religion (Tuan 1989).

Historians such as William McNeill (1976) and Roderick Nash (1967) provided perspectives from world history and American history for understanding the mutual influences involved in human interactions with ecosystems. Theologians such as John Cobb and Gordon Kaufman (1985) brought together theoretical and engaged perspectives by suggesting ways in which Christian beliefs can be more effectively expressed theologically and in environmental action. Ecofeminists such as Rosemary Radford Ruether (1992), Sallie McFague (1993) and Heather Eaton (2005) illustrated the contested nature of the treatment of the Earth and the exploitation of women, as discussed in Chapter 10 by Amanda Baugh. Writers such as Robert Bullard (1990) and Dieter Hessel (1992) have made important contributions to understanding the linkages between social injustice and environmental pollution, some of which are described in Chapter 12 by Richard Bohannon and Kevin O'Brien. In this same spirit Roger Gottlieb has made distinctive contributions in his numerous books and anthologies, especially *A Greener Faith* (2006a), *The Sacred Earth* (2003), and *The Oxford Handbook of Religion and Ecology* (2006b).

Another forerunner of the field of religion and ecology is Steven Rockefeller, who first convened a conference on "Spirit and Nature" at Middlebury College in 1990. This was made into a film and a book of the same name in 1992 (Rockefeller and Elder 1992). Steven was broadly trained in philosophy and world religions and went on to lead the drafting committee for the *Earth Charter*. Expanding on this important work, a comprehensive theoretical and historical examination of religious traditions and ecology was undertaken by historians of religions, theologians, and environmentalists in the Harvard conference series on World Religions and Ecology from 1996 to 1998. The *Earth Charter* in its draft form was also part of these conferences.

At the same time, Christian process theologians, such as John Cobb, Jay McDaniel (1995), and Catherine Keller (1986), and engaged Christian ethicists, such as Larry Rasmussen (1996) and Ron Engel (1990), have been working to formulate an expansion of religious and ethical sensibilities across time (intergenerational) and across space (to include other species and the planet as a whole). Gary Snyder (1999), Joanna Macy (1991), Ken Kraft, Stephanie Kaza (Kraft and Kaza 2000), and Chris Queen (2000) have been leaders of engaged Buddhism, a movement with a longstanding commitment to the environment. Indigenous traditions embody environmental sensibilities that are now being much more widely appreciated. Drawing on their spiritual relationships with the natural world, indigenous elders have led resistance to environmental projects that are adversely impacting their communities and land. In addition, there has emerged a lively exploration of responses to nature experienced as sacred outside the religious traditions through the works of Catherine Albanese (1990), Graham Harvey (1997), and Bron Taylor (2009). It is not only the institutional religions, but also eco-spiritual movements and nature religions that are contributing to the growth of religion and ecology.

Ethical roots of the field

Of course the field of religion and ecology has been prompted not only by these varied intellectual lineages, but also by concern regarding pressing environmental issues. The global environmental challenges that we face are becoming better understood by scientists, but it is often difficult to break through media hype to build greater public awareness of environmental issues. The anthropogenic, or human-induced, character of the environmental crisis remains difficult to comprehend and, hence, it is challenging to mount a significant response that could reverse or diminish the deleterious effects of our current consumer-driven, petroleum-based culture. We humans currently affect the Earth on a macrophase level, yet we continue to think about our presence on the Earth in microphase cultural contexts. We face global challenges such as climate change, biodiversity loss, and population pressures. On every side we see the degradation and diminishment of soils, air, renewable energy, and clean water, especially for local, indigenous, and marginalized peoples.

The complex nature of our global environment crisis is increasingly evident as weather patterns are becoming more severe, as species are becoming endangered and becoming extinct, as nonrenewable resources such as oil are being wantonly used up, as forests and fisheries are being depleted, and as water is becoming polluted or scarce. The problem of climate change is becoming more visible to a larger public, while the massive extent of species extinction still remains invisible to most people. Yet these two global challenges suggest that our burgeoning population and industrializing presence are altering not only the face of the planet and its climate, but also the process of natural selection itself. Human decisions will determine which species will live and which will die. This is because in the twentieth century we exploded from two billion to six billion people and increased the pace of economic development beyond the boundaries of what is sustainable.

As the developing world attempts to raise its standard of living with unrestrained industrialization and rapid modernization, there is an inevitable impact on the environment and natural resources. The result is that severe pollution of water, air, and soil is becoming more widespread in places such as India and China. Similarly, the high level of consumption of energy and resources by the developed world is causing serious problems of inequity and injustice. The tension between environmental protection and economic development is thus a source of increasing conflict between the developed and developing world. Since the United Nations Conference on Environment and Development in Rio in 1992 there have been a series of major UN conferences and negotiations to redirect the course of development to be more equitable and sustainable. Regrettably, the worldwide increase in military spending, especially by the United States, means that less money is available for the pressing issues outlined in the Millennium

Development Goals regarding poverty and the environment (www.un.org/millenniumgoals).

Thus, the human community is still struggling to reinvent the idea of "sustainability," as discussed by Willis Jenkins in Chapter 8. It is becoming clear that a broader definition is needed for more effective practice—one that integrates efforts at poverty alleviation with environmental protection. Many religious communities have been involved in efforts to mitigate poverty, hunger, and disease, but now they are recognizing this cannot be done adequately without attention to the environment. Sufficiency of food, shelter, and health for humans will depend on a thriving biosphere to support life for the Earth community. This linking of environmental and justice concerns can be seen in the 20-volume book series on "Ecology and Justice" from Orbis Books that we edited along with Leonardo Boff and Sean McDonagh. The aim of that series is described as publishing books that "seek to integrate an understanding of Earth as an interconnected life system with concerns for just and sustainable systems that benefit the entire Earth."

The litany of environmental and development problems has been frequently described, but what is becoming ever more clear is that they cannot be solved by science, technology, law, politics, or economics alone. That is because we are more aware that environmental and development issues are, in large measure, social issues. Thus, "fixing" the environment through technology or regulating development through legislation will not be sufficient. These are necessary approaches, but more is needed, especially the connections around eco-justice. We are being pressed to see the linkage between environment and people, between healthy ecosystems and healthy social systems, between environmental protection and poverty alleviation.

A huge challenge has been the misperceived conflict between economics and ecology. As Laura Hartman discusses in Chapter 11, neo-classical economic thinking has equated economic growth with progress, largely ignoring harms caused to the environment. While this thinking drives our industrial processes, economists are shifting, however gradually, to a realization that the environment can no longer be seen as an externality to be ignored. While profits have been the principle traditional indicators of economic growth, ecological economists are developing a new field of study and practice, pioneered by Herman Daly, Robert Costanza, Richard Norgaard, Hazel Henderson, and others. They have formed an international Society for Ecological Economics (www.ecoeco.org), and are challenging models of economic growth and development along with conventional methods of cost accounting that disregard the environment (Costanza et al. 1997.)

Thus, in discussing the topic of sustainability and the contribution of religions, we may need a broader basis for analysis than simply "sustainable development," which may still be viewed too narrowly as measured by economic indicators of growth. As defined by the Bruntland Commission report *Our Common Future* (World Commission on Environment and Development

1988), it is development that meets present needs while not compromising the needs of future generations. This ethics of intergenerational equity is a necessary criterion that emphasizes balancing environmental and economic growth, but it does not always take into account the full range and interaction of human–Earth flourishing. Such a broad context may be enhanced by the contribution of the world's religions, both in theory and in practice, regarding poverty alleviation and environmental protection. We may be able to draw on shared values as well as diversified practices of the religions.

The world religions can broaden the category of sustainability to include past, present, and future concerns. Such long-term perspectives will be needed to understand sustainable ecosystems that have developed over billions of years, a necessary perspective if we are to create sustainable living for humans at present, and for all life in the future.

Institutional roots of the field

With the assistance of many other scholars of religion, we organized a three-year conference series at Harvard from 1996 to 1998 in order to explore elements of the world's religions that highlight human–Earth relations in scripture, in ritual, and in ethics. A major goal of the series was to begin a process of retrieving, reevaluating, and reconstructing the ecological dimensions of the world's religions so as to contribute to a sustaining and flourishing future for the Earth community. Over 800 international scholars and theologians of world religions participated in the conferences that included the western religions (Judaism, Christianity, and Islam), the Asian religions (Jainism, Hinduism, Buddhism, Confucianism, Daoism, and Shinto), and indigenous religions. We served as series editors for the ten volumes published by the Harvard Center for the Study of World Religions as a result of these conferences (Tucker and Grim 1997–2004). The contributions of scholars and theologians from around the world made visible the dynamic interaction of ideas and practice, worldviews and ethics. The Harvard volumes on Confucianism, Daoism, and Buddhism have been translated into Chinese and published in the People's Republic of China. Plans are underway to translate the other volumes as well.

The final gathering of that series was a culminating conference in spring 1998 that brought together scientists, economists, and policy experts along with historians of religion and theologians. That autumn, the Forum on Religion and Ecology was formed at a conference at the United Nations and the American Museum of Natural History, with more than 1,000 people in attendance.

In 1999, the Forum organized a conference at the Harvard Yenching Institute on "Religion and Animals" that was later published as *A Communion of Subjects* by Columbia University Press. Paul Waldau and Kimberly Patton were the conference organizers and editors of the volume (Waldau and Patton 2009). Paul has gone on to found the Religion and Animals group at the American Academy of Religion along with Laura Hobgood Oster. The Humane Society of the US (HSUS) was instrumental in this as well as the conference series as a whole, due to the leadership of Rick Clugston, who directed the Center for Respect of Life and Environment at HSUS for nearly 20 years.[3] The current co-chair of that group, Dave Aftandilian, provides an important summary of the area of "religion and animals" in Chapter 9 of this volume.

Since the conference series began, the field of religion and ecology has grown within academia and other organizations such as the American Academy of Religion (AAR). At the AAR a Religion and Ecology group began with the efforts of David Barnhill and Eugene Bianchi and has grown steadily in size and vitality. Moreover, colleges and universities are now offering courses in this area, as are divinity schools and seminaries that focus on training Christian ministers (www.webofcreation.org). High school teachers have developed creative curricula as well (www.rsiss.net/rsissfore.html). There are graduate programs being offered at the University of Florida as well as at Drew University, the University of Toronto, and the University of Hawaii. In addition, there is a joint Master's degree program in religion and ecology at Yale between the Forestry and Divinity Schools. Moreover, many environmental studies programs are encouraging the participation of religious studies and the humanities in what have been predominantly science and policy-oriented programs. A new generation of younger scholars is putting its stamp on the field, as evident in this book, *Grounding Religion*.

A two-volume *Encyclopedia of Religion and Nature* was edited by Bron Taylor, who also founded the Society for the Study of Religion, Nature, and Culture (www.religionandnature.com/society) (Taylor 2005), which held its first three meetings in Florida, Mexico, and the Netherlands. Two academic journals have been launched: the first was *Worldviews, Global Religions, Culture, and Ecology*, founded in 1996; the second, *Journal for the Study of Religion Nature and Culture*, was founded in 2007 (and was formerly the journal *EcoTheology*). A Forum for the Study of Religion and the Environment has been created in Europe by Sigurd Bergmann (2000). He has organized conferences and published several books in this field. A partner organization called the Canadian Forum on Religion and Ecology (www.cfore.ca) has also emerged and sponsored several conferences in Canada. These emerging institutions reflect the fact that religion and ecology is influenced both by the spread of ideas made possible by globalization (discussed by Lois Ann Lorentzen in Chapter 13) and by a commitment to the unique cultures and ecologies of particular places (discussed by Brian Campbell in Chapter 14).

To support this newly emerging academic field, one of the first tasks of the Forum was to create a major international website to assist research, education, and outreach. This took more than seven years and is still being updated, with the help of many scholars. (www.yale.edu/religionandecology). There is also a monthly online newsletter that reaches some 8,000 people. The newsletter provides current information on news, publications, and events related to religion and ecology and to climate change. This newsletter was initiated by Whitney Bauman, who served as the Forum webmaster, and has been continued by the present webmasters, Elizabeth McAnally and Sam Mickey.

Though much work has been done within academic institutions, the field of religion and ecology also depends on work done within religious institutions. Statements on the environment and on eco-justice have been released by the major world religions and indigenous traditions, and are posted on the Forum website. Leaders such as the Ecumenical Patriarch, the Pope, and the Dalai Lama have spoken out regarding the urgency of these issues. The Ecumenical Patriarch, Bartholomew, has presided over eight international symposia focused on water issues (www.rsesymposia.org). Rowan Williams, the head of the Anglican Church in England, has written sermons on this topic (www.archbishopofcanterbury.org) and the US Presiding Bishop for the Episcopal Church, Katherine Jefferts Schori, has testified before Congress on the risks of climate change. Moreover, ministers and lay people are organizing projects such as fighting mountain top removal, educating children in ecology, conserving energy in the Interfaith Power and Light project (www.theregenerationproject.org). Many of these activities are depicted in the film *Renewal*, which features eight case studies of religious environmentalism across the United States (www.renewalproject.net). Moreover, Catholic nuns have been active in projects on sustainable agriculture and ecological literacy (http://sistersofearth.net/). Of particular note is the work of Mirriam MacGillis, the founder and director of Genesis Farm in New Jersey (www.genesisfarm.org). These efforts have been documented in Sarah McFarland Taylor's *Green Sisters* (2007). In addition, the National Religious Partnership for the Environment has been working for 15 years with Jewish and Christian groups in the United States (www.nrpe.org), while the Alliance for the Conservation of Nature in England has established numerous ecological projects around the world (www.arcworld.org).

The public voice of religion and ecology

As this field has expanded, so has the recognition of the importance of religion in environmental programs and concerns. For example, scientists have for years asked religious communities to play a more active role in environmental issues. These scientists observe that moral authority has played an important role in many transformations of values and behavior, such as the abolition of slavery in nineteenth-century England and in the civil rights movements by religious leaders in the United States and South Africa in the twentieth century. They also recognize the large number of people around the world who are influenced by religion: one billion Muslims, Christians, Hindus, and Confucians, respectively.

This scientific call to religion was articulated by more than 2,000 scientists in "A Warning to Humanity" in 1992 (Kendall *et al.* 1992) and more recently in E.O. Wilson's book *The Creation* (2006). Similarly, the biologists Paul Ehrlich and Donald Kennedy have proposed a Millennium Assessment of Human Behavior (2005). In addition, policy think tanks, such as the Worldwatch Institute in Washington, DC, have encouraged the role of religions. One of their principal researchers, Gary Gardner, published a chapter on this topic in the State of the World report of 2003 and a book called *Inspiring Progress: Religious Contributions to Sustainable Development* (2006). Moreover, the policy expert and the former Dean of the School of Forestry and Environmental Studies at Yale, James Gustav Speth, also called for the participation of the world's religions in his book *Bridge at the Edge of the World* (2008).

In this mix of programs and policies for sustainability that have emerged around the world, there is a growing recognition that cultural and religious values may have a significant role to play in helping to shape a sustainable future. While religions have their problematic dimensions, including intolerance, dogmatism, and fundamentalism, they have also served as wellsprings of wisdom, as sources of moral inspiration, and as containers of transforming ritual practices. Thus, they can serve as both conservators of continuity and agents of change. Religions have always played this role of conserving and transforming, balancing the dynamic tension of continuity and change for cultures over long spans of time. Indeed, human cultures are profoundly shaped by this dialectic, and civilizations endure by navigating the delicate balance between tradition and modernity. Moving too deeply into traditional patterns leads to fossilization and fundamentalism, while focusing solely on "the new and different" can lead to superficial and inadequate responses to change.

A central challenge of our present moment is to bring the depths of the world's religious traditions into meaningful dialogue with modernity. Such an effort needs especially to be focused on the growing environmental crisis. This is a key task for religions and scholars of religion, a necessary contribution to a sustainable future. It reflects the growing calls for spiritual insight and moral energy to be brought to bear in the discussions on sustainability. Many significant groups focusing on sustainability are seeking just such intersection with values and ethics. These include Mikhail Gorbachev's Green Cross, which has sponsored a series of conferences on "Earth Dialogues: Is Ethics the Missing Link?" The Club of Rome (www.clubofrome.org) and the Tällberg Foundation (www.tallbergfoundation.org) are also interested in defining the moral boundaries and conditions for a sustainable future. Moreover, there was a significant effort made by the World Bank under James Wolfensohn to create a discussion with religions around development issues, called World Faith Development Dialogue (www.wfdd.org.uk).

The force of religion and ecology in dialogue with science and policy is also evident in a series of conferences and engaged activities that have occurred over several years. We have participated in five of the symposia on "Religion, Science and the Environment" led by the Ecumenical Patriarch, Bartholomew. At the World Conservation Congress of the International Union for the Conservation of Nature (IUCN) in Barcelona we organized the first panel on "Spirituality and Conservation," featuring presenters from the world's religions.

Interest in the work on religion and ecology is growing significantly in East Asia as well. In the spring of 2008 we participated in conferences in South Korea, China, and Japan. In South Korea the Academy of Korean Studies hosted a conference titled "Global Forum on Civilization and Peace." In Japan we participated in a conference featuring the *Earth Charter*. In January 2009 we attended a conference at the major academic center in Taiwan, the Academia Sinica, which focused on Confucianism and ecology.

These are just a few of the many events that give evidence to the force of the public voice of religion and ecology in international conversations. For a list of other events (past and future) taking place, please visit the Forum's website (http://fore.research.yale.edu/).

Conclusion

We are at a moment of immense significance for the future of life on the planet, a moment when the world's religions may be of assistance as they move into their ecological phase. The integration of the virtues for human–Earth flourishing of the world's religions provides a unique synergy for rethinking sustainability and our relationship to the rest of the natural world. Such a synergy can contribute to the broadened understanding of sustainable development as including economic, ecological, social, and spiritual well-being. This broadened understanding may be a basis for long-term policies, programs, and practices for a planetary future that is not only ethically sustainable, but also sustaining for human energies. At present we face a crisis of hope that we can make a transition to a viable future for the Earth community. The need for the world's religions to provide moral direction and inspiration for a flourishing community of life is ever more urgent.

Notes

1 Mary Evelyn's specialty is Confucianism in East Asia and John's special field is Indigenous Religions, especially among Native North American Peoples. John did his Ph.D. at Fordham with Thomas Berry, while Mary Evelyn did an M.A. with him. She then pursued her Ph.D. work at Columbia with Wm. Theodore de Bary, one of the pioneers in Asian studies in the West, a noted scholar of Confucianism, and a close friend of Thomas Berry.

2 The influence of Ted de Bary should not be ignored, either. Ted was instrumental in establishing courses in Asian classics, history, and civilizations at Columbia. To

provide texts for these courses, he helped translate and edit major works on the Sources of Indian, Chinese, Korean, and Japanese Traditions for Columbia University Press. In addition to this remarkable achievement, his comparative studies of human rights in China and the West have been a source of great inspiration.

3 We also convened several conferences at the American Academy of Arts and Science in Cambridge, MA. These included one with major nature writers and religious thinkers in 1999 and two others that prepared a volume focusing on world religions and climate change in 2000 and 2001. This resulted in the first issue of *Daedalus* to be published both in print and online. (See "Religion and Ecology: Can the Climate Change?", *Daedalus*, Fall 2001, www.amacad.org/publications/fall2001/fall2001.aspx).

References

Albanese, C. (1990) *Nature Religion in America: From the Algonkian Indians to the New Age*, Chicago, IL: University of Chicago Press.

Bergmann, S. (2000) *Creation Set Free: The Spirit as Liberator of Nature*, trans. Douglas Stott, Grand Rapids, MI: Wm. B. Eerdmans.

Berry, Thomas (1988) *Dream of the Earth*, San Francisco, CA: Sierra Book Clubs.

Bullard, R. (1990) *Dumping in Dixie: Race, Class, and Environmental Equality*, Boulder, CO: Westview.

Callicott, B. and R. Ames (1989) *Nature in Asian Traditions of Thought: Essays in Environmental Philosophy*, Albany, NY: SUNY Press.

Costanza, R., J. Cumberland, H. Daly, R. Goodland, and R. Norgaard (1997) *An Introduction to Ecological Economics*, Boca Raton, FL: CRC Press.

Dawson, C. (1929) *Progress and Religion: An Historical Inquiry*, London: Sheed and Ward.

Eaton, H. (2005) *Introducing Ecofeminist Theologies*, London: T&T Clark.

Ehrlich, P. and D. Kennedy (2005) "Sustainability: Millennium Assessment of Human Behavior," *Science* 309(5734) (July 22): 562–63.

Engel, R. (1990) *Ethics of Environment and Development: Global Challenge, International Response*, Berkeley: University of California Press.

Gardner, G. (2006) *Inspiring Progress: Religious Contributions to Sustainable Development*, Washington, DC: Worldwatch Institute.

Glacken, C. (1967) *Traces on the Rhodian Shore: Nature and Culture in the West from Ancient Times to the End of the Eighteenth Century*, Berkeley: University of California Press.

Gottlieb, R. (2003) *The Sacred Earth*, New York: Routledge.

——(2006a) *A Greener Faith: Religious Environmentalism and Our Planet's Future*, Oxford: Oxford University Press.

——(2006b) *The Oxford Handbook of Religion and Ecology*, Oxford: Oxford University Press.

Harvey, G. (1997) *Contemporary Paganism: Listening People, Speaking Earth*, New York: New York University Press.

Hessel, D. (1992) *After Nature's Revolt: Eco-Justice and Theology*, Minneapolis, MN: Fortress.

Kaufman, G. (1985) *Theology for a Nuclear Age*, Manchester, UK: Manchester University Press.

Keller, C. (1986) *From a Broken Web: Separation, Sexism, Self*, Boston, MA: Beacon.

Kendall, Henry *et al.* (1992) "World Scientists' Warning to Humanity," available at http://www.ucsusa.org/about/1992-world-scientists.html.

Kraft, K. and S. Kaza (eds) (2000) *Dharma Rain: Sources of Buddhist Environmentalism*, Boston, MA: Shambala.

McDaniel, J. (1995) *With Roots and Wings: Christianity in an Age of Ecology and Dialogue*, Maryknoll, NY: Orbis.

McFague, S. (1993) *The Body of God: An Ecological Theology*, Minneapolis, MN: Fortress.

McNeill, W. (1976) *Plagues and Peoples*, New York: Anchor Books.

Macy, J. (1991) *World as Lover, World as Self: Courage for Global Justice and Ecological Renewal*, Berkeley, CA: Parallax.

Naess, A. (2008) *The Ecology of Wisdom: Writings by Arne Naess*, Berkeley, CA: Counterpoint.

Nash, R. (1967) *Wilderness and the American Mind*, New Haven, CT: Yale University Press.

Queen, C. (2000) *Engaged Buddhism in the West*, Somerville, MA: Wisdom.

Rappaport, R. (1979) *Ecology, Meaing and Religion*, Berkeley, CA: North Atlantic Books.

Rasmussen, L. (1996) *Earth Community, Earth Ethics*, Maryknoll, NY: Orbis.

Rockefeller, S. and J. Elder (eds) (1992) *Spirit and Nature: Why the Environment Is a Religious Issue*, Boston, MA: Beacon.

Rolston III, H. (1989) *Environmental Ethics: Duties to and Values in the Natural World*, Philadelphia, PA: Temple University Press.

Ruether, R. (1992) *Gaia and God: An Ecofeminist Theology of Earth Healing*, New York: HarperCollins.

Snyder, G. (1999) *The Gary Snyder Reader: Prose, Poetry and Translations*, Washington, DC: Counterpoint.

Spengler, O. (1923). *The Decline of the West*, 2 vols., trans. Charles Francis Atkinson, New York: Alfred A. Knopf.

Speth, J. (2008) *Bridge at the Edge of the World*, New Haven, CT: Yale University Press.

Steward, J. (1972) *Theory of Cultural Change: The Methodology of Multilinear Evolution*, Champaign, IL: University of Illinois Press.

Taylor, B. (ed.) (2005) *The Encylopedia of Religion and Nature*, 2 vols., New York: Continuum.

——(2009) *Dark Green Religion: Nature Spirituality and the Planetary Future*, Berkeley: University of California Press.

Taylor, S. (2007) *Green Sisters: A Spiritual Ecology*, Boston, MA: Harvard University Press.

Teilhard de Chardin, P. (2003) *The Human Phenomenon*, trans. Sarah Appleton-Weber, Brighton, UK: Sussex Academic Press.

Toynbee, A. (1949) *Civilization on Trial*, Oxford: Oxford University Press.

Tuan, Y. (1989) *Morality and Imagination: Paradoxes of Progress*, Madison, WI: University of Wisconsin Press.

Tucker, M. and J. Grim (series eds.) (1997–2004) *Religions of the World and Ecology*, 10 vols., Boston, MA: Center for the Study of World Religions/Harvard University Press.

Vico, G. (1999 [1744 first edition]) *New Science*, New York: Penguin.

Voegelin, E. (1952) *The New Science of Politics: An Introduction*, Chicago, IL: University of Chicago Press.

Waldau, P. and K. Patton (2009) *A Communion of Subjects: Animals in Religion, Science, and Ethics*, New York: Columbia University Press.

Wilson, E.O. (2006) *The Creation: An Appeal to Save Life on Earth*, New York: W.W. Norton.

World Commission on Environment and Development (1988) *Our Common Future*, Oxford: Oxford University Press.

Chapter 8

Sustainability

Willis Jenkins

The relation of religion and sustainability pairs one ambiguous, absorptive concept with another equally contested. As the editors of this book make clear in Chapter 1, the study of religion covers a broad range of social phenomena and contains multitudes of human experience. The emerging study of sustainability covers a narrower range but its central concept seems almost as susceptible of contrary worldviews and competing moral agendas. Sustainability has been used to argue for and against climate treaties, for and against free markets, for and against development spending, even for and against environmental preservation. Thinking through the relation of religion and sustainability therefore requires understanding how the pluralism and ambiguity of each concept create important questions.

Answers to those questions shape how societies interpret and respond to global problems such as climate change and persistent world poverty. Views on the relation of religion and sustainability thus bear practical significance for addressing some of society's most difficult challenges. Those views help determine, for example, whether and how biodiversity loss is perceived as a moral issue; whether cultural values and moral traditions must change, and, if so, which ones and how extensively; how human poverty relates to economic systems and what difference human suffering should make in environmental policies. Those are normative issues concerning how persons and societies will address grave problems, so the conceptual ambiguity here cannot remain merely a matter of speculative inquiry. Relations of religion and sustainability shape how humans will make their future, how the human future will affect life on earth, and—perhaps most importantly—what hope and meaning cultures will make from the task of addressing global problems. This chapter therefore focuses on questions that arise as moral communities draw from religious traditions or use religious resources in order to respond to sustainability problems.

History of sustainability ideas

In its rudimentary sense, sustainability means a capacity to maintain some entity, outcome, or process over time.[1] The term was first employed by resource managers to refer to maintaining yield over time; hence, agriculture, forest management, and financial investments are sustainable if the costs and extractions of the activity do not exhaust the material resources on which it depends. In recent decades the concept has been used to assess threats posed by human action to the economic, ecological, and political systems on which humanity depends. Sustainability in this broader sense involves the connection of specific social and environmental problems to the functioning of human and ecological systems.

The broader sense puts the topic of religion and sustainability in ancient perspective, introducing a critical question from environmental history. In the view of some theorists and historians, religion has always been a function of a society's ecological relations. For example, some interpret the religious aspects of hunter-gatherer cultures, ancient and contemporary, as cultural habits that reproduce sustainable environmental relations. As cultures acquired different ways of dwelling, and especially greater powers over nature, their religions changed accordingly. In some situations, religions may have contributed to civilizational collapse when they prevented social change in response to unsustainable land and water uses (Diamond 2005: 472). A strong version of this view claims that religion amounts to a symbolic expression of a culture's ecological relations; a more modest version holds that enduring religions depend on and accommodate themselves to sustainable societies (Radkau 2008: 77–85). So perhaps the topic of religion and sustainability is universal in human society and as old as its history.

On the other hand, contemporary human powers and the global problems they create are historically unprecedented. Humanity has no experience of consciously deciding the fate of species or of managing the earth's atmosphere, certainly not of trying to do so collectively as a global species. Does religion function differently in an era in which human civilization exercises planetary impact? Some think that religion must function in new ways to help guide a globalizing civilization. On this view, the challenge of sustainability involves powers and perils unknown to previous ages, which creates unique pressures for religious change in ours, perhaps even giving rise to new forms of religious experience.

8A

Does the relation of religion and sustainability imply something unprecedented in cultural history, or is it universal to the relation of culture and nature?

In any case, public use of sustainability as a concept for reflecting on humanity's planetary impacts is recent and has been religiously involved from the outset. Religious communities and theological debates attended the public emergence of the sustainability idea well before its first major international use as a guiding concept, which was in a 1980 report from the International Union for Conservation of Nature (IUCN). The IUCN report extended the notion of sustainable resource yield to a broader context of environmental management. Certainly many earlier organizations and global conferences discussed related concepts in their growing concern with humanity's planetary impacts, but sustainability was not used as an organizing guideline.[2] It is somewhat remarkable, then, that the World Council of Churches (WCC) in 1974 was already discussing the idea of sustainability, by 1975 had initiated a major program on a "Just, Participatory, and Sustainable Society," and by 1983 had generated sufficient internal debate over the concept to change the third term of its program to "the Integrity of Creation" (Hallman 2001).

The publication which may have done the most to provoke public thinking of earth systems in terms of sustainability never uses the term. The 1972 *Limits to Growth* report issued by the Club of Rome (Meadows *et al.* 1972) argued that human economies had reached the planet's biophysical limits and called for a scaling back of economic activity. Although the term "sustainability" appears nowhere in it, the report's account of an approaching conflict between ecological limits and human growth was influential for subsequent appeals to sustainability. That same year the Stockholm Declaration, issued by the conference which established the UN Environment Programme, appealed to the need to safeguard natural resources for future generations. Stockholm argued that "the capacity of the earth to produce vital renewable resources must be maintained," yet also established priority for the poor in economic development.[3]

Sustainability did not publicly appear as the concept for integrating those two commitments—safeguarding ecological capacity and creating development for the poor—until the 1975 WCC assembly in Nairobi, which inaugurated the "sustainable society" program. It was a religious gathering, then, that helped transform the idea of sustainability from a concept of resource management into a social principle and moral project. The WCC was able to achieve that transformation in part because it used the concept to connect its established support for pro-poor liberation theologies with emerging international concerns about environmental problems (Bakken *et al.* 1995: 9ff).

The inclusive social scope of sustainability was thus already established when the 1980 IUCN report proposed sustainability as a guiding principle in its World Conservation Strategy. The strategy report noted that excess consumption by the affluent and struggles for survival by the poor were cumulatively undermining conditions of flourishing for all, and proposed conservation measures to protect ecological and social goods. In 1987 sustainability came to worldwide prominence through the World Commission on Environment and Development publication *Our Common Future*, often called the "Brundtland Report," after the name of its chair (former Norwegian Prime Minister Gro Harlem Brundtland). The Brundtland Report directly addressed tensions between the global project of economic growth and emerging concerns with sustainability by proposing the hybrid concept "sustainable development." In its famous definition, "sustainable development is development that meets the needs of the present without compromising the ability of future generations to meet their own needs" (World Commission on Environment and Development 1987: 43).

Brundtland succeeded in placing sustainable development on the international political agenda, setting a basic principle to integrate environmental, economic, and social commitments in a coherent framework. The integrative capacity helped create political support for a major global conference addressing environmental issues, thus opening the way for the 1992 "Earth Summit" in Rio de Janeiro. Rio produced an extensive set of strategies for realizing sustainable development over the coming century in its Agenda 21 program. A decade later, in 2002, the UN held the World Summit on Sustainable Development in Johannesburg. By calling for an international agreement on fundamental ethical principles of sustainable development, Brundtland also helped set in motion an extensive cross-cultural and interfaith initiative that led to the Earth Charter.

However, by combining environmental and economic agendas into one guiding principle, Brundtland also created controversy. Some critics charged that "sustainable development" was an oxymoron, while others observed that it at least stood for a chronic argument between those who would prioritize growth and those who prioritize conservation. Others noted the vagueness of its definition: Just what are the needs of the present and how are they met? How do we know the needs of future generations and what abilities they will require?

In its optimism about combining economic and environmental goals, the Brundtland Report constructs a much different perspective than *The Limits to Growth*, which outlines a stark conflict between continued growth and ecological health. The difference in perspectives derives from differing views about a central issue for any idea of sustainability: whether natural resources can be replaced or substituted through technological ingenuity. Judgments on that issue lead to competing models of sustainability, which may involve different moral worldviews, as I will discuss on pp. 104–8. So while the sustainability idea can reconcile multiple normative commitments, it also creates further controversies, which is illustrated by its fate within the WCC.

While the WCC was one of the first adopters of the term "sustainability," by 1983 its program focus on the "sustainable society" had been replaced by the "integrity of creation" in a new program unit on "Justice, Peace, and the Integrity of Creation," which has endured since. Within the WCC, theological discussions anticipated that if sustainability were combined with prevailing pro-growth economic policies it could compromise concerns both for the liberation of the poor and for nature's intrinsic value. The new program clearly identified the WCC's basic moral values: social justice and the integrity of creation. By the time of the World Summit on Sustainable Development, the WCC joined other religious communities in insisting on "sustainable communities" rather than "sustainable development." Thus the same religious institution that helped launch the public career of sustainability also discovered religious reasons to criticize its success (Rasmussen 2005).

By contrast, the global initiative for an Earth Charter was more approving of sustainability discourse, using it to gather and articulate cross-cultural, interfaith consensus on "principles for a sustainable way of life as a common standard" (Earth Charter, Preamble). Some of the Charter's drafting consultations encountered misgivings about development-focused concepts, but in the end the Charter uses the terms "sustainable development," "sustainable livelihood," and "human development" when connecting protections of ecological integrity with social justice (Principles 5, 9, and 10). More important than the terms it employs is the Charter's vision of human unity and sense of historical crisis. The Charter presents its principles not as mere policy guidelines but, in the face of unprecedented global problems, as "an ethical foundation for the emerging world community." It speaks on behalf of "the peoples of Earth" to declare that "we are one human family and one Earth community with a common destiny. We must join together to bring forth a sustainable global society founded on respect for nature, universal human rights, economic justice, and a culture of peace" (Preamble).

The Earth Charter was not created by a religious institution, but it intentionally draws from the ideas of many religious and cultural traditions in order to create a holistic vision, a common cosmology, and a corresponding call for change in moral consciousness. The Charter thus responds to the challenge of sustainability with some conventional tropes of religion. The Charter's lead drafter, Steven Rockefeller, explains that "the objective is to give the emerging global consciousness the spiritual depth—the soul—needed to build a just and peaceful world community" (Rockefeller 2001: 103).

8B

Does a global ethic of sustainability need spiritual depth? Can it establish shared religious foundations? Could a worldview of sustainability support an ethic or spirituality independent of any particular tradition?

The idea of sustainability

The involvement of religious institutions and thinkers in developing the idea of sustainability raises questions about how to think of the relation between religion and sustainability. Consider first the kind of questions raised by sustainability studies. Investigating the connection between social problems and ecological systems represents a scientific research program as well as a project of cultural and ethical reflection (e.g. Lubchenco *et al.* 1991; Palmer 2004). Focusing on the ecological dependency of economic and social systems, sustainability concepts can illuminate mutual effects between environmental degradation caused by human activities and systemic perils presented by environmental problems. That means that scientific research must find ways to investigate complex feedback between dynamic systems in the context of an unavoidable political question: Can human activity successfully maintain itself and its goals without exhausting the resources on which it depends? By tracing the connection of problems caused by cultural practices to degradation or jeopardy of larger systems, the idea of sustainability thus directs reflection to basic values and comprehensive goals. Perhaps a research program that pushes toward basic cultural values and entire worldviews enters the realm of religious reflection, or attains similar scope. Either way, relations of religion and science face a new challenge with sustainability.

8C

If the idea of sustainability reflects on an entire pattern of life, is it inherently religious? How can science-based sustainability research programs take account of the roles of religion in cultural and political systems?

Researching the planetary impact of human activity and evaluating its durability provokes reflection on the purpose of human life and forms of human society. Problems like climate change and biodiversity loss point to the planetary reach and evolutionary impact of human powers, even while the persistence of extreme poverty within a globalized economy points to stark inequality among humans. All three problems pose new scales of obligation and risk. Mitigating their impact, let alone resolving these problems, requires reform across many human systems—financial, political, legal, energy, transportation, communication, and more. Any proposals for reform will encounter controversy over which goals and goods receive priority, and how social objectives can best be achieved. There is a long-running debate over whether economic development must precede human rights protections and environmental conservation, or vice versa. What are the most important goals of global cooperation, the basic minimum needed to sustain the systems of a decent civilization? How do we decide which interests to prioritize, which values to protect, what goals to pursue?

The idea of sustainability confronts societies with a new kind of moral question: What, above all else, must be sustained? The idea does more than point to goods and values imperiled by the expansion of human powers; by connecting specific problems to human and ecological systems, the idea of sustainability directs the practical imagination toward integrating those goods and values into a coherent social vision. How do we simultaneously address development for the poor, protection of biodiversity, management of carbon emissions, and population stability? Reflecting on sustainability requires creative ideas about the interaction of economic health, ecological integrity, and social justice in the context of responsibilities to the future.

8D

What is the moral status of the future? Do we have obligations to future generations? Responsibilities for the future of life on this planet? How should we understand the moral future of decades and centuries within the billion-year epochs of deep time?

Its inclusive scope and aspirational vision make the concept of sustainability ideologically absorptive and politically popular. Who could be against it? That is precisely its weakness, argue its critics: Sustainability seems conceptually meaningless, or at least too susceptible of competing ideas to be practically useful (e.g. Palmer 1994). Others argue, however, that so long as the various ideas recognize the basic connection between social problems and human and ecological systems, they represent important responses to the question of what to sustain over time. On this view, the concept of sustainability produces a discursive arena for political debate and for the practical moral imagination (Robinson 2004). The argument here depends on whether the idea of sustainability is successful in shaping public deliberation. Here religious imagination may have a role to play. Religious symbols, metaphors, narratives, and practices may invoke ways of integrating multiple goods or may orient social imaginaries toward a harmony of moral values. "Eco-justice," for example, has been used by some religious communities to insist on ecological respect through social solidarity.

The idea of sustainability presents a challenge to political deliberation, a challenge which is odd for appearing at once minimal and comprehensive. By investigating the relation of social problems to systemic functioning it seems to consider merely the prospects for a decent human survival. Yet because those prospects rest on the connection of social goals to ecological functioning, evaluating them forces reflection on the value of nonhuman life, the goals of economy, the role of humanity within Earth's systems and creatures, and the kind of futures we want to make possible. As we begin to consider what humans should sustain, we are eventually forced to reflect on what sustains humanity.

Those may be properly religious reflections, but they also pose a question about religion: How do specific beliefs and practices depend on specific ecological conditions, or even places? For many indigenous peoples their way of life—including their stories, cosmologies, identities, and much else that we might put under the (perhaps alien) heading of "religion"—depends on intimate connection to specific creatures and particular places. Inuit ways of life, for example, may be endemic to the Arctic. What it means to be Inuit may be so dependent on membership in Arctic communities that their stories and spiritualities begin to lose their intelligibility in other biotic contexts, or if the Arctic ecosystems degrade. A decent survival for a certain people may then entail whatever is required for long-term inhabitation of a certain land. That may explain the outspoken resistance of many indigenous peoples to thin notions of sustainability, including Inuit outspokenness on climate change. It may also explain the relatively weaker resistance to sustainability concepts from leaders of the global religions; perhaps global religious expressions depend less on intimate relations with specific places.[4] How deeply a religion is wounded by environmental degradation indicates something of how Earth matters for its way of life.

There is, then, a paradoxical depth to the idea of sustainability. Although it inquires merely about the moral minimum of a decent survival, answering the questions it raises invites reflection on the totality of our dependency and relations. It requires an accounting of the goods that we pursue—on what those goods depend and what their pursuit costs. It makes visible the actual answers our actions give to the question of what sustains us, and places those answers in the complexity of human poverty, other-than-human suffering, and ecological degradation. As sustainability confronts political societies with decisions about how to protect what sustains us, it pushes sweeping moral questions into public deliberation. The idea of sustainability can be overwhelming and paralyzing.

Exploring the religious dimensions of those questions or drawing from religious traditions may empower responses to overwhelming challenges. Religious communities may offer hope in the face of evil, anxiety, or death. Within political deliberations tempted to embrace some historical fatalism— that economies develop by ungovernable forces, that governments interact by inexorable conflicts of power, or that cultures progress by inevitable technological intensification—religious resources can help publics face complex and overwhelming ideas. Treating sustainability as a problem of religious profundity lets publics consider possibilities that our economic, political, and technological systems might work differently and better, that human societies still have important choices to make.

At the same time, however, religion can trouble the possibility of pluralist public discussion. Global problems seem to require a global ethic with at least some shared ground of values and commitments from which to construct collaborative responses and perhaps institutions of global governance. Religious visions may seem too narrow and inaccessible, if not divisive. What kind of religion or religious engagement helps make sustainability an ethical question for a global public, and what sort undermines possibilities for a global ethic?

8E

How might the religious imagination inform, shape, or distort public discussion of sustainability? Can religion help facilitate development of a global ethic, or does cross-cultural collaboration require an ethic without religious roots? What new moralities, new religious expressions, and/or new spiritualities might a sustainable civilization require?

The very fact of global political debate about what humanity should sustain indicates new dimensions of human responsibility and new conditions for culture. Humanity's technological and economic powers expanded so dramatically in the twentieth century that, for at least for the next few human generations, the course of life on the planet will be significantly shaped by human society. Some scientists have called this era of human power over the planet a new geological epoch: the Anthropocene. If greater responsibility comes with greater power, human civilization must develop new moral capacities in order to fulfill its Anthropocene role. In the fitful twentieth-century emergence of a global society with at least some shared commitments, perhaps such development has begun. If the survival of civilization depends on stories, practices, and worldviews that support different ecological patterns, perhaps the future of religion will be shaped by ecological realities (Tucker 2003).

Three models of sustainability

So far we have seen that the idea of sustainability absorbs and integrates competing moral values. This section illustrates how differences in thinking about competing moral values create different models of sustainability. One of the most important points here is whether resources and values can be substituted and replaced. Two opposing views and an attempt to mediate them lead to three different models of sustainability.

Consider again the basic question: What must we sustain? Do you think that answers to that question should be measured by a common standard, or must they turn out irreducibly multiple? From one perspective, societies aim to preserve one key value, human welfare, through one central action, development (which includes consumption and production). The opposing perspective holds that societies must aim to preserve multiple values, possibly including human welfare, other species (some or all), ecosystems (some or all), political goods such as democracy or human rights, and cultural goods such as artistic creation.

Those two different perspectives turn on the question of whether resources are substitutable for one another, such that exhaustion of one resource can be justified if it creates another of equal or greater value for human welfare. If they are substitutable, then the question of sustainability appears as an investment problem: How can consumption of resources most efficiently provide welfare now while investing for the sake of continuing production opportunities for coming generations? If, on the other hand, blue whales, forest ecosystems, and food commodities cannot be measured against one another, but instead represent three different *kinds* of value, then human activity faces a more complex moral situation.

Decisions about the kind of value question societies face may hinge on background pictures of the relation between economic and ecological systems. If one thinks that ecological systems pose limits to human economy, one may endorse a non-substitutable view in order to describe normative limits on human action. If one thinks that economic development creates more resources as it uses others, then one is more likely to endorse a substitutable view, on the view that production overcomes limits and reduces scarcity. Unfortunately for non-specialist citizens, those background pictures often correspond to professional knowledges; economists tend to adopt the latter and environmental scientists the former.

Related to those two general perspectives is the differentiation between "strong" and "weak" sustainability. "Strong sustainability" requires preservation of multiple goods, like the existence of species and the functioning of particular ecosystems. "Weak sustainability" espouses a general principle to leave future generations no worse off than we are. In terms of protecting old growth forests, for example, a strong view might argue for protection, even if it requires foregoing development that could increase opportunities for future generations. A weak view would take into account the various benefits old growth forests provide, and would then attempt to measure the future value of those benefits against the values created by development that consumes them now.

A third approach mediates these two perspectives on value: A pragmatic view argues that in the face of irreconcilable views of the world, perhaps we must sustain conditions for political argument over them. Perhaps preserving some opportunities for future generations requires the enduring existence of particular ecological and social goods. For example, the opportunity to decide whether or not old growth forests matter for human dignity depends on their preserved existence. Allowing the massive loss of species would close down that option for humanity, effectively ending the debate. This approach effectively proposes that we must sustain conditions for the ongoing debate over sustainability (Barry 1997; Norton 2005).

These three approaches correspond to three basic models of sustainability, each of which constructs a way to prioritize among competing values and proposes ways of thinking about the ethical future.

Economic models of sustainability

Economic models propose to sustain welfare, as expressed in the form of capital, which offers a universal currency for exercising preferences. In the classic definition of Robert Solow, sustainability poses an investment problem, in which societies must use returns from the use of natural resources in order to create new opportunities of equal or greater value. Social spending on the poor or on environmental protection, while perhaps justifiable on other grounds, takes away from this investment and so competes with a commitment to sustainability.

This neo-classical version of an economic model offers a powerful guide to social policy by making values commensurable across kind and across time according to an index of welfare that is defined by individual choice. However, the neo-classical model suffers from three chronic vulnerabilities. First, many natural resources and ecological functions cannot easily be valued because markets do not adequately account for them, leading to market behavior that threatens public goods. Second, risks and benefits to future generations are often discounted at rates that seem intuitively unacceptable to many. Third, individuals seem to make choices for reasons other than maximizing welfare, and, moreover, do even that imperfectly and irrationally. Because of those weaknesses, many religious communities hesitate to endorse economic sustainability without some moral qualification, often in reference to principles of justice or some view of the common good.

With a non-substitutable view of values, however, the economic model might look different. If we do not assume that "natural capital" is always interchangeable with financial capital, argues Herman Daly (1990), sustaining opportunity for the future requires strong conservation measures to preserve ecological goods and to keep economies operating in respect of natural limits. These considerations lead toward an ecological model.

From a different perspective on the relation between opportunity and capital, spending on the poor might be regarded as its own kind of investment in the future. According to Amartya Sen's "development as freedom" dictum, we create options for the future by creating options for today's poor because more options will drive greater development. In this political model of sustainability, sustaining opportunity for the future requires social spending on the poor today. This approach leads toward a political model.

Ecological models of sustainability

Ecological models propose to sustain biological diversity and ecological integrity. Rather than focusing on welfare or capital as the key unit of sustainability, they focus directly on the health of the living world. Within this approach, there are two major ways of deciding which ecological goods to sustain. From an anthropocentric point of view, essential natural resources should be sustained, as should those ecological systems and regenerative processes on which human systems rely. From an ecocentric point of view, species should be sustained for their intrinsic value, as should ecological systems as generators of creatures with intrinsic value. On specific policies, strong and weak views may converge.

Interdisciplinary religious and economic reasoning in support of an ecological model can be found in the collaboration of process theologian John Cobb and ecological economist Herman Daly. In *For the Common Good* (1994), they argue against not only the valuation in dominant economic frameworks but also the view of human personhood they assume. Cobb and Daly argue for a more relational view of human personhood, shaped in human community and sustained through ecological relations.

Political models of sustainability

Political models propose to sustain social systems that realize human dignity. Concerned with the way local and global environmental problems jeopardize human dignity, these models focus on sustaining the environmental conditions of a fully human life. Environmental justice and civic environmentalism represent one strategy of this model; by focusing on environmentally mediated threats to human life they point to necessary ecological goods or sustainable environmental management schemes. Another subset of the political model includes those pragmatist approaches that propose sustaining conditions for open debate about sustainability. Here sustaining a political system of deliberative democracy effectively requires sustaining ecological and economic goods along with political goods like procedural rights.

Significant religious involvement within this model includes the various uses and appearances of religion in environmental justice movements. In perhaps the most famous example, the Chipko Movement in India drew on Hindu symbol and Ghandian values as villagers protested logging of local forests. Their protests can and have been interpreted according to cultural, political, ethical, and religious values.

Many other movements around the world interpret sustainability as a dimension of political justice. They may draw on concepts such as "ecological debt" and "ecological footprint" in order to illustrate the outsized impact of global North societies in relation to global South societies. Fairness and temporality matter here not only in terms of obligations for the future but culpabilities for past actions. In regard to climate change, for example, some poorer countries insist that the industrialized nations that exhausted the atmosphere as a carbon sink bear proportionate responsibility for mitigating climate effects and/or distributing adaptive technologies. A political notion of justice may then shape what they consider an appropriate response.

Advocates of all three models can be found within many religious communities, which makes the debates over sustainability within religious traditions especially interesting to observe. The future of human civilization is debated and imagined through contests over the future of a religious community, conducted through various uses of religious and cultural resources. The contests are especially interesting to observe within the global religious traditions because they include among their members constituents from both North and South, from many cultures, and from wealthy and poor classes. One obvious example of that tension may be seen in how global religious communities exhibit ambivalence in regard to globalizing social relations and, consequently, uncertainty about whether to take contextual or universalist approaches to global problems.

Conclusion

This chapter has shown that the task of interpreting sustainability encounters dimensions of religious thought and inquiry in multiple ways. Making sense of sustainability requires at least recognizing the religious responses and questions that this challenge to humanity provokes. It may not be possible to offer a full account of humanity in its planetary context without some recourse to religion, if not in tradition and symbol, at least in cultural function. Yet whether global society needs a full account or a shared account remains an open question. The variety, creativity, and wildness of religious forms in the coming century may be assessed by this basic question: Do they sustain hope?

Case study: the Misali Ethics Project[5]

A few years ago, the catch was becoming scarce in the overfished waters around Pemba, an island off the coast of Tanzania. Fishermen ignored government regulations set in the Tanzanian capital, and as fish became inaccessible to their nets, they began resorting to dynamite and poison, with destructive consequences for the coral. Why such obviously destructive practices?

Pemba's inhabitants are nearly all Muslim, and while Islamic law includes many restrictions protecting land species and waterways, conservation of marine animals has been an underdeveloped arena of Islamic ethics. Moral behavior in Islam is regulated through law (*shari'a*), so if some aspect of life is unaddressed by *shari'a* the faithful may find themselves without explicit moral guidance. Animals that live in water are exempt from most protections that apply to terrestrial animals, because the Qur'an states: "Lawful to you is the pursuit of water-game and its use for food." The Qur'an asserts that the water of rivers, streams, and seas is pure, and it permits eating animals from such water. Furthermore, it sets no explicit restrictions on how they may be hunted. Consequently, Islamic law has traditionally imposed few restrictions on the use of water-dwelling wildlife.

After centuries of fishing the marine area of Misali (about five miles off the coast of Pemba) without protections, improved technology—better boats and finer nets—and increased demand—from tourists and mainland fishmongers—began to threaten fish stocks. As the fish became harder to catch, fishermen resorted to more aggressive techniques, with negative consequences for both fish stocks and the marine ecosystem. Attempts by the government (distantly located on the mainland) to impose regulations were ignored. In this case, resistance from a community that had relied on traditional practices of open access to a resource may have been further animated by the perception of marine regulations as un-Islamic.

In 1998 the Islamic Foundation for Ecology and Environmental Sciences, CARE International, the World Wide Fund for Nature, and the Alliance of Religions and Conservation developed an environmental education program based on Islamic principles. In a series of workshops for local fishermen, juridical authorities worked with marine specialists to highlight Qur'anic verses on conservation of natural resources. While the leaders could not point to the strongest normative proscriptions—an explicit statement from the Prophet or a saying of his Companions forbidding some activity—they could point to general principles that shape the expression of *shari'a*. The workshops therefore focused on general legal principles of stewardship (*khilafa*), prohibition of waste, and maintenance of balance (*mizan*), or public benefit (*maslahah*). Such general jurisprudential principles orient ethical objectives of the law as a whole, regulating its expression in everyday context. The workshops helped participants to discover normative criteria for acceptable fishing (especially maintaining balance and public benefit) even in the absence of a specific Qur'anic code of fishing.

Since the workshops, local religious leaders have become involved as environmental guardians. As a result, the fishing practices of the community have changed (no dynamite, no poison, no tightly woven nets), with a resulting upsurge in the community's fish reserves. Furthermore, some of the waters may be designated as a *hima* (protected reserve under Islamic law), which would entail additional protections for the fishery.

The Misali Ethics Project is presented by its supporting non-governmental organizations (NGOs) as an example of dramatic and powerful normative change achieved by working with the religious tradition of a particular community. They claim that it has helped approximately 10,000 villagers on the islands of Pemba and nearby Zanzibar to develop new social practices that will ensure the stability of the fishery and assist the communities in continuing to develop sustainably. The case seems to show that a contextual, traditionalist approach can be effective even when there is a prevailing, environmentally harmful practice (overfishing and dynamiting) reliant on a religious principle (free access to marine resources).

Discussion questions

1   What conditions or factors facilitated religious change in this case? Was that change appropriate? Sufficient? What else would you need to know to make a judgment?
2   What seems to have been the relation between the change in religious norms and the change in fishing practices? What other factors may have been at play?
3   What model of sustainability does the Misali fishing community seem to have adopted? What criticisms could be raised about that model?
4   Does the change on a pervasively Muslim island offer hints for the cultural changes needed in more pluralist societies? Could Islamic principles of *khilafa* or *mizan* have a role to play in interfaith or secular discussions of sustainability?
5   Are there environmental problems that would pose a more difficult challenge for traditional Muslim communities? How might they, for example, address the global problem of climate change? What changes in the tradition and/or the community would be required to address that problem?

Notes

1   Some of the following has been adapted from Jenkins (2009).
2   Among the precursors is the 1974 Cocoyoc Declaration, issued in a UN environmental symposium, which observed that increasing demands of humanity could not be endlessly sustained.
3   Report of the UN Conference on the Human Environment (Stockholm 1972), Principles 2 and 3.
4   Despite the contrast here, note that membership in an indigenous way of life and a global religious tradition is possible, as many of the Gwich'in people of Northern Alaska prove.
5   Case adapted from Ahmad and Bruch (2002) and Khalid (2003).

References

Ahmad, A. and C. Bruch (2002) "Maintaining Mizan: Protecting Biodiversity in Muslim Communities," *Environmental Law Review* 32: 10020–37.
Bakken, P.W., J.G. Engel, and R.J. Engel (1995) *Ecology, Justice, and Christian Faith: A Critical Guide to the Literature*, Westport, CT: Greenwood Press.
Barry, B. (1997) "Sustainability and Intergenerational Justice," *Theoria* 45: 43–65.
Daly, H.E. (1990) "Toward Some Operational Principles of Sustainable Development," *Ecological Economics* 2(1): 1–6.

Daly, H.E. and J. Cobb (1994) *For the Common Good: Redirecting the Economy Toward Community, the Environment, and a Sustainable Future*, Boston: Beacon Press.

Diamond, J. (2005) *Collapse: How Societies Choose to Fail or Succeed*, New York: Penguin.

The Earth Charter (2009) http://www.earthcharterinaction.org/content/pages/Read-the-Charter.html (accessed December 1, 2009).

Hallman, D. (2001) "Climate Change and Ecumenical Work on Sustainable Community," in D. Hessel and L. Rasumssen (eds) *Earth Habitat: Eco-Injustice and the Church's Response*, Minneapolis: Fortress Press.

International Union for Conservation of Nature (1980) "World Conservation Strategy," Gland: World Conservation Union, United Nations Environment Programme, World Wide Fund for Nature.

Jenkins, W. (2009) "Sustainability Theories," in W. Jenkins (ed.) *The Spirit of Sustainability*, Great Barrington, MA: Berkshire Publishers.

Khalid, F. (2003) "Practical Islamic Environmentalism," available at http://ifees.org.uk/index.php?option=com_content&task=view&id=40&Itemid=55 (accessed December 1, 2009).

Lubchenco, J., A.M. Olson, L.B. Brubaker, S.R. Carpenter, M.M. Holland, S.P. Hubbell, S.A. Levin, J.A. Macmahon, P.A. Matson, J.M. Melillo, H.A. Mooney, C.H. Peterson, H.R. Pulliam, L.A. Real, P.J. Regal, and P.G. Risser (1991) "The Sustainable Biosphere Initiative: An Ecological Research Agenda," *Ecology* 72.2: 371–412.

Meadows, D.H., D.I Meadows, J. Randers, and W.W. Behrens (1972) *The Limits to Growth: A Report for the Club of Rome's Project on the Predicament of Mankind*, New York: Universe Books.

Norton, B.G. (2005) *Sustainability: A Philosophy of Adaptive Ecosystem Management*, Chicago: University of Chicago Press.

Palmer, C. (1994) "Some Problems with Sustainability," *Studies in Christian Ethics* 7(1): 52–62.

Radkau, J. (2008) *Nature and Power: A Global History of the Environment*, trans. T. Dunlap, Washington, DC: Cambridge University Press.

Rasmussen, L. (2005) "Christianity and Sustainable Communities," in B. Taylor (ed.) *The Encyclopedia of Religion and Nature*, New York: Thoemmes Continuum.

Robinson, J. (2004) "Squaring the Circle? Some Thoughts on the Idea of Sustainable Development," *Ecological Economics* 48: 369–84.

Rockefeller, S. (2001) "Global Interdependence, the Earth Charter, and Christian Faith," in D.T. Hessel and L. Rasmussen (eds) *Earth Habitat: Eco-Injustice and the Church's Response*, Minneapolis: Augsburg Fortress.

Tucker, M.E. (2003) *Worldly Wonder: Religions Enter Their Ecological Phase*, Chicago: Open Court Publishing.

World Commission on Environment and Development (1987) *Our Common Future*, New York: Oxford University Press.

Further reading

Agyeman, J. (2005) *Sustainable Communities and the Challenge of Environmental Justice*, New York: New York University Press.

Daly, H.E. (1996) *Beyond Growth: The Economics of Sustainable Development*, Boston: Beacon Press.

Jenkins, W. (2008) "Global ethics, Christian theology, and Sustainability," *Worldviews: Global Religions, Culture, and Ecology* 12: 197–217.

Jonas, H. (1984) *The Imperative of Responsibility*, Chicago: University of Chicago Press.

Plumwood, V. (2002) *Environmental Culture: The Ecological Crisis of Reason*, New York: Routledge.

Rolston, H. (1994) *Conserving Natural Value*, New York: Columbia University Press.

Sen, A. (1999) *Development as Freedom*, New York: Random House.

Solow, R.M. (1993) "Sustainability: An Economist's Perspective," in R. Dorfman and N.S. Dorfman (eds) *Economics of the Environment*, New York: Norton.

Wirzba, N. (2003) *The Paradise of God: Renewing Religion in an Ecological Age*, New York: Columbia University Press.

Chapter 9

Animals and religion[1]

Dave Aftandilian

Introduction

For as long as we have been human, and perhaps well before that, animals have played key roles in our religious beliefs.[2] More than 30,000 years ago, for example, the Paleolithic peoples of western Europe painted carefully detailed, naturalistic images of Ice Age animals on the walls of caves like Chauvet and Lascaux in France (Bahn and Vertut 1997; Chauvet *et al.* 1996). Without written records, we cannot know for certain what these animal images meant to the people who painted them. Nevertheless, we can be sure that these images, and the animals they depicted, were central to Paleolithic religious beliefs and practices. This is true because of both the very high quality of the paintings and their location in the spiritually charged, liminal spaces of caves, which are so often connected with death and rebirth for peoples around the world.

Moving to more recent times, animals have been important subjects and objects of religious belief for indigenous peoples around the world, from the Earth Diver duck of the creation stories of the Cheyenne people in North America (Grinnell 1962 [1926]: 242–44) to the Ancestral Kangaroo of the Yolngu Aboriginal people of Australia (Morphy 1989: 155–57). Animals also figure prominently in other religious traditions, from the symbolic lamb of Christianity to the sacred Mother Cow of Hindu religions. We should also note that human beings ourselves are animals, and so even when religions seem fully anthropocentric or speciesist, they are nonetheless also discussing animals—human ones.

Yet despite their importance in nearly every human religion, the roles of other than human animals in religious beliefs have received little sustained, critical study until very recently. For example, the Animals and Religion Consultation of the American Academy of Religion was not officially founded until 2003 (Van Horn, forthcoming), and *A Communion of Subjects*, the first comprehensive survey of the roles of animals in world and indigenous religious traditions, was not published until 2006 (Waldau and Patton 2006a).[3] Why has there been so little interest in studying animals and religion for so long?

As editors Paul Waldau and Kimberley Patton point out in their introduction to *A Communion of Subjects*, part of the answer lies in contemporary Western cultures' difficulty understanding animals on their own terms (Waldau and Patton 2006b: 13). Western thinkers have long focused on drawing a dividing line between us and other animals. For example, the ancient Stoics and later Cartesian-inspired scientists argued that the capacity to reason separated humans from other animals (Steiner 2006).

However, more recent ethological and cognitive research has shown that other animals are able not only to think, but also to feel emotional states we might recognize and accurately describe in human terms such as "joy," "grief," and more (Bekoff 2006; Griffin 2001). Individual animals also have characteristic personalities that differentiate them from other members of their species, as anyone who has lived with a companion animal knows (perhaps all too well!; see also Waldau and Patton 2006b: 13–14). Furthermore, Marc Bekoff, Frans de Waal, and others have even shown that animals possess a highly developed sense of morality (Bekoff and Pierce 2009; de Waal 2009; Hauser 2006). As older scientific notions of our difference from other animals have begun to break down, many have come to see animals as ethically important beings, fellow travelers on our spiritual as well as terrestrial journeys, and therefore worthy of our study and care.

Moreover, just as ethological studies have been shifting to ask new questions about other animals in recent decades, so too have studies of animals in other disciplines. Scholars from anthropology, art history, critical theory, history, literary studies, philosophy, semiotics, sociology, and other disciplines have begun to focus on understanding the meanings of animals in past and present human societies, texts, and artworks. A new field of study has been born from this intellectual ferment, variously known as "animal studies," "critical animal studies," or "human–animal interactions." Scholars of animals and religion are inspired by, draw from, and contribute to these new humanistic and social scientific studies of animals, along with cognitive, ecological, ethological, and evolutionary studies of animals from the natural sciences. And, of course, personal observations and experiences of real animals also undergird the study of animals and religion—even if some scholars may be uncomfortable making this connection explicit in their works for fear of ridicule from differently inclined colleagues (e.g. Aftandilian 2007b: xi).

9A

Which academic disciplines do you think are most relevant to helping us better understand other than human animals? Which disciplines are most relevant to helping us decide how human beings ought to treat and live alongside animals?

Thus far, studies of animals and religion have focused primarily on uncovering the roles of animals within existing faith traditions. Through this work of recovery, we can learn not just about animals as religious subjects or objects within a given religion, but also about deeper aspects of that religion itself. Such aspects might include the meaning of sacrifice or the afterlife, or who a religion sees as members of—or set apart from—its own religious community (Van Horn, forthcoming). Such studies also have a practical dimension: They may inspire people of faith within a given tradition to change their own personal or congregational approaches to animals. For example, studies of the importance of animals as worthy objects of religious concern in Jewish and Christian traditions have led many members of these faiths to become vegetarians (see, e.g., www.jewishveg.com and www.all-creatures.org/cva/), and have inspired many congregations to include more humane foods in their potluck dinners and to support animal welfare.

Once the meanings of animals within a given tradition have been fleshed out, we can then undertake comparative studies of animals and religion in various faith traditions in terms of categories such as creation stories, sacrifice, or the question of whether animals have a soul. Such studies can further illuminate the roles of animals, as well as the roles of real versus symbolic animals, within particular traditions. And of course they can highlight similarities and differences in approaches to animals in different faith traditions.

As with the study of other "Others" such as women or people of color within religious traditions, studying animals and religion can also help us better understand foundational concepts for religious studies in general. Such concepts include, for example, who counts as a "person" capable of religious subjectivity in various traditions. Studies along these latter lines are taking the field of animals and religion in intriguing new directions, including the study of other animals as themselves potentially religious.

Tradition-based approaches

In his book *A Greener Faith*, Roger Gottlieb identifies four paths that religious environmentalists have taken to respond to the environmental crisis: *recovery* of neglected pro-environmental parts of their spiritual traditions; *reinterpretation* and/or critique of existing traditions; *evolution* of new models within existing traditions; or radical *innovation*, creating entirely new liturgies, rituals, stories, etc. (Gottlieb 2006: 21ff). Although Gottlieb did not develop this framework specifically for the study of animals and religion, it nevertheless offers a useful structure by which to understand the various approaches scholars and traditions have taken to animals.

Recovery

Scholars have been exploring the roles of animals within nearly every world and indigenous religious tradition, past and present (see Waldau and Patton

2006a for a sense of the range of these studies). Some studies are primarily theological or historical, while others focus on sacred art, narratives, or lived practices, ritual and otherwise (see the lists in the References and Further reading sections at the end of this chapter for examples). These studies have revealed a wide range of often neglected roles that animals play in religions, including serving as sources of spiritual power, mediators of the divine, teachers, spiritual agents or companions, and objects of religious concern.

In indigenous traditions, for instance, animals often serve as sources of spiritual power for humans. Bears and beavers have been seen as bringers of healing powers by native peoples throughout North America (Aftandilian 2007a: 234–37; Rockwell 2003: 74–89), while raptorial birds give humans the power to become better hunters and warriors (e.g. Brown 1992: 40–45). These beliefs are based at least in part on close observations of the actual behaviors of real animals: owls, for instance, are peerless and silent hunters of the night (Aftandilian 2007a: 422–23), while beavers may be seen to bring healing powers because of the wide range of medicinal plants that they eat.[4]

Animals also serve as mediators who help awaken and connect humans to the divine presence. For example, in the Hebrew Bible's story of Balaam and his donkey (Numbers 22:21–35), the donkey was able to see the angel that God had placed in the road to block Balaam's path, while Balaam was not. Because his donkey turned aside, obeying God rather than Balaam, God spared both Balaam's and the donkey's life (Roy 2007: 206).

In many traditions, animals act as teachers, modeling proper religious and social behavior. Christian stories about Saint Francis are particularly rich in examples of the piety of other animals (Hobgood-Oster 2008: 67–69). In one story, a multitude of birds listen attentively to Francis's sermon about their need to praise God; after he gives them leave to depart by making the sign of the cross, the birds soar up into the air and divide into four parts like the cross Francis signed over them. Their songs carry and spread the word of God to the four quarters, just as proper Christians are supposed to do. In another story, Francis arises before dawn and goes out to pray. Because the world is covered in snow, none of the other brothers joins him in morning prayers, but a faithful cricket does, offering an example of how animals can attend to the sacred office of prayer better than many humans.

This view of animals as teachers also occurs in many other religious traditions. For example, an early Buddhist *Jataka* tale describes a goat which was about to be sacrificed by the presiding Brahman (Chapple 1993: 24). The goat suddenly laughed, and then let out a mournful cry. When the Brahman asked the goat to explain, the goat said that he laughed because he realized he had suffered as a goat in his last 500 births, but would be reborn as a human in his next life. But he wept with compassion for the Brahman, who would suffer the same fate as soon as he sacrificed the goat. The Brahman freed the goat, which trotted away; the goat was struck by lightning a few moments later, and thereby freed of his suffering. The Brahman was also saved, thanks to the goat's teaching about the spiritual dangers of sacrificing animals.

As this example shows, many religious traditions also view animals as spiritual companions connected with humans through shared creation, reincarnation, and/or possession of a soul. In the traditions of many Native American tribes, for example, animals are understood to have souls. The Oglala Lakota say that animals and humans share the same four souls (Brown and Cousins 2001: 89–90), and the Ojibwe of Parry Island explain that "not only men, but animals, trees, even rocks and water are tripartite, possessing bodies, souls, and shadows" (Jenness 1935: 20).[5] Furthermore, instead of being described as lower on the spiritual or evolutionary ladder than humans, animals rank *above* humans in most, if not all, Native American cosmologies. Ojibwe writer Basil Johnston explains that in the beliefs of his tribe "creation was conducted in a certain order: plants, insects, birds, animals, and human beings. In the order of necessity, humans were the last and the least; they would not last long without the other forms of beings" (Johnston 2003: ix).[6]

However, many religious traditions do not share Native Americans' views of animals as superior to humans in terms of their spiritual ranking. In Abrahamic traditions, animals and other humans are all created by God, and are therefore of concern to God (DeWitt 2000; Patton 2000: 409–10; Wennberg 2003: 289–92; see also Romans 8:18–25). But the first creation story in Genesis makes it clear that humans are superior to other animals, because only humans are made in God's image: "Then God said, 'Let us make humankind in our image, according to our likeness; and let them have dominion ... over all the wild animals of the earth.'" (Genesis 1:26).

Furthermore, traditional interpretations of both Jewish and Christian theology indicate that animals do not have souls (Linzey and Cohn-Sherbok 1997: 1–16). Even in Hindu traditions, which almost universally agree that animals and humans have qualitatively similar souls (*ātman*s), humans are still ranked above animals, because only humans can receive revelation through sacred texts (Vedas); therefore only humans normally have access to spiritual liberation (*moksa* or *mukti*) (Nelson 2006: 181–85).

9B

What roles have animals played in world and indigenous religions? How might the recovery of and new attention to these roles be influenced by the increasing recognition of other animals as thinking, feeling subjects like ourselves?

Reinterpretation, evolution, innovation

How do we respond to hierarchical, speciesist, anthropocentric conceptions of animals in religious traditions like these? For many contemporary theologians and people of faith, the answer has been to criticize and/or reinterpret such traditions. The meaning of "dominion" in Genesis 1:26, for example, has been extensively reinterpreted. Most often, such reinterpretations read "dominion" as referring to a stewardship responsibility on the part of humans toward animals, not *carte blanche* to do with the rest of creation as we like (Fowler 1995: 80–86; Gottlieb 2006: 24–30). Islam speaks of a similar stewardship responsibility for humans; the Qur'an describes humans as Allah's "vice-regents" (*khalifa*) on Earth (Sura 2:30), trustees who are responsible for caring for the creation (Foltz 2006: 15–16; Izzi Dien 2000: 74–77).

9C

How might differing theological understandings of humans as responsible for dominion and/or stewardship over the Earth influence our conceptions of religious duties toward animals?

British theologian Andrew Linzey has developed one of the more far-reaching reinterpretations of Christian theology regarding animals. In his pivotal book *Animal Theology*, Linzey argues that humans not only have a stewardship responsibility toward creation, but actually are charged with service and self-sacrifice on behalf of other animals, "co-operating with God in the healing and liberating of creation" (Linzey 1995: 45). On this reading of Christian theology, humans are still unique among God's creations, but mainly because of our moral capacity to care for all other beings. For Linzey, in other words, humans are unique in our "ability to become the servant species" (1995: 57).

Recovery and reinterpretation of religious traditions regarding animals have also led to the evolution of new approaches within these traditions, and to the creation of entirely new liturgies, rituals, and stories. For example, Rabbi Arthur Waskow has led the search among Jews for a new understanding of what it means to keep kosher in the contemporary world; he calls this new practice "eco-kosher" (Waskow 1995). Traditional kosher laws cover approved and non-approved slaughtering practices (Cohn-Sherbok 2006: 85–86), but they do not address the issue of factory farming, whose horrendous consequences for the lives of animals certainly seem to violate the Jewish ethical principle of kindness to animals (*tsa'ar ba'alei chayim*) (Kalechofsky 2006: 96–98). To keep eco-kosher in this context, then, might mean not eating meat from factory farmed animals, or perhaps even not eating meat at all. Other examples of new approaches to animals being developed within existing traditions include adaptations of traditional Buddhist memorial services in Japan for deceased companion animals (Ambros forthcoming; Kenney 2004) and the rapid spread of Christian blessings of the animals during the late twentieth century from Catholic churches into many denominations that had not sponsored such services before (Hobgood-Oster 2008: 107–28).

Innovative approaches to animals are also being created *de novo* within and outside religious traditions. For example, while Jewish and Christian theologies traditionally have not attributed a soul to animals, a few theologians and many ordinary believers have long questioned this view (see, e.g., Shanahan 2002). Even so eminent a theologian as Martin Luther could not bear the thought of an afterlife without his beloved canine companion Tölpel; when asked whether he expected to find dogs in heaven, Luther replied, "[C]ertainly" (Bainton 1957: 8–9). Today, many Christians grieving the loss of their beloved companion animals take solace in the new story of the Rainbow Bridge. There animals who have passed on are said to wait for their human companions to join them, so that they can cross the Rainbow Bridge to heaven together (see www.rainbowbridge.org).

9D

Why do you think many religions have taught that animals do not have souls? What would be at stake in changing such a teaching?

New rituals are also being developed outside mainstream religious traditions to help people reconnect to animals and express concern for their welfare. The Council of All Beings ritual, for example, arose out of the deep ecology movement in the 1980s. In this ritual, humans take on the role of some aspect of the natural world, often an animal, and express the being's anger and sadness at environmental devastation. Later in the ritual, participants also draw on the being's spiritual power to help humans resolve the problems about which each being had spoken (Fleming and Macy 1995; Seed *et al.* 1988). During the 1990s, various online communities began to coalesce around the concept of spiritual therianthropy—mentally transforming into an animal with whom one feels a special bond as a way to connect more closely both with that species and with one's own spirituality (Aftandilian and Copeland 2007: 610). Rather than fearing the intense spiritual connection that humans can feel to animals (Sax 2009: 329), participants in rituals like these instead are seeking new ways to rediscover and strengthen these human–animal spiritual bonds.

Thinking animals, rethinking religion

While important work on the meanings of animals within religious traditions continues today, other scholars are turning to new and potentially more fundamental questions about how taking animals seriously as thinking, feeling subjects might reshape the study of religion itself. Recent work in cognitive ethology has shown us that animals think and feel, just as humans do (see p. 114). How might these facts affect our understandings of religion?

Contemporary western scientific views of animals as subjects are coming closer to what many indigenous peoples have been saying for thousands of years: animals are people, too. Different peoples, to be sure, because each species of animal is unique; but similar in that animals can all think, feel, and possess spiritual powers and insights from which humans can benefit. For example, the Ojibwe peoples of North America do not class just humans as people, but also consider spiritually powerful beings from the world of nature to be people, including certain kinds of animal beings. Irving Hallowell, an anthropologist who worked with the Ojibwe, refers to these kinds of animals as "other than human persons" (Hallowell 1960; see also Harvey 2006: 17–20). These other than human persons think and act in the world just as humans can. They also have souls, just like us (e.g. Jenness 1935: 20). Most Native American tribes share a similar conception of animals (Grim 2006), and so do many other indigenous peoples (see, e.g., Bird-David 1999; Willerslev 2007: 73ff).

This concept of animals not just as subjects, but as *persons*, suggests that humans can enter into meaningful relationships with animals, just as we do with other human persons. For people of faith and others, then, the question becomes: What sorts of relationships ought we to enter into with animals? "Geologian" and Passionist monk Thomas Berry suggested that we ought to recognize that all modes of life have value, and that humans are not superior to other animals, but just one species among many; in other words, he recommends a *communal* relationship with other animals (Berry 2006).[7] Feminist ethicists and philosophers, in turn, have proposed a *caring* relationship with animals. Such a relationship would include grieving with animals who are suffering because of human actions such as destroying their habitat or factory farming them for meat (Adams 2006; Donovan and Adams 2007), and even praying on their behalf (Adams 2004).[8]

9E

How might this view that animals are "other than human persons," which is common among many indigenous peoples, influence ethical and religious conceptions of animals in industrial and globalized cultures? How might it influence religious responses to environmental problems?

Furthermore, if animals are thinking, feeling persons who also have souls, could they enter into *religious* relationships? Asking such a question takes us into *terra* that at first glance looks very much *incognita*—how can we possibly tell if animals are religious, given the difficulties scholars have long encountered in trying to understand animals on their own terms (Nagel 1974; Waldau and Patton 2006b: 13–14)? Yet the problem is not insurmountable. As mentioned earlier, Marc Bekoff, Frans de Waal, and others have demonstrated that animals have a moral sense; because morality is often seen as a prerequisite for religion, the presence of a moral sense in animals suggests they have the potential to be religious.

Other ethologists have also noted behaviors in animals that seem analogous to human ritual practices, which again suggests the possibility of religiosity in animals. For example, elephants not only recognize dead elephants, but grieve for the loss of family members (sometimes at the risk of their own lives) and bury their dead (Moss 2000: 73–74, 269–71). Jane Goodall has observed chimpanzees dancing in awe and wonder beneath the spray of a waterfall in the Kakombe Valley (Goodall 2003: 188–89), and Jill Pruetz has seen a savanna chimpanzee in Senegal making a similar dance-display toward a slow-moving brush fire (Pruetz and LaDuke 2009: 3). Walter Burkert (1986: 40–42) has argued that the practice in some human cultures of ritually sacrificing body parts developed out of analogous sacrificial behaviors of animals, such as a fox gnawing off its own leg to escape a trap.

There are also numerous examples of world and indigenous religions recognizing the potential of animals to be religious (Patton 2000: 417–21). We have already discussed saints' stories from Catholic traditions that describe animals as pious (Hobgood-Oster 2008: 66–69). Psalm 148 provides another example from the Judaeo-Christian tradition; in this psalm, all the wild animals of creation are called to praise God, as are humans. In Islamic traditions, animals are described as praising God, receiving divine revelation, and even being the first to observe the fast (Foltz 2006: 16–20). For example, it is written in the Qur'an, "Don't you see that it is Allah Whose praises all things in the heavens and earth do celebrate, and the birds (of the air) with wings outspread? Each one knows its own (mode of) prayer and praise" (Sura 24:41). Similarly, the Prophet forbade the killing of frogs, since he believed they praised God through their croaking. And in a Buddhist *Jataka* tale, we meet a hare who keeps a monthly fast and encourages his fellow animals to do the same (Patton 2000: 420).

9F

Can other than human animals themselves be religious? Why or why not?

Finally, thinking through this question of whether animals themselves might be religious subjects (not just objects of religious interest) compels us to rethink some of the most foundational concepts in religious studies. We must, for example, reflect critically on what we really mean by terms that are often too vaguely defined, such as "religion," "religious," "ritual," and "sacrifice" (see Taylor 1998 for essays on several of these critical terms; for critical analyses of "sacrifice" through the lens of animals and religion, see Klawans 2006; Patton 2006). The study of animals and religion, then, leads us to rethink not just what animals mean in traditional or new religions, but also what the category of religion itself means to us.

Case study: creation stories and views of animals

Stories are one of the most powerful ways that humans make sense of the world around us, including our relationship to the divine. The stories we tell about animals profoundly affect our understandings of their importance in the human and supernatural realms; therefore, changing the stories we tell about animals can change how we view and treat them (Aftandilian 2007b: xvi; Hobgood-Oster 2007: 199). Conversely, since every society's stories about animals are deeply affected by its attitudes towards them, we can better understand a given culture's or religion's views of animals by critically analyzing such stories.

If we want to understand how people of faith understand animals in relation to the divine, we would do well to focus on creation stories involving animals. Such stories play an especially important role in constructing people's perceptions of animals because they lay the foundations for how each people sees the world and its proper place in it, as well as its duties toward the world and other beings. Because they are set in the mythic era at the dawn of time, such accounts of origins are "both explained and validated as part of a design built into the world from its very beginnings" (Hiebert 1996: 30). The roles animals play in creation stories, then, profoundly influence the ways the people who tell those stories view and treat animals.

Below are excerpts from two different creation stories involving animals. The first is from the Yuchi, a Native American people who originally lived in the Southeastern United States, but who now live in Oklahoma. The second is from the Judaeo-Christian Bible. Read both stories, and then consider the comparative questions at the end of this case study.

Yuchi creation story excerpt (Lankford 1987: 107)

In the beginning not a thing existed; there was only water and some animal creatures, as the old people used to tell. The fowl of the air and the sun met together: they held council [on] what they could do to find the earth. The sun took the lead at their meeting. They asked the animals in the water to search for earth; they expected the beaver could find some earth, but he could not. And then they expected the fish-otter to dive, but he also could not do it. Thereupon they asked the crawfish, who said, "If I dive into the water, the following signs will show you: if I cannot come back to the surface of the water, blood will rise up. If, however, I come back with earth, some dirty yellow water will rise to the surface." He did not know whether he could get to where the earth was, but they sent him anyway. He went down into the water, and after they had waited for a long time, they saw some dirty yellow water coming to the surface, and then the crawfish himself appeared with a little dirt between his claws. It was only very little dirt; they took it and hit it against something that was sticking out of the water, and the earth was made. Some storytellers, however, say that they just threw the earth upon the water and then the earth was made. The crawfish had dived for earth for a long time, and when he came back to the surface of the water the dirt had almost melted, just a little was left over; after the earth was made, the other animals were also created.

Genesis 1 creation story excerpts (New Revised Standard Version, NRSV)

In the beginning when God created the heavens and the earth, the earth was a formless void and darkness covered the face of the deep, while a wind from God swept over the face of the waters. ...

And God said, "Let the waters under the sky be gathered together into one place, and let the dry land appear." And it was so. God called the dry land Earth, and the waters that were gathered together he called Seas. And God saw that it was good. Then God said, "Let the earth put forth vegetation: plants yielding seed, and fruit trees of every kind on earth that bear fruit with the seed in it." And it was so. The earth brought forth vegetation: plants yielding seed of every kind, and trees of every kind bearing fruit with the seed in it. And God saw that it was good. ...

And God said, "Let the waters bring forth swarms of living creatures, and let birds fly above the earth across the dome of the sky." So God created the great sea monsters and every living creature that moves, of every kind, with which the waters swarm, and every winged bird of every kind. And God saw that it was good. God blessed them, saying, "Be fruitful and multiply and fill the waters in the seas, and let birds multiply on the earth." ...

And God said, "Let the earth bring forth living creatures of every kind: cattle and creeping things and wild animals of the earth of every kind." And it was so. God made the wild animals of the earth of every kind, and the cattle of every kind, and everything that creeps upon the ground of every kind. And God saw that it was good.

Then God said, "Let us make humankind in our image, according to our likeness; and let them have dominion over the fish of the sea, and over the birds of the air, and over the cattle, and over all the wild animals of the earth, and over every creeping thing that creeps upon the earth."

Discussion questions

1 What roles do animals play in each creation story? What role do humans play in each creation story?
2 How might the relative importance of the roles played by animals and humans in these two stories affect how the readers/listeners view the relative subjectivity and power of animals and humans?
3 For whom was the Earth created in each story? How might the differing answers to this question in each story affect the views of animals and humans held by the people who tell them?
4 In the Yuchi story, what does it mean that it was the crawfish who succeeded at finding the earth? What does this suggest about how the Yuchi view different kinds of animals?
5 What duties do humans have toward animals in the Genesis story? How might the answer to this question affect how humans view and treat animals?

Notes

1 Thank you to Sarah F. Rose and the volume editors for their close readings of this chapter. Laura Hobgood-Oster and Aaron Gross also provided valuable feedback. Any errors or infelicities that remain are, of course, my own responsibility.
2 For convenience, throughout this chapter I will refer to other than human animals simply as "animals."
3 Informal discussions about proposing an Animals and Religion Consultation to the American Academy of Religion began in 1997, and the Forum on Religion and Ecology sponsored a conference on "World Religions and Animals" in 1999. This conference, in turn, led to the publication of *A Communion of Subjects* in 2006. I am most grateful to Gavin Van Horn for sharing his research on this subject.
4 For example, beavers are fond of willow bark, which contains salicylic acid, the active ingredient in aspirin. Humans who observed and then copied beaver food habits may have discovered the analgesic properties of willow bark, and used it as a medicine (Müller-Schwarze and Lixing Sun 2003: 43).
5 For more on Native American conceptions of the soul, see Hultkrantz 1997.
6 In part this ranking of animals above humans in the cosmological scheme of things is probably due to a traditional respect for elders in Native American cultures (Beck and Walters 1977: 204–06; Brown and Cousins 2001: 50–53; McNally 2009). Since the animals were created first, they are our *elder* brothers and sisters, with more knowledge about how to live in the world and spiritual power than humans possess.
7 The Judaeo-Christian story of Noah's ark and the flood (Gen. 6–9) also suggests that humans and animals are literally in the same boat, in an ecological sense.
8 The Council of All Beings ritual discussed earlier is partly intended to help humans cope with our shame and grief regarding how human actions have harmed other animals.

References

Adams, C. (2004) *Prayers for Animals*, New York: Continuum.

——(2006) "'A Very Rare and Difficult Thing': Ecofeminism, Attention to Animal Suffering and the Disappearance of the Subject," in P. Waldau and K. Patton (eds) *A Communion of Subjects: Animals in Religion, Science, and Ethics*, New York: Columbia University Press.

Aftandilian, D. (2007a) "Animals, Agriculture, and Religion among Native Americans in Precontact Illinois: An Interdisciplinary Analysis of Perception and Representation," unpublished Ph.D. thesis, Department of Anthropology, University of Chicago.

——(2007b) "Introduction: Of Bats, Animal Studies, and Real Animals," in D. Aftandilian, M.W. Copeland, and D. Scofield Wilson (eds) *What Are the Animals to Us? Approaches from Science, Religion, Folklore, Literature, and Art*, Knoxville: University of Tennessee Press.

Aftandilian, D. and M.W. Copeland (2007) "Shapeshifting," in Marc Bekoff (ed.) *Encyclopedia of Human–Animal Relationships: A Global Exploration of Our Connections with Animals*, vol. 2, Westport, CT: Greenwood Press.

Ambros, B. (forthcoming) "Memorials for Pets," in John Nelson and Inken Prohl (eds) *The Handbook of Contemporary Japanese Religions*, Leiden: E.J. Brill.

Bahn, P.G. and J. Vertut (1997) *Journey through the Ice Age*, Berkeley and Los Angeles: University of California Press.

Bainton, R.H. (1957) "Luther on Birds, Dogs, and Babies: Gleanings from the 'Table Talk'," in *Luther Today*, Martin Luther Lectures vol. 1, Decorah, IA: Luther College.

Beck, P.V. and A. L. Walters (1977) *The Sacred: Ways of Knowledge, Sources of Life*, Tsaile, AZ: Navajo Community College Press.

Bekoff, M. (2006) "Wild Justice, Social Cognition, Fairness, and Morality: A Deep Appreciation for the Subjective Lives of Animals," in W. Waldau and K. Patton (eds) *A Communion of Subjects: Animals in Religion, Science, and Ethics*, New York: Columbia University Press.

Bekoff, M. and J. Pierce (2009) *Wild Justice: The Moral Lives of Animals*, Chicago: University of Chicago Press.

Berry, T. (2006) "Prologue: Loneliness and Presence," in P. Waldau and K. Patton (eds) *A Communion of Subjects: Animals in Religion, Science, and Ethics*, New York: Columbia University Press.

Bird-David, N. (1999) "'Animism' Revisited: Personhood, Environment, and Relational Epistemology," *Current Anthropology* 40(S): S67–91.

Brown, J.E. (1992) *Animals of the Soul: Sacred Animals of the Oglala Sioux*, Rockport, MA: Element.

Brown, J.E. and E. Cousins (2001) *Teaching Spirits: Understanding Native American Religious Traditions*, Oxford: Oxford University Press.

Burkert, W. (1986) *Creation of the Sacred: Tracks of Biology in Early Religions*, Cambridge, MA: Harvard University Press.

Chapple, C.K. (1993) *Nonviolence to Animals, Earth, and Self in Asian Traditions*, Albany: State University of New York Press.

Chauvet, J.-M., E.B. Deschamps, and C. Hilaire (1996) *Dawn of Art: The Chauvet Cave, the Oldest Known Paintings in the World*, New York: Harry N. Abrams.

Cohn-Sherbok, D. (2006) "Hope for the Animal Kingdom: A Jewish Vision," in P. Waldau and K. Patton (eds) *A Communion of Subjects: Animals in Religion, Science, and Ethics*, New York: Columbia University Press.

de Waal, F. (2009) *Primates and Philosophers: How Morality Evolved*, Princeton, NJ: Princeton University Press.

DeWitt, C. (2000) "Behemoth and Batrachians in the Eye of God: Responsibility to Other Kinds in Biblical Perspective," in D. Hessel and R. R. Ruether (eds) *Christianity and Ecology: Seeking the Well-Being of Earth and Humans*, Cambridge, MA: Harvard University Press.

Donovan, J. and C. Adams (eds) (2007) *The Feminist Care Tradition in Animal Ethics: A Reader*, New York: Columbia University Press.

Fleming, P. and J. Macy (1995) "The Council of All Beings," in A. Drengson and Y. Inoue (eds) *The Deep Ecology Movement: An Introductory Anthology*, Berkeley, CA: North Atlantic Books.

Foltz, R. (2006) *Animals in Islamic Tradition and Muslim Cultures*, Oxford: Oneworld.

Fowler, R.B. (1995) *The Greening of Protestant Thought*, Chapel Hill: University of North Carolina Press.

Goodall, J. (2003) *Reason for Hope: A Spiritual Journey*, New York: Grand Central Publishing.

Gottlieb, R. (2006) *A Greener Faith: Religious Environmentalism and Our Planet's Future*, Oxford: Oxford University Press.

Griffin, D. (2001) *Animal Minds: Beyond Cognition to Consciousness*, Chicago: University of Chicago Press.

Grim, J. (2006) "Knowing and Being Known by Animals: Indigenous Perspectives on Personhood," in P. Waldau and K. Patton (eds) *A Communion of Subjects: Animals in Religion, Science, and Ethics*, New York: Columbia University Press.

Grinnell, G.B. (1962 [orig. pub. 1926]) *By Cheyenne Campfires*, New Haven, CT: Yale University Press.

Hallowell, A.I. (1960) "Ojibwa Ontology, Behavior, and World View," in S. Diamond (ed.) *Culture in History: Essays in Honor of Paul Radin*, New York: Columbia University Press.

Harvey, G. (2006) *Animism: Respecting the Living World*, New York: Columbia University Press.

Hauser, M. (2006) *Moral Minds: How Nature Designed Our Universal Sense of Right and Wrong*, New York: Ecco.

Hiebert, T. (1996) *The Yahwist's Landscape: Nature and Religion in Early Israel*, New York: Oxford University Press.

Hobgood-Oster, L. (2007) "Holy Dogs and Asses: Stories Told through Animal Saints," in D. Aftandilian, M.W. Copeland, and D. Scofield Wilson (eds) *What Are the Animals to Us? Approaches from Science, Religion, Folklore, Literature, and Art*, Knoxville: University of Tennessee Press.

——(2008) *Holy Dogs and Asses: Animals in the Christian Tradition*, Urbana: University of Illinois Press.

Hultkrantz, Å. (1997) *Soul and Native Americans*, ed. Robert Holland, Woodstock, CT: Spring Publications.

Izzi Dien, M. (2000) *The Environmental Dimensions of Islam*, Cambridge: Lutterworth Press.

Jenness, D. (1935) *The Ojibwa Indians of Parry Island, Their Social and Religious Life*, Ottawa: Canada Department of Mines and National Museum of Canada.

Johnston, B. (2003) *Honour Earth Mother*, Lincoln: University of Nebraska Press.

Kalechofsky, R. (2006) "Hierarchy, Kinship, and Responsibility: The Jewish Relationship to the Animal World," in P. Waldau and K. Patton (eds) *A Communion of Subjects: Animals in Religion, Science, and Ethics*, New York: Columbia University Press.

Kenney, E. (2004) "Pet Funerals and Animal Graves in Japan," *Mortality* 9(1): 42–60.

Klawans, J. (2006) "Sacrifice in Ancient Israel: Pure Bodies, Domesticated Animals, and the Divine Shepherd," in P. Waldau and K. Patton (eds) *A Communion of Subjects: Animals in Religion, Science, and Ethics*, New York: Columbia University Press.

Lankford, G.E. (1987) *Native American Legends, Southeastern Legends: Tales from the Natchez, Caddo, Biloxi, Chickasaw, and Other Nations*, Little Rock, AK: August House.

Linzey, A. (1995) *Animal Theology*, Urbana: University of Illinois Press.

Linzey, A. and D. Cohn-Sherbok (1997) *After Noah: Animals and the Liberation of Theology*, London: Mowbray.

McNally, M. (2009) *Honoring Elders: Aging, Authority, and Ojibwe Religion*, New York: Columbia University Press.

Morphy, H. (1989) "On Representing Ancestral Beings," in H. Morphy (ed.) *Animals into Art*, London: Unwin Hyman.

Moss, C. (2000) *Elephant Memories: Thirteen Years in the Life of an Elephant Family*, Chicago: University of Chicago Press.

Müller-Schwarze, D. and Lixing Sun (2003) *The Beaver: Natural History of a Wetlands Engineer*, Ithaca: Cornell University Press.

Nagel, T. (1974) "What Is It Like to Be a Bat?" *Philosophical Review* 83(4): 435–50.

Nelson, L. (2006) "Cows, Elephants, Dogs, and Other Lesser Embodiments of Ātman: Reflections on Hindu Attitudes toward Nonhuman Animals," in P. Waldau and K. Patton (eds) *A Communion of Subjects: Animals in Religion, Science, and Ethics*, New York: Columbia University Press.

Patton, K. (2000) "'He Who Sits in the Heavens Laughs': Recovering Animal Theology in the Abrahamic Traditions," *Harvard Theological Review* 93(4): 401–34.

——(2006) "Animal Sacrifice: Metaphysics of the Sublimated Victim," in P. Waldau and K. Patton (eds) *A Communion of Subjects: Animals in Religion, Science, and Ethics*, New York: Columbia University Press.

Pruetz, J.D. and T.C. LaDuke (2009) "Reaction to Fire by Savanna Chimpanzees (*Pan troglodytes verus*) at Fongoli, Senegal: Conceptualization of 'Fire Behavior' and the Case for a Chimpanzee Model," *American Journal of Physical Anthropology*, available at http://www.interscience.wiley.com (accessed February 26, 2010).

Rockwell, D. (2003) *Giving Voice to Bear: North American Indian Myths, Rituals, and Images of the Bear* (rev. ed.), Lanham, MD: Roberts Rinehart.

Roy, S.C. (2007) "Paw Prints on Preaching: The Healing Power of Biblical Stories about Animals," in D. Aftandilian, M.W. Copeland, and D. Scofield Wilson (eds)

What Are the Animals to Us? Approaches from Science, Religion, Folklore, Literature, and Art, Knoxville: University of Tennessee Press.

Sax, B. (2009) "The Magic of Animals: English Witch Trials in the Perspective of Folklore," *Anthrozoös* 22(4): 317–32.

Seed, J., J. Macy, P. Fleming, and A. Naess (1988) *Thinking Like a Mountain; Toward a Council of All Beings*, Philadelphia: New Society Publishers.

Shanahan, N.B. (2002) *There Is Eternal Life for Animals: A Book Based on Bible Scripture*, Tyngsborough, MA: Pete Publishers.

Steiner, G. (2006) "Descartes, Christianity, and Contemporary Speciesism," in P. Waldau and K. Patton (eds) *A Communion of Subjects: Animals in Religion, Science, and Ethics*, New York: Columbia University Press.

Taylor, M.C. (ed.) (1998) *Critical Terms for Religious Studies*, Chicago: University of Chicago Press.

Van Horn, G. (forthcoming) "The Buzzing, Breathing, Clicking, Clacking, Biting, Stinging, Chirping, Howling Landscape of Religious Studies," in *Inherited Land: The Changing Grounds of Religion and Ecology*, edited by W. Bauman, R. Bohannon and K. O'Brien. Eugene, OR: Pickwick.

Waldau, P. and K. Patton (eds) (2006a) *A Communion of Subjects: Animals in Religion, Science, and Ethics*, New York: Columbia University Press.

——(2006b) "Introduction," in P. Waldau and K. Patton (eds) *A Communion of Subjects: Animals in Religion, Science, and Ethics*, New York: Columbia University Press.

Waskow, A. (1995) "What Is Eco-Kosher?" in *Down-to-Earth Judaism: Food, Money, Sex, and the Rest of Life*, New York: W. Morrow, available at http://www.theshalomcenter.org/node/1284 (accessed February 5, 2010).

Wennberg, R.N. (2003) *God, Humans, and Animals: An Invitation to Enlarge Our Moral Universe*, Grand Rapids, MI: William B. Eerdmans.

Willerslev, R. (2007) *Soul Hunters: Hunting, Animism, and Personhood among the Siberian Yukaghirs*, Berkeley: University of California Press.

Further reading

Deane-Drummond, C. and D. Clough (eds) (2009) *Creaturely Theology: On God, Humans, and Other Animals*, London: SCM Press.

Gross, A. (2010) "The Question of the Animal and Religion," unpublished Ph.D. thesis, Department of Religious Studies, University of California, Santa Barbara.

Harrod, H.L. (2000) *The Animals Came Dancing: Native American Sacred Ecology and Animal Kinship*, Tucson: University of Arizona Press.

Linzey, A. and T. Regan (eds) (1990/2007) *Animals and Christianity: A Book of Readings*, Eugene, OR: Wipf & Stock.

Linzey, A. and D. Yamamoto (eds) (1998) *Animals on the Agenda: Questions about Animals for Theology and Ethics*, Urbana: University of Illinois Press.

McDaniel, J. B. (1989) *Of God and Pelicans: A Theology of Reverence for Life*, Louisville, KY: Westminster/John Knox Press.

Martin, C.L. (1999) *The Way of the Human Being*, New Haven, CT: Yale University Press.

Perlo, K.W. (2009) *Kinship and Killing: The Animal in World Religions*, New York: Columbia University Press.

Spittler, J.E. (2008) *Animals in the Apocryphal Acts of the Apostles*, Tübingen: Mohr Siebeck.

Walters, K.S. and L. Portmess (eds) (2001) *Religious Vegetarianism: From Hesiod to the Dalai Lama*, Albany: State University of New York Press.

Webb, S.H. (1998) *On God and Dogs: A Christian Theology of Compassion for Animals*, New York: Oxford University Press.

Chapter 10

Gender

Amanda Baugh

What images come to mind when we consider the relationship between gender and nature?[1] The lone male hunter of Theodore Roosevelt's wilderness cult in nineteenth-century America, escaping the constraints of city life to have an experience of "real" wilderness? Women in India providing for their families by collecting firewood and carrying water from a river? Catholic sisters breaking into a nuclear missile site to symbolically sabotage the facility?[2]

These are some of the many ways in which men and women have fulfilled, contested, and remade gender norms through their relationships with nature. Many feminist scholars have pointed out connections between women and nature, and ways that both have been devalued compared to men and culture throughout Western history. While some, like anthropologist Sherry B. Ortner (1972), argue that the association between women and nature is socially constructed and derogatory, others, such as the late radical separatist feminist Mary Daly, embrace the notion that women have a special connection to nature. Radical and cultural feminists mark women's relationship to the earth through rituals like women's celebration of the solstice or the new moon (Eller 1993: 83–103). White Western men are often identified with a very different expression of nature that involves hunting, fishing, camping, and other forms of wilderness experiences, while both women and men of color often have been excluded from privileged access to outdoor space (Filemyr 1997: 160).

Within the field of religion and ecology, an overwhelming majority of thought on gender has focused on women, and especially ecofeminism. This chapter begins with an overview of the history and development of ecofeminism, followed by examples of other approaches to gender analysis within religion and ecology. We will conclude by considering why the field has tended to limit its gender analysis to women.

Ecofeminism

Ecological feminism, or ecofeminism, is a feminist perspective based on the assumption that women and nature are linked and mutually denigrated.

A term coined in 1972 by the French feminist Françoise d'Eaubonnes in *Le Feminisme ou la mort (Feminism or Death)*, ecofeminism posits a connection between abuse of the natural world and the oppression of women. It is feminist because it is committed to recognizing and ending male gender bias and offering practices and ideas not tainted by gender bias; it is ecological because it is committed to preserving ecosystems (Warren 1994: 1–2).

Drawing from a variety of disciplines and approaches, including humanities, social sciences, natural sciences, theology, grassroots organizing, and political activism, ecofeminists agree that it is impossible to solve the ecological crisis without considering women, just as it is impossible to achieve justice for women without considering the environment. Beyond that unifying point, ecofeminists offer a wide array of perspectives. Whereas some make an essentialist argument that women inherently are closer to nature than men, others insist that woman–nature connections are socially constructed as a product of social arrangements and the division of labor. Some ecofeminist analyses are empirical, showing how women's experiences are linked to nature through child rearing and daily subsistence tasks such as growing food, obtaining water, and collecting firewood. Others are cultural-symbolic, showing how women and nature have been symbolically linked and mutually denigrated in numerous Western cultural forms, such as the Bible.[3] In addition to empirical and cultural-symbolic approaches, many ecofeminists see a connection between women and nature through the lens of global politics, pointing out that women have little power to contribute to decision-making processes that affect their daily lives.[4] Rather than perceive these examples as isolated instances, most ecofeminists agree that the domination of women and the domination of nature are both manifestations of a patriarchal worldview in Western culture, which is also spreading across the globe through economic globalization and Western development practices.

Because there are numerous distinct approaches to ecofeminism, it is difficult to provide a single, coherent narrative describing its history and development. Heather Eaton describes the concept as "an intersection point of multiple pathways," as "[p]eople come to ecofeminism from many directions, and have taken it to other disciplines and actions" (Eaton 2005: 12). We will follow her model of dividing ecofeminism into four distinct pathways—activism and social movements, academia, religion, and global ecofeminism—and consider these approaches separately, even as we recognize that the pathways are deeply intertwined.

Activism

Ecofeminst theologian Ivone Gebara has written that "[e]cofeminism is born of daily life, of day-to-day sharing among people, of enduring together garbage in the streets, bad smells, the absence of sewers and safe drinking water, poor nutrition, and inadequate health care" (Gebara 1999: 2). Indeed, the earliest ecofeminist activity was related to women's daily struggles. In the early to mid-1970s, women in America and Western Europe increasingly noticed a series of calamities connecting women and environmental degradation. During the Vietnam War, women protested the use of the poisonous herbicide Agent Orange to destroy the Vietnamese landscape, linking this violent destruction of the earth to the rape of women and the abuse of children burnt by napalm. Just a few years later, in 1978, Lois Gibbs, a homemaker in upstate New York, identified a connection between toxic waste dumping and poor children's health in her neighborhood. She gathered other mothers and led the successful Love Canal movement, which held the state of New York accountable for toxic dumping in their neighborhood. Ecofeminist activity also emerged during an international protest in the early 1980s, when Women for Life on Earth began an eighteen-year campaign against the proposed housing of American missiles in London. Developing into the Greenham Common Women's Peace Camp, this protest group brought together more than 30,000 women from Britain and the United States, who opposed patriarchal militaristic agendas.

Widespread feminist organizing on environmental issues also developed through a series of conferences on women and the environment in the mid-1970s, the growth of green politics, and the emergence of grassroots movements responding to local environmental issues. Feminist authors published books pointing out the many connections between the oppression of women and the earth. Out of these activities emerged a loose network of activists who began to recognize themselves as ecofeminists.

Academia

As many women engaged in grassroots organization to protest the mistreatment of women and the earth, others searched for theories to explain the origins and development of that mistreatment. Much of that theorizing pointed toward a series of false dualisms ingrained in Western culture, first identified in 1953 by the famous French feminist Simone de Beauvoir. In *The Second Sex*, de Beauvoir theorized that Western cultural forms associated masculinity with freedom, rationality, pure consciousness, intellect, transcendence, and activity, while femininity was associated with the opposites of each of those traits, coded as inferior in Western culture: life, the body, nature, immanence, and passivity.

Ecofeminist scholars built upon this type of analysis in the late 1970s. For example, feminist writer Susan Griffin offered a provocative presentation of the history of Western patriarchal ideas in *Woman and Nature: The Roaring Inside Her* (1978). Combining poetry with prose, Griffin problematized the ways Western theology and philosophy link and denigrate the female and the natural. In the Prologue, Griffin suggested that men understood themselves as separate from nature. Discussing "man" in the abstract she wrote,

"He says he is not part of this world, that he was set on this world as a stranger. He sets himself apart from woman and nature" (Griffin 1978: 3). In the first half of the book, Griffin represented men's understanding of the world, showing parallels between instructions for clear-cutting a forest and instructions for training an efficient secretary, and suggesting links between the way a man breaks a horse and the way he loves a woman. In the second half of the book, Griffin offered a woman-identified interpretation of the world, implying that women know what men refuse to admit—that we are all deeply connected to the earth. In contrast to men's false idea that they are separate from the earth, Griffin ended with the statement: "I know in this earth, the body of the bird, this pen, this paper, these hands, this tongue speaking, all that I know speaks to me through this earth and I long to tell you, you who are earth too, and listen *as we speak to each other of what we know: the light is in us*" (1978: 229). According to Griffin, women have a special, intuitive understanding of all humans' connections with the earth.

Ecofeminist scholar-activists Carolyn Merchant and Vandana Shiva put forward similar ideas about women's ways of understanding and living in the world. In *The Death of Nature* (1980), Merchant argued that the sixteenth-century image of an organic cosmos and a nurturing female earth was displaced during the Scientific Revolution by a mechanistic worldview of the earth as matter to be controlled by humans. This new worldview, Merchant wrote, "resulted in the death of nature as a living being and the accelerating exploitation of both humans and natural resources in the name of culture and progress" (1980: xxii). The death of nature, according to Merchant, left a negative legacy for the environment and the status of women throughout Western history. Merchant argued that a dual concept of nature as female developed—nature as nurturing mother and nature as wild and uncontrollable—and this view became pervasive as patriarchal society sought to control nature rather than living with and within its confines.

Vandana Shiva also contended that a mechanistic worldview was responsible for environmental destruction across the globe, and that women had special knowledge for living sustainably within nature. In *Staying Alive: Women, Ecology, and Development* (1988), she commented on the irony of Western development practices. While Third-World women had successfully innovated in agriculture to provide food for their families and communities for centuries, Shiva notes, the "green revolution" of fertilizer and genetically modified crops changed everything. "[F]orty centuries of knowledge of agriculture began to be eroded and erased as the green revolution, designed by multinational corporations and western male experts, homogenized nature's diversity and the diversity of human knowledge on a reductionist pattern of agriculture" (Shiva 1988: 98–99). Like Merchant, Shiva argued that integrating women's ways of knowing into Western science and development practices would counter environmentally destructive habits.

Religion

Just as Merchant, Griffin, and Shiva wrote about ways in which Western patriarchal worldviews have caused enormous devastation to the environment, numerous scholars and theologians have written about the negative legacy of Western Christianity's treatment of both women and the earth. Some ecofeminist theologians have combined these critiques to show how the denigration of women and the earth are related and how new theologies can uplift both women and the earth. Other ecofeminists who searched for a religious practice concluded that Western Christianity was beyond reform, and they turned to feminist and goddess spiritualities.

Theologian Rosemary Radford Ruether provided an early ecofeminist voice from within Christianity. In *New Woman, New Earth* (1975), Ruether critiqued the sexism of Christian theology and classical philosophy. She called for a new prophetic vision of genuine social justice, based on her assertion that "women must see that there can be no liberation for them and no solution to the ecological crisis within a society whose fundamental model of relationships continues to be one of domination" (Ruether 1975: 204). To end the dual domination of women and the earth, Ruether argued, society must undergo a fundamental restructuring. Developing these ideas in her many subsequent ecofeminist publications, Ruether called for symbolic changes, such as "reshap[ing] our dualistic concept of reality as split between soulless matter and transcendent male consciousness," and altering our concept of God so that "instead of [humans] modeling God after alienated male consciousness, outside of and ruling over nature," God would become "the immanent source of life that sustains the whole planetary community" (Ruether 1993: 21). Along with these symbolic changes, Ruether also pressed for new social practices that would allow women and men to have equal roles in society. Providing an optimistic vision for the future, Ruether suggested that "these conversions, from alienated, hierarchical dualism to life-sustaining mutuality, will radically change the patterns of patriarchal culture. Basic concepts, such as God, soul-body, and salvation will be reconceived in ways that may bring us much closer to the ethical values of love, justice, and care for the earth" (1993: 22).

Sallie McFague is another feminist theologian who offered a vision of God that supported the equality of women and the value of the earth. In *The Body of God: An Ecological Theology* (1993a), McFague made the radical claim that Christian theologians must deconstruct any metaphors that contribute to the oppression of the earth, and offer in their place models and metaphors that support the well-being of the earth and all its systems and creatures. McFague especially criticized the image of God as a king ruling over the earth for two reasons. That image contributed to a dualistic separation between God's kingdom and the earth, and it deprived human beings of responsibility for the earth. In place of this problematic image,

McFague proposed that Christians learn to see the universe as the body of God. "Rather than viewing God as an external, separate being ruling over the world," McFague wrote, "it is appropriate to see God as in, with, and under the entire evolutionary process" (McFague 1993b: 93). Along with this model, McFague proposed the Big Bang and the development of the universe as a common creation story around which all people could unite. She hoped that this shared story would teach that "we are radically interrelated with and dependent on everything else in the universe and especially on our planet ... In this story we feel profoundly connected with all other forms of life, not in a romantic way, but in a realistic way" (McFague 1993b: 94). In addition to emphasizing human responsibility to care for the earth, McFague pointed out that the image of the universe as the body of God "underscores what our tradition has seldom allowed: that matter is of God and is good, that, indeed, if God is embodied, then matter, the natural world, is not only 'good' but in some sense sacred—a place where God is present" (1993b: 95). McFague's theology is ecological because it underscores the sacramental nature of caring for the earth, the very body of God. It is feminist because it counters the hierarchal dualisms that diminish women and the earth, making matter and bodies—coded as feminine and inferior within Western hierarchal dualisms—sacred elements inhabited by God.

Whereas Ruether and McFague strove to reform Christianity, other ecofeminists in the West rejected this tradition entirely in favor of feminist forms of spirituality that celebrate women and the earth. Since the 1970s, feminist spirituality has grown into a loosely connected movement comprising women (and occasionally some men) in the United States, Canada, and a few other Western societies who seek forms of religious expression that empower women. While no particular beliefs are required for participation in feminist spirituality, scholar of religion Cynthia Eller identifies five characteristics that apply to many spiritual feminists: "valuing women's empowerment, practicing ritual and/or magic, revering nature, using the feminine or gender as a primary mode of religious analysis, and espousing the revisionist version of Western history favored by the movement" (Eller 1993: 6). While some spiritual feminists may belong to covens or other small groups, most practice their spirituality alone. By celebrating ecological and feminist images such as Gaia and Mother Earth, practitioners of feminist spirituality assume that the earth is sacred and all living beings are worthy of respect.[5]

Scholars have applied ecofeminist concepts to other religions as well: Judith Plaskow (1993) offered a Jewish feminist vision of social change that involves environmental concern, and Johanna Macy (1991) offered a Buddhist ecofeminist perspective based on the Buddhist concept of dependent co-arising. Moreover, Carol Adams' edited volume *Ecofeminism and the Sacred* included contributions in dialogue with Judaism, Hinduism,

Buddhism, and Shamanism. However, the vast majority of ecofeminist dialogue with religious traditions has focused on Christianity and newer forms of feminist spiritualities.

What do ecofeminists mean by "woman" and "nature"?

To analyze these first three approaches to ecofeminism, we might start with an approach that should be familiar to readers of this text: asking what each approach means by "nature" and what each means by "women." Ecofeminists who celebrate a connection between women and nature uphold images of nature as life-sustaining and nurturing but also identify with nature's wild and uncontrollable side. Others write about the toil and drudgery of a life in unhealthy nature—farming in severe conditions of drought and desertification, or breathing air polluted by dangerous toxins. Sallie McFague's nature involves the entire cosmos, and she encourages us to see all of nature as sacred, from breathtaking mountain ranges to tiny insects.

Categories and constructions of "nature" in ecofeminist writing have gone largely unexamined, but ecofeminist constructions of "woman" have been critiqued widely. What is the basis for the special relationship between women and nature than many ecofeminists claim? Many maintain that women inherently are different from men and have a special intuition and relationship with the natural world, but *why* do women have that special connection? Likewise, essentialist understandings of the woman–nature connection assume that *all* women feel this special connection with nature, that they share a common feminine understanding of the earth that transcends the many significant differences between women from different races, classes, backgrounds, educations, and cultures. What's more, these approaches assume that women's proximity to nature is unequivocally good, ignoring any possible negative implications of tying women to the earth. Some critics accuse ecofeminism of creating a romanticized, idyllic image of women working the earth, ignoring the toil, drudgery, and poverty that can be connected to farming.

To address these issues, many theorists have called on ecofeminists to interrogate the categories of masculinity and femininity more fully. For example, feminist philosopher Victoria Davion argued that "a truly feminist perspective cannot embrace either the feminine or the masculine uncritically, as a truly feminist perspective requires a critique of gender roles, and this critique must include masculinity and femininity" (Davion 1994: 9). Rather than focusing solely on women and the earth, ecofeminists might consider constructions of masculinity and femininity and how they relate to the division of labor and assumed gender roles. Moreover, theorists like Greta Gaard have challenged ecofeminists to include more social and cultural analysis, such as critiques of capitalism and racism (Gaard 2003: 207). Davion, Gaard, and other critics of ecofeminist essentialism agree that ecofeminists are correct to challenge hierarchal dualisms, but the solution is not simply to reverse the hierarchy, valuing all things coded feminine.

10A

What are some problems with essentializing a connection between women and nature? Why might some feminists nonetheless uphold that connection?

Related to an essentialist critique, some women have challenged ecofeminism for its failure to account for the experiences of women of color. While some African American women have identified with ecofeminism—Delores S. Williams (1993) compared the treatment of the bodies of enslaved women in nineteenth-century America to the destructive practice of strip mining, and Shamara Shantu Riley wrote that "ecology is a sistah's issue too" (Riley 1993: 191)—white Western women have been the face of ecofeminism. According to African American environmental sociologist Dorceta E. Taylor, ecofeminism "as it is currently conceived ... does not adequately consider the experiences of women of color; neither does it fully understand or accept the differences between white women and women of color" (Taylor 1997: 62). Taylor extended this critique to the environmental movement as a whole, showing that issues primarily affecting people of color were historically not considered "environmental,"[6] and suggesting that black women cannot identify with ecofeminism because "women of color do not fight for sexual equality without fighting for racial equality" (1997: 63). Taylor and others have pointed out that there can be no simple dichotomy between women, "the oppressed," and men, "the oppressors," because white Western women often have been the oppressors of women and men of color, just as women of color have endured oppression at the hands of both white men and men of their own race. Moreover, Taylor charged that ecofeminists "have not paid enough attention to the ways in which the issues they explore have disproportionate impacts on people of color" (1997: 68), as women working in factories or as subsistence farmers, for example, face much more immediate environmental threats than women working as lawyers or CEOs. As Taylor and many others have pointed out, there can be no simple category of "women" in ecofeminist analyses. Instead, ecofeminist analyses must recognize significant differences among women, based on factors like culture, race, and class.

Global ecofeminism

While essentialism is a significant limitation, many scholars have offered constructive criticisms and proposed alternative viewpoints that underscore ecofeminism's enduring relevance. Work in the area of ecofeminism and globalization has been especially active in pointing out problems and offering solutions. As Heather Eaton and Lois Lorentzen (2003) have pointed out, globalization—the dissemination of a Western capitalist agenda and technology to the rest of the world through transnational corporations and development practices—presents numerous concrete problems for women and the earth. Eaton and Lorentzen brought together essays that apply ecofeminist ideas to concrete places and situations, because, they wrote, "the insistence upon the primacy of a woman–nature connection, while illuminating symbolic and cultural constructs, doesn't help us adequately analyze globalization as an extension of patriarchal capitalism" (Eaton and Lorentzen 2003: 5). For example, in her examination of both male and female Mijikenda farmers in Kenya, anthropologist Celia Nyamweru challenged the ecofeminist assertion that women are more earth-friendly than men. Examining the efforts of an international conservation organization to help the Mijikenda use their sacred *kaya* forests sustainably, Nyamweru found that both women and men used the forest unsustainably. In contrast to ecofeminist writings that show women's special connections to nature, Nyamweru wrote, "the perception of the *kaya* forests in Mijikenda culture cannot be interpreted in terms of benevolent space or of specifically female space. They are places of potential danger that have to be approached according to proscribed behaviors and to which women's access is strictly controlled" (Nyamweru 2003: 54). Nyamweru showed that ecofeminist assertions of women's special relationship with nature do not apply across all cultures, and in the case of the Mijikenda ecofeminist analysis is not helpful in analyzing the effects of patriarchal capitalism.

10B

How does global ecofeminism address some of the problems of earlier ecofeminist analyses? What problems remain?

New directions in religion, gender, and nature

While Eaton, Lorentzen, and Nyamweru have provided constructive criticism of ecofeminist analyses, other scholars have challenged religion and ecology's exclusive focus on ecofeminism. In "Has Ecofeminism Cornered the Market?" feminist scholar of religion Tovis Page suggested that scholars have overly emphasized ecofeminist understandings to the exclusion of other approaches to women and nature. While Page recognized the positive contributions of ecofeminism, she argued that the exclusive focus on eco-feminism creates problems because it assumes ecofeminism applies in all situations, tends to neglect concrete reality in favor of abstract concepts, and "highlights particular types of religion—namely those that are liberal or progressive in orientation ... cordoning off conservative and orthodox forms of religion from serious engagement in the study of religion, gender, and nature" (Page 2007: 303). Page proposed other routes for analyzing the relationship between these concepts, such as "more particularized and empirically based studies that examine the complex dynamics between religion, gender, and nature in specific cultural and historical contexts *and* over time" (Page 2007: 304). We now turn to two different studies that model that type of approach.

Women and nature in American religion

In *Green Sisters: A Spiritual Ecology* (2007), Sarah McFarland Taylor's historical-ethnographic study of ecologically activist Catholic sisters, Taylor showed how "green" sisters in North America both conserved and challenged traditional gender norms through their work to protect the earth. Taylor described a burst of new religious energy among green sisters since the mid-1990s and showed that much of their activity grew out of the women's movement. Reporting the influence of various ecofeminist authors upon their ecological consciousnesses, the sisters shared many affinities with the women's spirituality movement. They valued women's knowledge, invoked images of the divine female, and even created gender-balanced prayers (Taylor 2007: 8). For example, Taylor noted that some sisters "pray the directions as 'the sign of the cross' with corresponding four directional dedications made to 'Father'; 'Son'; 'Holy Spirit'; 'One God, Mother of us all.' This variation conserves a Trinitarian framework but creatively finds a way to infuse that framework with greater theological gender balance" (2007: 234). While these women carefully stayed within the boundaries of their expected gender roles, Taylor showed that their activities actually expanded the role of women within the Catholic Church. While many seem to reinscribe traditional expectations for submissive women by wearing the habit and working in the kitchen, Taylor argued that the picture was much more complicated. She wrote: "within the lives of green sisters the dualism of being either 'out of the kitchen' (and thus liberated) or 'in the kitchen' (and thus confined to a regressive gender-defined sphere) is fundamentally a false one ... the sisters have created a third way" (Taylor 2007: 179). Through their activities related to the earth—running community-supported organic farms, teaching children about the environment, protesting nuclear missile sites, and interrupting shareholder meetings of environmentally irresponsible companies—green sisters both reinforced and rebuffed expectations of submissive Catholic sisters.

While Taylor showed how green sisters challenge gender norms even as they strive to uphold them, Rebecca Kneale Gould's study of modern homesteaders in America shows how women who consciously reject traditional gender roles end up reinscribing them, albeit with new meanings and in new ways. Based on historical research on American homesteaders from the 1920s to the 1940s, as well as her contemporary ethnographic fieldwork, Gould asked intriguing questions about the role gender plays when men and women choose to live a life in nature, away from the conveniences, technology, and consumer culture of modern American society. "Does 'back to the land' mean 'back to the kitchen' for homesteading women?" Gould asks. "And, if so, with what consequences?" (Gould 2005: 205). Originally drawn to the study of homesteading because of her admiration for the "tough as nails" reputation of the mid-twentieth-century homesteader and writer Helen Nearing, Gould recalled her initial surprise when she saw the extent to which heterosexual homesteading couples maintained traditional gender roles. Despite some exceptions, Gould wrote, "it is more often the case that women ... spend more time cooking, cleaning, sewing, and child rearing than they spend chopping wood, doing carpentry, digging wells, and tending the grounds" (2005: 301, n. 2). While many couples embarked upon their homesteading experiments with idealized hopes for shared labor and gender neutrality, most couples found themselves forced back into traditional gender roles, especially when they began to have children.

Nonetheless, Gould pointed out that the decision to homestead, with all of its gendered implications, has to do with nature and culture as well as gender. She suggested that, for women, "making the decision, say, to wash diapers by hand may feel alternatively like entrapment or liberation, depending on which cultural norms (consumer society or 'women's sphere') they see themselves working against—and who on the homestead is actually making the decision" (Gould 2005: 216). Just as Taylor demonstrated that green sisters' work in the kitchen did not imply a regressive and restrictive women's sphere, Gould suggested that the ideals of homesteading require feminists to reconsider their distrust of homemaking. While many second-wave feminists found homemaking meaningless and boring, Gould suggested that for many homesteaders homemaking becomes the most important profession, because it "has as its ultimate goal, 'the blossoming of human

---

10C

How do you interpret the decisions of women growing up in the era of second-wave feminist America, such as Taylor's green sisters and Gould's homesteaders, to return to traditional gender norms? What role might religion play in their decision-making processes?

culture,' the creation of 'an Eden on earth'" (2005: 17). Through their richly detailed studies of two groups of women living their daily lives in direct relation to nature, Gould and Taylor showed the complex negotiations of gender as women work out their relationships to men and other women, societal expectations, and the natural environment in the decades surrounding the turn of the twenty-first century.

Evaluating the field

Scholars in the field of religion and ecology have paid careful attention to women from its beginning, but, as Tovis Page pointed out, the field's gender analysis largely is restricted to women, and especially ecofeminism. How would conversations about religion and nature change if we expanded our inquiry to include *gender*, not just *women*?

In an article about how ideas of masculinity and femininity shaped the modern environmental movement in the wake of Rachel Carson's publication of *Silent Spring*, environmental historian Maril Hazlett suggested that conservationism and ecology have different gender codings. "Since its beginning around the turn of the century," she writes, "the conservation movement had focused on the environment primarily in terms of resource management or wilderness preservation. In contrast, Carson used ecology to define people's homes, gardens, and health as part of the natural world" (Hazlett 2004: 701). If Hazlett is correct that ecological efforts are more associated with femininity while conservation efforts are related to masculinity, can we conclude that the field of religion and ecology is concerned more with women because it tends to focus on particular kinds of environmental activity that include mostly women? Is there a place for conversations about masculinity, hunting, camping, and conservation within religion and ecology? And what about sexuality? Some scholars have challenged ecofeminism for assuming that all subjects are heterosexual. Is this the case for all gender analyses within religion and ecology? What about the relationships between gender and nature stemming from conservative religious traditions, such as the Boy Scouts of America's policy on homosexuality?[7] While ecofeminist analyses have offered fertile ground for the consideration of women, religion, and nature, a host of other fascinating questions about gender and nature remain to be explored.

10D

Why might men be so absent from considerations of gender within the field of religion and ecology? What other groups or ideas remain to be explored?

Case study: Women and Life on Earth

Women and Life on Earth (WLOE) is a non-profit organization and internet project whose stated goal is to support "women in international cooperation for peace, ecology, and social justice." The project developed out of the Women and Life on Earth organization of the early 1980s, which formed following the nuclear meltdown at Three Mile Island. WLOE was an important force in early ecofeminist activities. Identifying as ecofeminists, WLOE leaders drafted a Unity Statement in 1979 to assert the group's goals:

> We see connections between the exploitation and brutalization of the earth and her people and the physical, economic and psychological violence that women face every day. We want to understand and try to overcome the historical divisions of race, poverty, class, age and sexual preference that have kept women apart and politically powerless. Our concerns are many, but understanding the problems that confront us helps us imagine how we would like to live.
>
> (Women and Life on Earth 1980)

The next year, at the spring equinox, the group hosted a conference during which 600 women discussed the connections between women, ecology, and nonviolence. WLOE women continued to organize for women and the environment for the next two years, including a Women's Pentagon Action in November, 1980, during which 2,000 women surrounded the Pentagon. A WLOE organizer of that event, Grace Paley, drafted a statement of the demonstration's goal:

> We are gathering at the Pentagon on November 17, 1980 because we fear for our lives. We fear for the life of this planet, our Earth, and the life of our children who are our human future ... We want to be free from violence in our streets and in our houses. The pervasive social power of the masculine ideal and the greed of the pornographer have come together to steal our freedom, so that whole neighborhoods and the life of the evening and night have been taken away from us. For too many women the dark country road and the city alley have concealed the rapist. We want the night returned, the light of the moon, special in the cycle of female lives, the stars and the gaiety of the city streets.
>
> (Paley 2007)

WLOE was inactive by 1982, but in 1999 the organization was restored when several of the original members launched Women and Life on Earth as an internet project dedicated to peace, ecology, and global justice. WLOE's website states that the war in Kosovo, the "war on terror," and the wars in Afghanistan and Iraq provide "proof of the need for international communication and solidarity for peace with justice" (Women and Life on Earth 2009). They send e-newsletters and alerts in English, German, French, and Spanish to women across the world, and their website includes contributions from well-known women writers and activists from India, the United States, and Western Europe.

Discussion questions

Spend some time perusing WLOE's website, http://wloe.org/, and consider the ways that the organization represents women, men, and the environment.

1 How does WLOE present the relationship of women to the earth? Is this an essentialist view?
2 Consider the organization's logos: the original 1980 version which appears on the main page, and more issue specific logos that appear on the pages devoted to "Women and Peace," "Women and Ecology," and "Women and Globalization." The original logo depicts women in the phases of the moon, but the later logos do not depict women at all. What might this change reveal about WLOE's changing attitudes toward women and the earth?
3 Look at the photographs of WLOE contributors and members. What women does the organization aim to attract? Who might feel excluded from the organization? What do you think might be the organization's attitude toward men?
4 WLOE's website does not mention anything specifically about religion. Is WLOE a strictly secular organization, unaffected by matters of religion? How might religion play a role in this international organization? What evidence do you see of feminist spirituality?
5 Are there definitions of "religion" that make WLOE's work clearer, or do they distract from understanding what WLOE is about?

Notes

1 Gender Studies scholars distinguish between sex, a biological assignment based on the body (reproductive organs, physiological traits, etc.), and gender, the culturally constructed roles, behaviors, traits, etc. that a society designates for masculinity or femininity. "Male" and "female" are sex categories whereas "masculine" and "feminine" are gender categories.
2 These examples are drawn from Nash (1982: 141–60), Philipose (1989: 67), and S. Taylor (2007: 55).
3 Ecofeminist theologian Heather Eaton, for example, suggests that in the story of Adam and Eve "[w]omen were blamed for bringing sin into the world. Eve was used as the exemplar of 'woman' and sin, as her nature was corrupt and needed redeeming" (Eaton 2005: 65).

4 Sociologist Mary Mellor suggests that "the most obvious way in which gender is linked to the environment is that most of the people who affect environmental decision making are men and most of the people who are at the mercy of those decisions are women" (Mellor 2003: 13).

5 Author and activist Starhawk (1999, 2004) is among the best-known voices in feminist and earth-based spirituality.

6 For example, Taylor argues that when the United Farm Workers organized to keep companies from spraying pesticides on workers, their struggles were not widely supported by environmentalists because they were identified as health and labor issues, not environmental concerns. However, the environmental community did become involved in protests against the use of the chemical malathion to prevent an outbreak of fruit flies in white neighborhoods (Taylor 1997: 51–53).

7 Notable exceptions to Religion and Ecology's exclusion of ideas about sexuality include the work of Greta Gaard (1997) and Daniel Spencer (1996).

References

Davion, V. (1994) "Is Ecofeminism Feminist?" in K. Warren (ed.) *Ecological Feminism*, New York: Routledge.

de Beauvoir, S. (1952, 2nd ed. 1989) *The Second Sex*, trans. H.M. Parshley, New York: Vintage Books.

Eaton, H. (2005) *Introducing Ecofeminist Theologies*, New York: T&T Clark International.

Eaton, H. and L. Lorentzen (2003) "Introduction," in *Ecofeminism and Globalization: Exploring Culture, Context, and Religion*, New York: Rowman and Littlefield.

Eller, C. (1993) *Living in the Lap of the Goddess: The Feminist Spirituality Movement in America*, New York: Crossroads.

Filemyr, A. (1997) "Going Outdoors and Other Dangerous Expeditions," Frontiers: A Journal of Women Studies 18(2): 160–77.

Gaard, G. (1997) "Toward a Queer Ecofeminsm," Hypatia 12.1: 114–37.

——(2003) "Ecofeminists in the Greens," in H. Eaton and L. Lorentzen (eds) *Ecofeminism and Globalization: Exploring Culture, Context, and Religion*, New York: Rowman and Littlefield.

Gebara, I. (1999) *Longing for Running Water: Ecofeminism and Liberation*, Minneapolis: Fortress Press.

Gould, R. (2005) *At Home in Nature: Modern Homesteading and Spiritual Practice in America*, Berkeley: University of California Press.

Griffin, S. (1978) *Woman and Nature: The Roaring Inside Her*, San Francisco: Sierra Club Books.

Hazlett, M. (2004) "'Woman vs. Man vs. Bugs': Gender and Popular Ecology in Early Reactions to *Silent Spring*," *Environmental History* 9(4): 701–29.

McFague, Sallie (1993a) *The Body of God: An Ecological Theology*, Minneapolis: Fortress Press.

——(1993b) "An Earthly Theological Agenda," in C. Adams (ed.) *Ecofeminism and the Sacred*, New York: Continuum.

Macy, J. (1991) *World as Lover, World as Self*, Berkeley, CA: Parallax Press.

Mellor, M. (2003) "Gender and the Environment," in H. Eaton and L. Lorentzen (eds) *Ecofeminism and Globalization: Exploring Culture, Context, and Religion*, New York: Rowman and Littlefield.

Merchant, C. (1980) *The Death of Nature: Women, Ecology and the Scientific Revolution*, San Francisco: Harper San Francisco.

Nash, R. (1982 [1967]) *Wilderness and the American Mind*, New Haven, CT: Yale University Press.

Nyamweru, C. (2003) "Women and Sacred Groves in Coastal Kenya: A Contribution to the Ecofeminist Debate," in H. Eaton and L. Lorentzen (eds) *Ecofeminism and Globalization: Exploring Culture, Context, and Religion*, New York: Rowman and Littlefield.

Ortner, S. (1972) "Is Female to Male as Nature Is to Culture?" *Feminist Studies* 1(2): 5–31.

Page, T. (2007) "Has Ecofeminism Cornered the Market? Gender Analysis in the Study of Religion, Nature, and Culture," *Journal for the Study of Religion, Nature and Culture* 1(2): 293–319.

Paley, G. (2007) "Women's Pentagon Action Unity Statement," in *Peacework Magazine* 379; available at http://www.peaceworkmagazine.org/womens-pentagon-action-unity-statement-0 (accessed November 15, 2009).

Philipose, P. (1989) "Women Act: Women and Environmental Protection in India," in J. Plaint (ed.) *Healing the Wounds: The Promise of Ecofeminism*, Philadelphia: New Society Publishers.

Plaskow, J. (1993) "Feminist Judaism and Repair of the World," in C. Adams (ed.) *Ecofeminism and the Sacred*, New York: Continuum.

Riley, S. (1993) "Ecology is a Sistah's Issue Too: The Politics of Emergent Afrocentric Ecowomanism," in C. Adams (ed.) *Ecofeminism and the Sacred*, New York: Continuum.

Ruether, R. (1975) *New Woman, New Earth*, New York: Seabury Press.

——(1993) "Ecofeminism: Symbolic and Social Connections of the Oppression of Women and the Domination of Nature," in C. Adams (ed.) *Ecofeminism and the Sacred*, New York: Continuum.

Shiva, V. (1988) *Staying Alive: Women, Ecology, and Development*, London: Zed Books Ltd.

Spencer, D. (1996) *Gay and Gaia: Ethics, Ecology, and the Erotic*, Cleveland: The Pilgrim Press.

Starhawk (1999) *The Spiral Dance: A Rebirth of the Ancient Religion of the Goddess*, 3rd ed., San Francisco: HarperCollins.

——(2004) *The Earth Path: Grounding Your Spirit in the Rhythms of Nature*, San Francisco: HarperCollins.

Taylor, D. (1997) "Women of Color, Environmental Justice, and Ecofeminism," in K. Warren (ed.) *Ecofeminism: Women, Nature, Culture*, Bloomington: Indiana University Press.

Taylor, S. (2007) *Green Sisters: A Spiritual Ecology*, Cambridge, MA: Harvard University Press.

Warren, K. (1994) "Introduction," in K. Warren (ed.) *Ecological Feminism*, New York: Routledge.

Williams, D. (1993) "Sin, Nature, and Black Women's Bodies," in K. Warren (ed.) *Ecofeminism and the Sacred*, New York: Continuum.

Women and Life on Earth (1980) "Unity Statement," available at http://wloe.org/unity-statement-1980.78.0.html.

——(2009) "Introducing WLOE," available at http://www.wloe.org/About-us.74.0.html.

Further reading

Eaton, Heather (2005) *Introducing Ecofeminist Theologies*, New York: T&T Clark International.

Eaton, Heather and Lois Ann Lorentzen (eds) (2003) *Ecofeminism and Globalization: Exploring Culture, Context, and Religion*, New York: Rowman and Littlefield.

Scharff, Virgina (ed.) (2003) *Seeing Nature Through Gender*, Lawrence: University of Kansas Press.

Stein, Rachel (ed.) (2004) *New Perspectives on Environmental Justice: Gender, Sexuality, and Activism*, New Brunswick, NJ: Rutgers University Press.

Chapter 11

Economics

Laura M. Hartman

Ecology derives from the Greek term *oikos*, meaning home. But there is another common word that stems from the same root: economy. How do ecology and economy relate to one another? What might they both have to do with religion? This chapter explores the intersection of these three fields of study: religion, ecology, and economy.

Economics: what is it, who gets to decide, and why does it matter?

At its most basic, economics is the study of the *oikos*, the household—how people acquire and manage the physical materials they need to live. At its most complex, economics is an esoteric discipline understood by only a few experts, treating complex global systems of supply, demand, production, distribution, and consumption of goods and services. Many of us listen to the news and take note of "the economy" but would freely admit that we don't understand the more complicated concepts—we leave that to the experts, the economists. Economists in industrial societies can hold a great deal of power, influencing major policy decisions that have a large-scale impact.

Economists, and economics as a discipline, have a tremendous amount of political power. But so do individual consumers, particularly when taken collectively. Our everyday economic decisions—how you and I choose to run our *oikos*—matter not just to us, but also to the global economy. The price we see for rice in the grocery store is shorthand for an astounding array of information—how much the growers were paid, how much the shipping cost, and how rare this sort of rice is, for starters. Some argue that if subsidies are involved prices actually obscure information: government-subsidized gas means cheap transportation and therefore cheap goods. Such prices mask the environmental cost associated with that transportation. Regardless, prices do communicate information to consumers, information that influences the everyday decisions we make. But this communication goes both ways. The store keeps track of what we buy; the information, in the form of orders from distributors, "trickles up" the supply chain all the way to the producers, who (if they can) adjust their production accordingly. If we all stopped buying rice or started buying much more, rice farmers, rice distributors, grocery stores, and the whole global economy would feel the effect.

We can picture the economy as a complex web of interconnections. When I buy a bag of rice, I'm tugging strings which are felt around the globe. But, of course, it's not a static web. New strands are being added all the time, while others are being removed. My tugging, with my purchase, is only one of billions of tugs that occur every day—the whole system is humming with countless vibrations.

IIA

Do you see economics as an esoteric discipline? Do you understand it? Are you comfortable with the level of power that economists hold?

But what about the *oikos* of the earth? In the eyes of most traditional economists, the human economy is the only one that matters. But some recognize that the nonhuman world has its own "household," of which the human economy is but a part. Wendell Berry has called this earth-scale economy "the Great Economy," meaning the entire system of water, air, earth, and energy, as these elements move about the planet. The human economy, according to Berry, is properly understood as "the ways by which the human household is situated and maintained within the household of nature" (Berry 2007: 52). Interestingly, Berry's original concept of earth's economy was not called "the Great Economy," but instead "the Kingdom of God" (Berry 1987: 55). Berry's instinct to see the large-scale workings of the planet in terms of God's management of the world reveals the intriguing link between ecology, economy, and religion. This chapter examines each intersection in turn: religion and economics, ecology and economics, and religion, ecology, and economics.

Religion and economics

Economics, as the study of the distribution of goods and services, can in a metaphorical sense be applied to religion. Theologian Kathryn Tanner's *Economy of Grace* marries the two, as she declares that "the whole Christian story is a vision of economy, a vision of a kind of system for the production and circulation of goods, beginning with God and extending to the world, from creation through redemption" (Tanner 2005: xi). Within Christianity, economic metaphors serve to enlighten difficult concepts relating to salvation: Jesus's death is often discussed as payment of a *debt*, something that *redeems* Christians (much as one might redeem a coupon).

There is, in Christianity and other religions, the concept that God engages in a divine version of a "gift economy": regardless of human "ability to pay," God bestows generous gifts on believers, giving to all with divine generosity.[1] In Islam, the Qu'ran contains many statements with economic metaphors likening belief in God to a "good deal" for the believer. Following God may seem to come at a price, but the reward in the hereafter outweighs the cost: "Surely they who recite the Book of God and keep up prayer and spend out of what We have given them secretly and openly, hope for a commerce that will never go bankrupt" (Qu'ran 35:29). This is a gift economy indeed.

A different kind of economic metaphor is at work in Hinduism and Buddhism. The law of *karma* offers a kind of "payback" to individuals over time, and through different lifetimes, based on their good or bad behavior. The term "karmic debt" refers to the difficulty and suffering (or pleasure and rewards) that one is justly due, based on one's bad (or good) actions in this or previous lifetimes.

Beyond economic metaphors, religions have important traditional practices and views on economic matters. Religions even frequently shape the economies of which they are a part. From Jewish traditions of Jubilee debt-remittance to Muslim traditions of almsgiving (*zakat*), Abrahamic traditions have a long history of attention to economics and the needs of the poor. Historically, Judaism, Christianity, and Islam have outlawed usury (charging interest). This ban on usury has persisted most successfully in Islam: Muslim countries house banks that are run without usury, according to the laws of *Shari'a*. These banks are reportedly performing well, even in difficult economic times (Schneider 2009).

Many religions practice some form of almsgiving or property redistribution through voluntary donations. Buddhism teaches *dana*, generous giving, as a way of encouraging healthy detachment from possessions. Buddhist monks are often pictured with begging bowls, as they acquire their living through the alms they receive from lay people. Almsgiving is present in Hinduism, too: Hindus may gain spiritual gifts and merit by offering food and other donations to temples and holy practitioners. Hindus pursue the virtue of *aparigraha*, the absence of acquisitiveness. In Islam, *zakat* is one of the five pillars, or central practices: a certain percentage of wealth and produce is to be delivered to the poor, the disabled, those in crisis, and religious workers. Judaism and Christianity promote a tithe, a 10 percent offering of one's goods or income to aid religious groups and the poor.

Religious traditions typically denounce greed in economic transactions. Judaism cautions against idolatry, which may occur if we grant supreme status to money or possessions rather than to God. Christianity sees greed and gluttony as injurious to the soul, since they perpetuate a distorted desire for worldly, rather than spiritual, values. From a Confucian perspective, greed ruptures the social fabric, since it is a self-indulgent pursuit at others' expense. Society must protect its poorer and less capable members: Truly magnanimous leaders are those who help the lesser, rather than puffing themselves up. Greed, from a Hindu perspective, denies the divine ownership of the world, shows a lack of trust, and injures one's fellows. From a Buddhist perspective, grasping and greed are a doomed attempt to please the ego-self, which is both insatiable and illusory. The Buddha teaches that chasing after desires is like drinking saltwater, which only serves to increase one's thirst. Succumbing to inordinate desire will make one resemble a "hungry ghost," a being in the Buddhist tradition who has a large, empty stomach and a pitiful pinhole mouth: always hungry, never satiated.

Though greed is denounced, work is typically commended by religious traditions. Judaism prescribes one day of Sabbath rest per week, but does not discount the value of human work that serves *tikkun olam*, or joining God in work that mends the world. Buddhism speaks of "right livelihood" as part of the eightfold path to enlightenment. This refers to work that promotes happiness for all beings, and that is consistent with Buddhist teaching. Many Christians discuss the concept of "vocation" when they discuss work as God's "call" to a certain livelihood. The concept of vocation figures prominently in the work of sociologist Max Weber, who observed the historical rise of capitalism in Protestant Christian Europe (particularly a specific form of Calvinism in Northern Europe) and hypothesized a connection. Weber argued that a strong sense of vocation, coupled with a belief in hard work, a tradition of world-denying austerity, and a desire to prove one's "elect" status by acquiring God's blessing of wealth, led Protestantism's "worldly asceticism" to spark the rise of capitalism.

Weber's thesis is controversial, but it raises important questions: Do religious views give rise to certain economic forms? And do economic realities influence religious practice, as well? Vincent J. Miller argues that consumer culture has a profound effect on the practice of religion. He defines consumer culture as "a way of relating to beliefs—a set of *habits of interpretation and use*—that renders the 'content' of beliefs and values less important" than their freely chosen consumption (Miller 2003: 1). Miller describes the impact of consumer culture as both democratizing—consumer choice is multiplied like never before—and abstracting—leading to sound-bite sized shallow understandings of religious ideas, typically divorced from practice. Miller is concerned about the effect of consumer culture on religious practice, both lauding the increased freedom and lamenting the shallowness of the consumer mindset.

The confluence of religions and economics does have its disadvantages and dangers. When the religiously powerful are also economically and politically powerful (as in the time of the Spanish Inquisition, for example), history often shows a rise in abuses of power. And religious beliefs that are too closely tied to unjust economic systems raise questions about the appropriateness of a link between religion and economics. The caste system in

India, justified and sanctified by some Hindu teachings, remains controversial because it seems to keep in place an unjust system of economic oppression. Christian Prosperity Theology teaches that economically impoverished believers need only pray in the right way, and give money to the church, in order to create great riches for themselves. This, too, is controversial, for it seems to prey on practitioners' economic insecurities, blaming the poor for their own problems and encouraging such large donations that the churches make a substantial profit.

There may be danger in mixing economics and religion too closely. David Loy has written that in our industrial societies, economics, in fact, *is* a religion, for which the market is god and the economists are theologians and priests (Loy 1997: 275). Using a functionalist definition of religion, which defines a religion by its function in human lives (e.g. it gives a sense of purpose, narrates how the world "really" is, dictates what matters and how to order our lives), Loy believes that free market capitalism could qualify. He describes two propositions on which this "market religion" rests: "that *it [the market] is right and just* (which is why 'the market made me do it' is acceptable as a defense of many morally questionable activities); and that *value can be adequately signaled by prices.*" Loy believes these are false and dangerous assumptions, and that other religions have a role to play in countering this false religion of economics (Loy 1997: 277–78). If they fail, economics threatens to eclipse other religions in its power and persuasiveness.

11B

Are you concerned, as Vincent Miller is, about the influence of consumerism on religious practice? Based on what you understand "religion" to be, do you agree with David Loy that economics may be seen as its own religion?

In sum, religion's relationship with the economy is mixed. While religions may use economic metaphors, spiritual concerns compete with economic concerns for adherents' primary loyalty. Religions have their own views on just distribution of resources, charging interest, and the role of greed and work; these views often conflict with contemporary market and banking systems, and the root discipline of economics itself.

Ecology and economics

Economic behavior certainly impacts ecologies around the globe. From the gas I buy for my car (oil extraction, pollution, global climate change) to the beef I eat for lunch (use of fossil fuels, factory farming, unsustainable agriculture), the ecological ramifications of my economic transactions are sometimes clear and dramatic.

Is the reverse true? Do ecological concerns impact economics? Increasingly, yes, and largely thanks to a group of "ecological economists," who belong to a field of scholarship developed in the 1970s and 1980s.[2] Not unlike the Protestant Reformation of Western Christianity, ecological economics seeks to transform the dominant ideology of its field. To extend the analogy, ecological economics is a different economic "theology," including a new cosmology (worldview), an altered anthropology (view of human nature), a different teleology (view of worthy goals), and a revised eschatology (vision for a better future).

The "cosmology" of ecological economics dethrones the view of traditional economics which envisions the human economy as a primary actor in an "empty" world. Rather, ecological economics affirms that the human economy—what humans produce, consume, and dispose of—occurs as a subset within a larger earth economy, in agreement with Berry's "Great Economy" concept discussed on p. 145. This Great Economy is not an "empty" world, with plenty of space for human activity, but rather it is a "full" world, filled nearly to bursting by the large scale of the human economy and the other creatures who live on the earth.

Consciously situating the human economy within the earth economy allows ecological economists to (1) attend to the question of proper scale for the human economy by comparison with the earth economy and (2) raise questions about the sustainability of resource use, focusing on the environment's function as source and sink. This may seem like common sense, but the notion of the earth as a living system within which the human economy operates constitutes a radical shift in worldview for traditional economics.

The "anthropology" of ecological economics redefines *Homo economicus*, the economic actor often referred to in economic theory. Traditionally, *Homo economicus* was modeled as a rational individual seeking to maximize his or her pleasure by choosing economic activity based on personal preferences. In ecological economics, by contrast, *Homo economicus* is a person-in-community (Daly and Cobb 1989: 7). This concept recognizes that economic choices are made not simply to maximize personal pleasure but also for reasons of generosity, relationship, concern for others, and so forth. Though traditional views of *Homo economicus* recognize that "he" is only a model and not as complex as a real human, the model has power: major economic theories and real-world decisions rest on this one-sided construal of human behavior. Economist Herman Daly and theologian John Cobb diagnose this as a fallacy of "misplaced concreteness," an instance where theorists attribute too much credibility to what is only a heuristic device, an oversimplified model (Daly and Cobb 1989: 25).

11C

Why do ecological economists want to conceive of *Homo economicus* as person-in-community? What, if anything, is ecologically desirable about the concept?

The "teleology" of ecological economics questions the personal goals of acquiring happiness through purchasing products; it questions the national goals of unlimited economic growth as the key to well-being; and it questions the planetary process of economic globalization. Ecological economics calls the very measures of economic well-being into question, arguing that markers such as GDP (gross domestic product) do not measure true fulfillment or happiness, though in policy discussions they often serve in this way (another example of misplaced concreteness).[3] Ecological economists argue that unlimited economic growth cannot continue in a closed system, and some, like Daly (1977), argue for small-scale enterprises in a "steady-state" economy. True prosperity for people, according to ecological economics, lies not in the consumption of products but in vibrant, healthy communities, genuine participatory democracy, and flourishing systems of ecological production.

Ecological economists even envision a better world, engaging in an "eschatology" of sorts, as they quest for the mutual well-being of nature and people.[4] Ecological economics addresses (1) the appropriate scale of the human economy within the earth economy, (2) the problem of just distribution of resources so that all have at least a basic minimum on which to survive, and (3) the allocation of resources above and beyond this basic minimum. In this third realm, the market plays a key role; the parameters of the first two, however, should instead be decided by genuine participatory democratic processes. Ecological economists believe that governments, guided by the people, should direct a fair distribution of resources. Ecological economists, then, call for sacrifices on the part of the rich for the sake of more just distribution to the poor, as well as for the sake of lightening the impact of the human economy upon the earth system. This is the "better world" they imagine.

From the above discussion, two things should be clear: first, this represents a genuine departure from traditional economics; and, second, ecological economics contains important areas of overlap and confluence with religious ideas.

Religion, ecology, and economics

We have examined "Religion and Economics" and "Ecology and Economics." What happens when all three areas overlap? At a basic level, what happens is this: People care for the earth and each other through economic means, for religious reasons. But this pattern may occur in multiple ways, depending on the particularities of the religion, history, and context. Below is a sampling of some practices, movements, thinkers, and concepts that arise in this fruitful confluence of religions, ecology, and economics.

Sabbath and Jubilee

Groups seeking a different way of living more lightly on the earth often invoke two concepts from the Hebrew Bible: Sabbath and Jubilee. The Sabbath teachings prescribe a day of rest once a week for all in the household (including animals); they also direct the Israelites to observe a year of rest once every seven years, including letting the land lie fallow; in the Jubilee Year, once every 49 years, slaves are set free, debts are canceled, and land is returned to its original owners, as outlined in the Hebrew Bible (see Leviticus 25). Both Sabbath and Jubilee are times of feasting and celebration, when the community comes together to praise God and enjoy mutual rest.

Observant Jews do not use electricity or fossil fuels on the weekly Sabbath. They walk to the synagogue and they eat food that has already been prepared. They refrain from many activities, including paid work. Abstaining from work, in most cases, also means abstaining from environmental degradation, since much human work harms the planet. The Sabbath is linked to God's rest on the seventh day of creation. On the Sabbath, observant Jews stop transforming creation through their work, but instead appreciate and savor creation, much as God did on the seventh day.

The Sabbath Economics Collaborative is a group of Christian theologians and scholars seeking to draw upon these concepts in order to envision a more humane and earth-friendly way of understanding and practicing economics.[5] Ched Myers, a member of this group, articulates three principles:

1 the world as created by God is abundant, with enough for everyone— provided that human communities restrain their appetites and live within limits;
2 disparities in wealth and power are not "natural" but the result of human sin, and must be mitigated within the community of faith through the regular practice of redistribution;
3 the prophetic message calls people to the practice of such redistribution, and is thus characterized as "good news" to the poor.

(Myers 2002: 5)

Here we see echoes of central concepts in ecological economics: the idea of the proper scale of the economy, just distribution, and allocation of resources. Myers and others maintain that these concepts arise from the Bible's delineation of proper economic activity within community.

Both Sabbath and Jubilee concepts, according to Richard Lowery, affirm that God owns the land, and that humans must interact with it on God's terms, rather than their own terms. "In the modern world," he admits, "the specifics of biblical Sabbath and jubilee are moot or impossible. But the principles of social solidarity, abundance and self-restraint, and concern for the long-term survival of families can be adapted and applied" (Lowery 2000: 149). This view questions traditional economic assumptions such as unlimited growth and inequality, focusing instead on better distribution, greater generosity and sharing among the peoples of the earth.[6]

Christian "eco-eco-theology"

There is eco-theology, Christian writing that links religious ideas with ecological concepts. And then there is "eco-eco-theology," Christian writing that links religious and ecological concepts with economic ideas. Two Christian eco-eco-theologians bear brief examination here.

One of the founding works of ecological economics was written by an economist and a theologian: Herman Daly and John B. Cobb, Jr. Their 1989 book *For the Common Good* set the agenda for the field of ecological economics and illuminated its connections with a religious perspective. They call for limited economic inequality and good community life, deriving this from biblical accounts of economic laws in the Hebrew Bible, such as those preventing usury and describing the year of Jubilee (Daly and Cobb 1989: 314). They describe their offering to the field as a "prophetic theistic point of view" (1989: 386). From this religious viewpoint, Daly and Cobb justify their vision of a better world, one that offers sufficiency for all in a context of proper scale and relationship within the earth's limits. In Cobb's later works he names a new form of idolatry, "economism," and offers, by contrast, a better priority-concept, in "earthism." "Economism," he writes, "is the belief that society should be organized for the sake of economic growth"; Earthism, by contrast, seeks to organize society for the sake of the well-being of the planet and all who reside here (Cobb 1999: 5, 38).

Another eco-eco-theologian joining in the discussion is Sallie McFague. In her 2001 book *Life Abundant: Rethinking Economy and Ecology for a Planet in Peril*, McFague connects traditional Christian theology with traditional economic theory. Without blaming Christianity for economic excesses, she nevertheless describes traditional theology as "a docile, non-threatening partner" to traditional economics: Both ignore the earth, are comfortable with inequality, and take refuge in individuality and abstraction (McFague 2001: 160). McFague prefers ecological economics to traditional economics, and bluntly proclaims: "whether we choose one or the other of the two economic models *is* a matter of life and death" (2001: 196–97). She shares ecological economics' vision of a better world, and argues that, having glimpsed this possibility, "we must individually and collectively devise alternative ways of working, eating, cultivating land, transporting ourselves, educating our children, entertaining ourselves, even of worshipping God" (McFague 2001: 198). Her prescription, in fact, is for "cruciform living"— sacrifices on the part of the well-off, in order to free up resources for the poor without devastating ecological systems.

Eco-kashrut and eco-halal

Jewish dietary laws, *kashrut*, instruct believers to avoid certain foods in order to remain pure and holy; these laws safeguard Jewish identity and distinctiveness, and are treated as revelations from God. Contemporary Jews concerned with environmental problems sometimes add an ecological dimension to their observance of *kashrut*. Samuel Weintraub writes: "We should ... question the *kashrut* of food that is the product of child or other oppressed labor, or the cause of natural perdition" (Weintraub 1991–92). Lynn Gottlieb envisions each community forming "an eco-*kashrut* council to ... develop a list of eco-*kosher* and eco-*treyfe* [forbidden or unclean] products" (Gottlieb 1995: 181, italics added).

Muslim eating restrictions are called *halal*, and eco-*halal* farms and slaughterhouses are arising around the country.[7] At these slaughterhouses, animals are raised and killed in ways that avoid cruelty and environmental harm. During the month of Ramadan, when Muslims fast during the day, some advocate practicing a "Green Ramadan." This may involve carpooling, reduced meat consumption, and other environmentally sensitive consumption habits (Krishnamurthy 2009). These practices of avoiding products that cause ecological and social harm are one individual-level way of living out the vision of ecological economics.

Gandhi's self-rule and Schumacher's Buddhist Economics

Mahatma Gandhi, the respected leader of the Indian resistance against British rule, had his own Hindu perspective on ecology and economics. Religion scholar Larry Shinn describes the "inner logic" of Gandhi's views as follows:

> Whatever else a Gandhian ecology may be, it will begin with individual and collective self-rule (*svaraj*) premised upon truth (*satya*), nonviolence (*ahimsa*), and self-sacrificial actions (*tapas*). It will insist upon respect and compassion for all creatures and for nature itself. It will encourage economic self-reliance and self-sufficiency at the local (village, town, or neighborhood) level. Finally, a Gandhian ecology will interweave religious, economic, and political dimensions of life on both the personal and corporate levels.
>
> (Shinn 2000: 236)

Gandhi envisioned a better life for India consisting of economic as well as political self-rule. Locally self-sufficient villages, connected in regional networks, constituted the economic basis of his vision. Gandhi was well aware of the earth's limited resources, and he counseled temperance and self-sacrifice to live within these limits; as he famously said, "Earth provides enough to satisfy every man's need, but not every man's greed" (Shinn 2000: 228). Gandhi also saw no need to separate religious ideas from economic and ecological considerations.

E.F. Schumacher, a British economist with experience in Asia, wrote *Small Is Beautiful: Economics as if People Mattered* in 1975. Schumacher, an avid student of Gandhi, developed a perspective about ecology and economics that foreshadows later works by ecological economists. One of its best-known chapters, "Buddhist Economics," treats the Buddhist concept of "right livelihood" as an alternate foundation for an understanding of the role of labor—and the proper parameters for treatment of labor—in economic theory (Schumacher 1975: 53–55). He also invokes the values of simplicity and nonviolence as precepts for a Buddhist Economics, praising local production for its simplicity, and encouraging simplicity in consumer desires, which would lead to fewer contested resources and therefore less violence (1975: 57–59).[8] Schumacher's title pays tribute to the idea that small-scale economic initiatives have a lesser environmental impact, and are more likely to be humane, than larger economic operations (1975: 36). Quite willing to call natural systems and creatures "sacred," Schumacher marshals religious concepts in the service of his vision of an ecological economy (1975: 106–07).

Buddhist responses to consumerism

There is more to Buddhism and economics than Schumacher seemed to realize, specifically in regard to consumerism. In Buddhism, the ego-based view of the self is understood to be fundamentally untrue, so consumer activity seeking to satisfy personal desires (typical activity of the traditional *Homo economicus*) is mistaken and will only lead to suffering. Buddhists advocate a practice of mindfulness, careful meditative attention to one's thoughts and actions, in order to "learn to unhook from the craving" for material possessions (Kaza 2005: 150). Rather than seeking to continuously stimulate desires, Buddhists seek non-attachment, cultivating the wisdom that allows humans "to be content with what we have" (Loy 2002: 59).

Buddhism teaches that all beings are interconnected and recognizes that harm can occur to distant beings because of economic activity; in response, Buddhism offers a precept of nonviolence, or *ahimsa*, and counsels compassionate action (Kaza 2005: 142). Buddhism responds to poverty not by advocating more free trade, as proponents of economic globalization would, but rather by prescribing *dana*, or holy generosity (Loy 2002: 63–64).

"Engaged Buddhists" respond to globalization by seeking a proper scale for economic activity, by recognizing interconnections, and by seeking to avoid desire and ignorance while practicing compassionate action toward others (Simmer-Brown 2005: 97–103). For many, this proper scale calls for small, local enterprises, a process that Buddhist scholar David Chappel terms "glocalization" (2005: 246). Schumacher and ecological economists would concur.

IID

To what extent do you think the ideas of David Chappel, David Loy, and E.F. Schumacher—all explicitly derived from the Buddhist tradition—would be applicable to a non-Buddhist audience? To Western cultures?

The confluence of ecology, economics, and religion is a rich source of provocative questions. What is the best way to value, care for, and distribute the material things of life? What religious tools and practices help us to be good stewards? What should be done when the *oikos* of human households and the *oikos* of the earth conflict with one another? To what degree does economics degrade religious ideals, and to what degree uplift them? Does the market, as a tool, help human and nonhuman flourishing? Are there limits to its usefulness? To what should humans attach themselves, and of what should they let go? Which economic models are best for the environment? Which are most appropriate from a religious perspective?

Religions offer partial replies to these questions, but their definitive answers remain elusive. Some practitioners observe a Sabbath, and others practice non-attachment to material possessions. Some seek "cruciform living," and others search out eco-*halal* foods. Regardless, religious practitioners can find guidance in their traditions for careful attention to both the *oikos* of the earth and the *oikos* of their households. Though the guidance is there, the practice may not be: Religious people, like everyone else, contribute to a share of the environmental degradation that characterizes our world. It is hard, it seems, to practice what we preach.

Case study: Food Not Bombs

Food Not Bombs (FNB) is a movement "based on the principle that food is a right, not a privilege." Activists obtain donated food (often from grocery stores, typically expired food that would otherwise be discarded), cook it in large quantities, and serve it in a public place, for free, to anyone who wants it. The "not bombs" part of FNB's mission typically manifests in peace-activism leaflets and community organizing that occurs at FNB's public meals. Local FNB chapters are run by consensus and the organization avoids hierarchical structures; it is all-volunteer labor, as there is no money with which to hire anyone to do or manage the work.

FNB activists are dedicated to nonviolence, which they pursue by addressing the violence of poverty (distributing free food) and by avoiding violence to animals (serving vegetarian food), in addition to organizing against war (protests, street theater, leaflets, political campaigns). FNB aims to "feed everyone without restriction," rich or poor: Whoever comes to a meal site is entitled to share the food, no strings attached.

Below are some excerpts from the Food Not Bombs online handbook, designed to coach would-be FNB organizers. Use these to guide your reading of what they have posted at www.foodnotbombs.net.

On "recovering" donated food and the food economy:

> The volume of food available to recover is immense, but be selective. Take what you can use from the highest quality. In many places, there is no need to recover commercial produce because there is plenty of organic produce to recover! ... One of our goals is to encourage the awareness of the food's abundance as well as the undermining of the market of scarcity that places profits before people.

On why they serve vegetarian food:

> If more people were vegetarian and demanded organically grown, locally produced foods, this would encourage organic farming practices and support smaller farms. This in turn would make it easier to decentralize the means of food production and to create democratic control over the quality of the food produced and the stewardship of the land. More people can be fed from one acre of land on [a] vegetarian rather than meat-based diet. Our society's current meat-based diet allows for huge "agribusinesses" and dependency on chemical fertilizers and pesticides, resulting in the declining nutritional value of the food produced and also destruction of the environment ... Teaching people about the health benefits of a vegetarian diet actually creates a healthy, caring attitude towards ourselves, others, and the planet as a whole. Therefore, all of the food we prepare is strictly from vegetable sources, that is, no meat, dairy, or eggs.

On poverty and participation:

> Food Not Bombs responds to poverty and the lack of self-esteem in two ways. First, we provide food in an open, respectful way to whomever wants it. We will not make people jump through any bureaucratic hoops designed to control, humiliate, and often punish people who are poor.

Second, we invite people who receive food to become involved in providing that food. This provides an opportunity for people to regain their power and recognize their ability to contribute and make a change.

Discussion questions

1   Food Not Bombs is a secular movement, more affiliated with anarchism and pacifism than any religion. However, there is a set of values at play here that seem in harmony with certain ideas that show up in religion and ecology. Which religious/economic concepts, articulated in this chapter, might work in concert with the philosophy of Food Not Bombs?
2   What is FNB's critique of market economics, and how do they seek to respond to it? In what ways do they highlight or make use of the given "ecology" or "economy" of food distribution in a given area?
3   How would you describe the likely environmental impact of a FNB operation? How might this practice connect with concepts such as a "gift economy," almsgiving, Sabbath, Jubilee, "cruciform living," "eco-*kosher*," "eco-*halal*," nonviolence, *dana*, or "glocalization"?

Notes

1   In the social sciences, the term "gift economy" typically refers to a culture whose primary mode of economic exchange is not a market economy or a barter system, but rather one of gift-giving. Sociologist Marcel Mauss is known for his work on the gift concept in traditional cultures. Mauss's gift concept has taken on new life in the hands of postmodern theorist Jacques Derrida and theologian John Milbank, who discuss a "true" gift's qualifications as non-reciprocal, unrecognized, and so forth. For this context, suffice it to say that religious practitioners often see God's generosity—in the form of spiritual or physical blessings—as a gift, and one that figures into the purposes of God's overall *oikos*.
2   Herman Daly published his highly influential work *Steady-State Economics* in 1977. The first meetings of ecological economists occurred in the 1980s, and the first book titled *Ecological Economics* was published in 1987. The International Society for Ecological Economics was founded in 1989 (website of the International Society for Ecological Economics, "About the ISEE," available at http://www.ecoeco.org/about.php [accessed December 28, 2009]).
3   Some ecological economists have sought to create an alternate, more "accurate" measurement for human and planetary well-being to replace the gross national product (GNP). (See Costanza *et al.* 1997: 133 ff.)
4   See Costanza *et al.* (1997: 177–78). Also, Norgaard, "Ecological Economics: A Short Description," Forum on Religion and Ecology, available at http://fore.research.yale.edu/disciplines/economics/index.html. (accessed December 28, 2009).
5   See "Sabbath Economics Collaborative," available at www.sabbatheconomics.org (accessed December 28, 2009).
6   The Jubilee movement, which emerged around the turn of the millennium, sought to convince the world's richer governments to cancel poorer governments' debts in a modern instance of the Jubilee.

7 One of the first is the Taqwa Eco-Halal Cooperative near Chicago, IL. See *Renewal*, "Food for Faith," available at http://renewalproject.net/film/story/food_for_faith (accessed December 28, 2009).

8 Nonviolence, or *ahimsa*, is a concept that Buddhists and Hindus share.

References

Berry, W. (1987) *Home Economics*, San Francisco: North Point Press.

——(2007) "Christianity and the Survival of Creation," in D. Rhoads (ed.) *Earth and Word: Classic Sermons on Saving the Planet*, New York: Continuum.

Chappell, D. (2005) "Mutual Correction: Seeing the Pain of Others," in S. Kaza (ed.) *Hooked! Buddhist Writings on Greed, Desire, and the Urge to Consume*, Boston: Shambhala.

Cobb, J. (1999). *The Earthist Challenge to Economism: A Theological Critique of the World Bank*, New York: St. Martin's Press.

Costanza, R., J.C. Cumberland, H.E. Daly, R. Goodland, and R. Norgaard (1997) *An Introduction to Ecological Economics*, Boca Raton, FL: St. Lucie Press.

Daly, H. (1977) *Steady-State Economics: the Economics of Biophysical Equilibrium and Moral Growth*, San Francisco: W.H. Freeman.

Daly, H. and J. Cobb (1989) *For the Common Good: Redirecting the Economy toward Community, the Environment, and a Sustainable Future*, Boston: Beacon Press.

Gottlieb, L. (1995) *She Who Dwells Within: A Feminist Vision of a Renewed Judaism*, San Francisco: Harper San Francisco.

Kaza, S. (2005) "Penetrating the Tangle," in S. Kaza (ed.) *Hooked!: Buddhist Writings on Greed, Desire, and the Urge to Consume*, Boston: Shambhala.

Krishnamurthy, M. (2009) "Muslim Leaders Urge 'Green' Ramadan," *Daily Herald*, August 22, 2009, available at http://www.dailyherald.com/story/?id=315522 (accessed December 28, 2009.)

Lowery, R. (2000) *Sabbath and Jubilee*, St. Louis, MO: Chalice Press.

Loy, D. (1997) "The Religion of the Market," *Journal of the American Academy of Religion* 65(2): 275–90.

——(2002) "Pave the Planet or Wear Shoes? A Buddhist Perspective on Greed and Globalization," in P. Knitter and C. Muzaffar (eds) *Subverting Greed: Religious Perspectives on the Global Economy*, Maryknoll, NY: Orbis Books.

McFague, S. (2001) *Life Abundant: Rethinking Economy and Ecology for a Planet in Peril*, Minneapolis: Fortress Press.

Miller, V. (2003) *Consuming Religion: Christian Faith and Practice in a Consumer Culture*, New York: Continuum.

Myers, C. (2002) *The Biblical Vision of Sabbath Economics*, Washington, DC: Tell the Word, Church of the Saviour.

Schneider, N. (2009) "Can Islam Save the Economy?" *Religion Dispatches*, January 26, 2009, available at http://www.religiondispatches.org/archive/economy/803/can_islam_save_the_economy (accessed December 28, 2009).

Schumacher, E.F. (1975) *Small Is Beautiful: Economics as if People Mattered*, New York: Harper & Row.

Shinn, L. (2000) "The Inner Logic of Gandhian Ecology," in C. Chapple and M.E. Tucker (eds) *Hinduism and Ecology: The Intersection of Earth, Sky, and Water*, Cambridge, MA: Harvard University Press.

Simmer-Brown, J. (2005) "Cultivating the Wisdom Gaze," in S. Kaza (ed.) *Hooked! Buddhist Writings on Greed, Desire, and the Urge to Consume*, Boston: Shambhala.

Tanner, K. (2005) *Economy of Grace*, Minneapolis: Augsburg Fortress.

Weintraub, S. (1991–92) "The Spiritual Ecology of Kashrut," *Reconstructionist* (Winter): 12–14.

Further reading

Berry, W. (1987) *Home Economics*, San Francisco: North Point Press.

Cobb, J. (1999) *The Earthist Challenge to Economism: A Theological Critique of the World Bank*, New York: St. Martin's Press.

Daly, H. and J. Cobb (1989) *For the Common Good: Redirecting the Economy toward Community, the Environment, and a Sustainable Future*, Boston: Beacon Press.

Kaza, S. (ed.) (2005) *Hooked!: Buddhist Writings on Greed, Desire, and the Urge to Consume*, Boston: Shambhala.

Weber, M. (2005) *The Protestant Ethic and the Spirit of Capitalism*, ed. T. Parsons, London: Routledge.

Chapter 12

Environmental justice and eco-justice

Richard R. Bohannon II and Kevin J. O'Brien

The sort of dialogue between religion and environmental issues demonstrated in this book represents something of a new phenomenon, at least in the West. The idea of a global environmental crisis emerged in the mid- to late twentieth century, and so it is only in recent decades that religious institutions, religious people, and scholars of religion have developed responses to this phenomenon.

However, the religious response to environmental degradation does not emerge from nowhere. Religious communities have weighed in on other sweeping and urgent issues throughout history, and religious people have long been concerned with the future and fate of this world. Thus, many religions draw on long traditions of moral argument and ethical imagination when responding to the new crisis of environmental degradation. More specifically, religions draw on longstanding commitments to *human* well-being and *human* liberation, and so building on these traditions means taking human beings seriously in environmental discussions. Thus, most religious responses to environmental issues assume that conservation and preservation are never only about nonhuman animals and ecosystems, but necessarily also include the human beings who impact, depend upon, shape, and are shaped by their environments.

This chapter is about one longstanding commitment in many religious traditions—justice—particularly focusing on the ways Christians have enhanced environmental conversations with an ideal of justice. In this context, arguments about justice assert that all members of a community should have fair and equitable access to that community's resources and participate in the community's decision-making processes, and that special moral attention should be paid to the "least among us," those who are poor or disadvantaged, and those who have been marginalized and oppressed. Inspired by this ideal, Christian environmentalists have dealt with ideas of "environmental justice" and "eco-justice,"[1] raising important questions for any study of environmental issues and the study of environment and religion in particular.

We will begin with key examples of environmental injustice, and then move to distinguish between two responses to the phenomenon:

environmental justice—a movement advocating the rights and participation of marginalized peoples in environmental concerns—and *eco-justice*—a theological and ethical ideal that harmoniously incorporates both social and ecological concerns. We will then discuss the tensions and commonalities between these two approaches to justice, and conclude with a discussion of the various roles of religion in the broad discussion of justice and environmental issues.

Readers should note that this chapter is focused on race, class and ethnicity, primarily in the United States. As chapters in this volume on globalization and gender describe, women have often also borne the brunt of environmental problems in many situations, and the problems of environmental injustice cross all national boundaries.

The reality of environmental injustice: two examples

Within the modern environmental movement, the connections between environmental issues and social justice began to focus on human-made chemicals, with particular early attention to the exposure of farm workers in California to the infamous pesticide DDT. In 1962, Rachel Carson published the environmental classic *Silent Spring* and argued that the rampant use of pesticides caused drastic and irreparable harm to animals and ecosystems. Carson's key example was that DDT destroys the reproductive capacity of many bird species, and so she suggested that its continued use would lead to spring seasons with no birdsong. Another disturbing finding was the serious impact of this pesticide on the physical and the mental health of those who handled it. Carson writes that such an impact on human health is "a heavy price to pay for the temporary destruction of a few insects, but a price that will continue to be exacted as long as we insist upon using chemicals that strike directly at the nervous system" (Carson 1962: 198).

Applying this argument, groups of farm workers responsible for spraying crops with DDT and later picking them began to advocate laws banning the chemical in the late 1960s. They argued that the use of DDT was both environmentally irresponsible and an unjust labor practice, emphasizing that its most immediate victims were the poor workers employed on California farms, most of them migrants from Mexico. Among such workers, instances of birth defects and cancers were dramatically higher than in the rest of the population, and this health concern established a clear link between the environmental issue of DDT and the labor issue of workers' rights.

A leader in this movement was the Mexican American organizer César Chávez, who co-founded (with Dolores Huerta) and ran a union, the United Farm Workers (UFW). Chávez was trained as a community organizer and inspired by a commitment to social justice from Catholic Social Teaching, which helped him to appeal to the faith of his workers and to request support from church leaders. Building on a Catholic commitment to social justice and appealing to the examples of Gandhi and Martin Luther King, Chávez led nonviolent marches, boycotts, and fasts to demand that workers be treated fairly, which included keeping them safe from the demonstrated harm of pesticides like DDT. He called attention to the fact that farm workers "have been cursed and ridiculed, they have been stripped and chained and jailed, they have been sprayed with the poisons used in the vineyards," but trained to resist nonviolently, "to overcome with love and compassion" (Chávez 1969: 211).

Chávez's campaigns were in many ways successful: the UFW secured more rights for farm workers and helped to establish a legal ban against DDT in the United States. However, this movement still continues to struggle for the rights and health of poor farm workers, paying special attention to the impacts of new pesticides on the land and people and the health of workers in other countries around the world that continue the legal use of DDT.[2]

Of course, environmental justice is not just an issue for farm workers, and includes a long list of issues that expand beyond exposure to manufactured chemicals. This was made clear in 2005 when the city of New Orleans became the nation's quintessential example of racism and urban poverty, as black residents spent horrifying days waiting for rescue from their flooded city in the wake of Hurricane Katrina. This was a clear example of environmental injustice, as the poor and minority communities of the city were disproportionately harmed and made homeless by the hurricane and the broken levees.

Katrina did not happen in a vacuum, however; in addition to the area being environmentally vulnerable due to hubristic management of the Mississippi River (see Colton 2005), the disaster struck a city and region that was already the home of numerous environmental injustices, and left new social and environmental problems in its path. Southeastern Louisiana has long been one of the most toxic areas in the United States, with pollution occurring on a different scale than what Chávez experienced.

Before 1950, there were no major industries located in the state of Louisiana; by 1971, however, the state had 60 major petrochemical plants. The state established lax environmental controls to attract economic development, confident that the enormous amount of water that passes through the Mississippi River was capable of handling an endless amount of industrial discharge (Colten 2000; Wright 2003). By the 1970s, the area between Baton Rouge and New Orleans had an average of one refinery or industrial plant per one-half mile. In 1998, that stretch of land—alternatively called the "chemical corridor" or "cancer alley"—gave off one-sixteenth of all emissions for the United States (Roberts and Toffolon-Weiss 2001).

Louisiana also contains a distinctive racial and ethnic makeup. Like other Southern states, the most prominent racial dynamic is between whites and blacks, but Louisiana also has a sizable Native American population, particularly in the far southern end of the state, as well as Cajuns, the descendants of French settlers in Canada. Environmental racism against these groups is certainly an issue (e.g. Roberts and Toffolon-Weiss 2001), but most of the environmental justice research in the area has been concerned specifically with the effects of industrial pollution on black neighborhoods. Today, the most polluted corridor along the Mississippi has an undeniably large black population: In a nine parish study of the area from Baton Rouge to New Orleans ("parishes" are the equivalent to counties in other states), 80 percent of black residents were found to live within three miles of a polluting facility (Wright 2005: 95).

The city of New Orleans is home to some of this industry, and downstream from much of the rest, but the city's environmental problems do not stop there. "The deeper we dig into the story of Katrina," writes Michael Eric Dyson, "the more we must accept culpability for the fact that the black citizens of the Big Easy ... were treated by the rest of us as garbage" (2006: 14). While Dyson does not develop this image of "garbage" explicitly, it is apt. The unequal burden of Hurricane Katrina on black residents was preceded by a deep history of housing discrimination and segregation, and followed by inequitable policies for rebuilding New Orleans. Before Katrina, the majority (67.9 percent) of the population in New Orleans was black, and the city poverty rate was 23 percent (Dyson 2006: 5). Hurricane Katrina and its aftermath laid bare an additional aspect of environmental injustice: Within the city of New Orleans and surrounding areas, low-income communities and poor people of color were segregated into the neighborhoods most vulnerable to excessive flooding, had poor access to transportation and limited involvement in public policy decisions, and lacked the economic means and the social capital to recover quickly or restore pre-Katrina standards of living.[3]

In light of Hurricane Katrina, then, it is clear that environmental injustice in southern Louisiana is not simply a matter of the siting of polluting industries—though that is certainly important—but is part of a deeply ingrained structure that affects a multiplicity of daily decisions, significantly limiting the options of the poorer, blacker neighborhoods to the advantage of a wealthier, whiter population.

Just as Chávez was motivated in part by his Catholic faith, activism around these issues in the South has often been led by the black church. In nearby southern Mississippi, for instance, Jesus People Against Pollution—a small organization that developed among African American Christians—has led a widely publicized campaign for the cleanup of significant toxic contamination from an Agent Orange military facility in the 1970s. As documented in the recent film *Renewal* (Ostrow and Rockefeller 2007), the Greater First Baptist Church of Escatawpa, in coastal Mississippi, has led a similar fight about the black community's exposure to toxic chemicals in the aftermath of Hurricane

Katrina. The black church also played a central role for activists fighting a uranium enrichment plant near the town of Homer, in northern Louisiana, providing both a social network and an organizing language of faith (Roberts and Toffolon-Weiss 2001). The central role of the church, black and white, also appears to be continuing in current rebuilding efforts in New Orleans (Evans *et al.* 2008).

The farms of California and the neighborhoods of Louisiana are unfortunately just two among many examples, but the broad trend is clear from these brief cases: marginalized people—the poor, people of color, and victims of historic injustices—tend to bear the burden of environmental destruction in their homes, their bodies, and their lives. Furthermore, these peoples tend to have the least access to healthy ecosystems and the benefits they provide, and often lack the political influence and wealth necessary to prevent and mitigate environmental and health hazards. This is the reality of environmental injustice, an undeniable phenomenon in contemporary human societies.

12A

Do you know of other examples of environmental injustice? What do you think are the most central injustices in the region where you live? How might they be connected to environmental concerns?

Mitigating the human cost of environmental problems: the environmental justice movement

The most concrete and direct response to this reality has been the environmental justice (EJ) movement, which took shape most formally when the United Church of Christ (UCC) became involved with a rural community in Warren County, NC. The black-majority community was protesting the proposed siting in their county of a waste dump for polychlorinated biphenyl (PCB), a highly toxic chemical. Church leaders helped to lead protests, organize congregations, and integrate prayers and religious songs into activism. Dollie Burwell, a member of a local UCC congregation and an active member of the Southern Christian Leadership Conference (SCLC), became the leader of the protests.

In 1986, the UCC's Commission for Racial Justice became involved and sought to link what was happening in Warren County to a wider national trend. They conducted a survey correlating every registered toxic waste facility in the United States to local racial demographics. This survey led to a watershed document, first published in 1987 (updated in 1994 and again in 2007), *Toxic Wastes and Race*. The key finding was that, even when socioeconomic factors are considered, race is the most statistically significant predictor in the siting of hazardous wastes. Throughout the country, zip codes which contain high concentrations of people of color are by far the most likely to contain toxic waste. The authors of the 2007 update (Bullard *et al.* 2007) to this report, using a more precise methodology, only helped to solidify these earlier findings, and in fact showed that in 2007 racial disparities were *higher* than previously estimated, at least in some instances.

Toxic Waste and Race was written to equip grassroots organizations with a solid resource and to influence public policy. Thus, the 1987 draft concludes with four pages of policy and organizational recommendations; the first one is for the "President of the United States to issue an executive order mandating federal agencies to consider the impact of current policies and regulations on racial and ethnic communities" (UCCCRJ 1987: xv). This proposal was an impressive success: Seven years later, President Bill Clinton signed executive order 12898, titled "Federal Actions to Address Environmental Justice in Minority Populations and Low-Income Populations," a landmark piece of government policy. Inspired by such success, the environmental justice movement continues to thrive and struggle today to respond to, raise awareness about, and overcome environmental injustices.

What motivates *Toxic Waste and Race* more than anything is a drive for data to prove the reality of environmental injustice. This emphasis on data has become a characteristic of the EJ movement, the literature of which is predominantly social scientific, with extensive quantitative analysis and carefully researched case studies of particular instances of environmental racism. This data collection is vital to the movement: in order to demonstrate the existence of environmental injustices in courts and legislatures (and thus effect systemic change), one must have solid, reliable data on which to base one's claims. For instance, EJ activists in New Orleans after Katrina have worked hard to both measure and publicize the reality of unjustly distributed burdens and access, and to use the data they gather to directly intervene in policy debates (see Bullard and Wright 2009).

12B

How helpful or important is quantitative data for making public policy arguments about justice? What does it help with? How might it limit the kinds of arguments an activist can make?

The same approach to measuring injustice and finding a way to make a concrete impact animated one of the earliest national meetings of EJ activists and scholars: the First National People of Color Environmental Leadership Summit in 1991. The summit featured strategy sessions and caucuses linking various grassroots activists into a coherent movement. The gathering also approved the organizing Principles of Environmental Justice (see the case study on pp. 176–77).

At his opening speech to this Summit, Benjamin Chavis, a key author of *Toxic Wastes and Race*, spoke of "environmental racism" as the problem around which the EJ movement should be organized. He defined this term as

> racial discrimination in environmental policy making and the enforcement of regulations and laws, the deliberate targeting of people of color communities for toxic waste facilities, the official sanctioning of the life threatening presence of poisons and pollutants in our communities, and the history of excluding people of color from the leadership of the environmental movement.
>
> (Lee 1992: 8)

This definition offers a helpful and clear perspective on what the environmental justice movement is about. It also points toward two controversies within the movement: whether environmental injustice must be *intentional*, and how much the movement should focus on *racial* discrimination in contrast to injustice more broadly.

Central to Chavis's definition are words like "deliberate" and "official sanctioning," which suggest that discrimination must be intentional in order to be considered an example of environmental racism. Chavis and many others in the movement are particularly focused on demonstrating that prejudicial ideas and beliefs cause practical harm, and so they focus on such discrimination. However, some worry that this can lead to challenges in proving environmental racism or convincing government agencies to make changes, because intentions are quite difficult to prove (e.g. McGurty 2007). Furthermore, the majority of empirical research on environmental justice (e.g. analyzing data on what racial communities live near toxic industrial facilities) is able to demonstrate *correlation* but not *causation*.

Thus, most scholars and activists in the EJ movement argue that discrimination is a reality whether anyone deliberately chooses to discriminate or not. As Larry Rasmussen comments, "all that is required—this is the point—is simply to be in business as business has evolved over the past few hundred years. It's the system's ways that matter, and the system regularly overrides intentions out of sync with market pressures and practices" (1996: 83). In other words, Rasmussen argues that the racially unjust *results* of an individual or institution's behavior should be central, not the *intentions* of that individual or institution. With a similar emphasis on results rather than intentions, the prominent environmental sociologist Robert Bullard offers this definition:

Environmental racism refers to any policy, practice, or directive that differentially affects or disadvantages (whether intended or unintended) individuals, groups, or communities based on race or color. Environmental racism combines with public policies and industry practices to provide benefits for whites while shifting industry costs to people of color. It is reinforced by governmental, legal, economic, political, and military institutions.

(Bullard 1994: 98)

Bullard's definition understands racism as a *structural* problem in society. Environmental racism thus exists wherever it can be shown that communities of color bear a disproportionate burden to the benefit of white communities; whether or not this is the result of intentional bigotry does not have to be determined.

12C

What is the difference between structural and intentional forms of racism? What would be the strategic implications for the EJ movement of deciding which form of racism to focus on?

George Lipsitz (2006) likewise portrays environmental racism as part of a much larger, institutional form of racism—encompassing housing policies, employment practices, and banking standards, among others—constructed to promote the properties and social positions of whites. To quote Micheal Eric Dyson, race is an "irreducible reality" that shapes how reality is experienced by both blacks *and* whites (Dyson 2004: 41). That is, environmental racism is not only about the disproportionate and unjust burdens placed on people of color, but also about securing a system of white privilege.

A second controversial aspect of Chavis's definition concerns the fact that he chose to focus on "environmental racism" rather than "environmental injustice." This is a common move, and many argue that a discussion of "injustice" broadly is too vague and unspecific, and so choose to use the more disturbing and energizing word "racism." Others argue that the term "environmental racism" can be "misleading" (Timney 1998) since it limits the problem to one of race, perhaps disguising the fact that, for instance, poor white communities in Appalachia have suffered disproportionate environmental problems from coal mining. Several other researchers do not make this explicit critique, but likewise subsume racism as one manifestation of environmental injustice. Bob Edwards, for instance, appeals to a broader idea of environmental injustice when he writes that "across the nation, low-income people, regardless of race, and people of color, regardless of economic status, are more likely to suffer poor health and quality of life due to environmental degradation" (Edwards 1995: 37).

Environmental racism, however, need not be an all-inclusive term, and Timney's concern inadvertently points to the need to clearly distinguish between environmental injustice and the more specific phenomenon of environmental racism. That is, class-based coal mining policies that discriminate against poor whites in places like Appalachia in no way invalidate the existence of racist waste-management policies that discriminate against blacks and Hispanics in places like Houston. Furthermore, as a grassroots movement focused on concrete political change, it makes sense for the EJ movement to distinguish distinct social problems and focus the energy of activists; rather than addressing all discrimination and poverty in the nation, many EJ activists argue, they should focus on the more concrete— although still incredibly pervasive—problem of the racist distribution of environmental burdens and benefits.

Imagining a global ethic: the ideal of eco-justice

Contemporaneous with the beginnings of the environmental justice movement, some North American Christian theologians and ethicists were developing another approach to emphasize the connection between environmental and social issues. This group of scholars coined the term "eco-justice" in order to emphasize the unity of God's creation and the resulting moral connections between humans and the nonhuman world. As a singular concept, eco-justice asserts that there is one moral stance to be taken toward social and environmental ethics: People of faith are called to treat all other creatures—human or otherwise—justly.

A key figure in the development of this idea was William Gibson, who developed and directed "The Eco-Justice Project" at Cornell University, where he organized scholarly conferences and published a journal on the subject.[4] Gibson was also the principle author of one of the first official church statements on eco-justice, a resource paper distributed by the Presbyterian Church, *Keeping and Healing the Creation*. This document urged Christians to recognize the "eco-justice crisis—the historic turning point at which the abuse of nature and the injustice to human beings place the future in grave jeopardy, both for natural systems and for human society." In response to this crisis, the paper argues, the church must reevaluate its life and mission to "fully incorporate the keeping and healing of the creation— the protection and restoration of the vulnerable and the oppressed, both human and nonhuman" (Presbyterian Eco-Justice Task Force 1989: 3, 60). The emphasis in this document is on the synthesis of social justice and environmentalism, a single mission of religious reform responding to both environmental degradation and human oppression.

Eco-justice combines the long Christian tradition of ethical reflection on justice—asserting that all members of a community should have fair and equitable access to the community's resources and participate in the community's decision-making processes—with a key insight from Christian eco-theology: that human beings are part of a community with the rest of creation. With this basis in moral theory and theology, eco-justice is a more abstract concept than environmental justice, asserting based on faith that social and environmental problems have common cause and can be addressed in united and complementary ways. However, this abstraction allows eco-justice to be a far more sweeping and global concept: While EJ advocates tend to focus on carefully studying particular cases of environmental injustice, eco-justice calls for a global commitment on behalf of all creatures everywhere.

The scholars who first developed the ideal of eco-justice sought a unifying principle, and so they were widely ecumenical and inclusive in spirit. From its foundations, this movement has sought to build a global ethic, a single principle applicable to the entire world and instructive for all persons. It is true that the theological basis of eco-justice is a Christian idea of creation—that God created the world, made the world good, and made human beings to live in harmony with the world. However, many advocates do not see this belief as exclusively Christian, and work toward an interreligious common ground about the idea and value of creation.

12D

Based on what you know and have read about religious traditions in this text, do you believe the ideal of eco-justice could be applicable in traditions other than Christianity? Why or why not?

The ideal of eco-justice has not been widely embraced outside of Christian contexts, but it has spread well beyond the Protestant Christians in the United States who first developed it. Eco-justice now animates the work of many of the Catholic nuns and sisters who have continued social ministries while adding a careful attention to environmental degradation as part of their calling of service to the church and the world. This is chronicled in Sarah McFarland Taylor's sociological analysis *Green Sisters*. For instance, Taylor discusses the work of Dominican nun Carol Coston, who worked in the peace and justice movement in the 1970s and has more recently extended that work to include environmental causes, helping to found a farm dedicated to "cultivating diversity: biodiversity and cultural diversity." This is one among many examples Taylor cites of nuns who believe and live as though "justice for humans and justice for the whole earth are inextricably linked" (Taylor 2007: 33–34). Such a holistic, unified ethic is the core of eco-justice.

Along similar lines, a group of South African theologians and ethicists appeal to eco-justice when they work to frame the growing awareness in their nation that "care for economic and social justice cannot be separated from the environment," because "human well-being is dependent on the well-being of the land" and "the problems poor people experience on a daily basis are essentially environmental problems" (Conradie *et al.* 2001: 138). These are eco-justice claims because they make broad assertions about the nature of the social and environmental problems faced by South Africans, assuming that these problems have a common root and must be solved together.

Religion in environmental justice and eco-justice: distinctions and dialogue

Environmental justice and eco-justice are distinct ideas, organizing principles for two movements with important differences. While eco-justice rallies a global community around an ideal of harmonious coexistence throughout the community of life, environmental justice focuses on the rights of human communities that bear disproportionate environmental burdens. While environmental justice tends to be motivated by concrete and quantifiable data about particular instances of race or class discrimination, eco-justice is animated by an abstract theological claim about the unity of human and nonhuman communities.

Among the important differences between these movements are very different roles for religious communities. In the EJ movement, religious institutions have played important roles by collecting and distributing data, offering meeting spaces and organizational networks, and funding programs of research and activism. The United Farm Workers protests in California were aided enormously by the support of Catholic clergy and volunteers. In Warren County, North Carolina, an office of the United Church of Christ helped provide leadership and gathered and analyzed the basic data quantifying inequities, while a local Baptist church functioned as an organizational hub for protesters. Religious traditions provide moral motivation and inspiration, but their primary role in the environmental justice movement has been more practical and concrete.

In the eco-justice movement, by contrast, religion primarily provides moral and theological guidance. Christian theology justifies the movement, emphasizing the singularity of God's creation and therefore the unity of human oppression and environmental degradation. Belief in the goodness of God's creation and the theological hope for harmony provide the primary justification for the movement's central, utopian ideal. Of course, Christian churches support eco-justice activism and teaching in practical and institutional ways, but the most important role of religion here is as a source of inspiration, hope, and ideology. In contrast to the EJ movement, eco-justice has not primarily been about bottom-up community organizing, but has instead worked to distribute the ideas and intellectual energy coming from theological and moral leaders in churches.

Distinguishing eco-justice and environmental justice is therefore a way to think about the different roles religion can play in the environmental movement. Religious institutions can be seen as social hubs fueling practical enterprises, or as intellectual hubs inspiring a new vision of life together. Religious belief can be seen as a motivating factor helping to engage people in a struggle to defend their neighborhoods and their health, or it can be seen as a source of conversion to make believers care more about their neighbors throughout the world. The distinction between eco-justice and environmental justice also helps to demonstrate the choices that environmental and religious activists must sometimes make: between dedicating themselves to local struggles or global ideals, between narrowly proving particular claims of injustice and degradation and encouraging broader commitments to justice and sustainability as ideals, between supporting change materially on the ground and motivating widespread support with inspiring ideas.

However, another reason to note the distinction between environmental justice and eco-justice is to raise the possibility of a religious environmentalism inspired by both.

12E

Is it possible to combine the concrete, local focus of environmental justice with the abstract, global ideal of eco-justice?

One Christian theologian who has incorporated both the particularity of environmental justice and the universality of eco-justice is Leonardo Boff. Boff is a liberation theologian, and he defines this approach as theology that necessarily seeks to "understand and take an active part in the real and historical process of liberating the oppressed" (Boff and Boff 1987: 9). Thus, he writes primarily about the Christian duty to liberate the poor and marginalized, and focuses on the communities of such people in his own country of Brazil.

In his book *Cry of the Earth, Cry of the Poor*, Boff notes that these communities are oppressed not only by economic systems and political violence, but also by environmental degradation. His environmental theology is most concretely a reflection on what is happening to the Amazonian rainforest in his country, and Boff expresses outrage that his government has entered into coalitions with multinational companies to harvest that forest, conducting what he calls a "war on the trees." Boff points out that this is not only a threat to biodiversity and ecological health, but also an attack on the Brazilian people—particularly the indigenous peoples who have lived with the rainforest for countless generations. Disturbed by this trend, he reports on a series of injustices: plans for hydroelectric dam projects to flood fully 2 percent of the Amazon, the construction of thousands of miles of road designed to truck resources out of the forest, and decimation of indigenous cultures whose lands and cultures are being taken away (Boff 1997: 92–100). Boff argues that the destruction of the Amazon is an act of violence against a particular group of poor and marginalized people. This is clearly an appeal to environmental justice.[5]

However, Boff's argument also tilts in the direction of eco-justice when he expands outward from the example of the Amazon to make more sweeping claims about the relationship of human beings to the entire planet's ecosystems. He asserts broadly that environmental degradation is not cleanly separable from human oppression, but that these two sets of problems

> stem from two wounds that are bleeding. The first, the wound of poverty and wretchedness, tears the social fabric of millions and millions of poor people the world over. The second, systematic aggression against the earth, destroys the equilibrium of the planet, threatened by the depredations made by a type of development undertaken by contemporary societies, now spread throughout the world.
>
> (Boff 1995: 67)

According to Boff, these two "wounds" were inflicted by the same weapon: domination, the use of power over others rather than power employed cooperatively with others. The two problems therefore also have a common solution: an ecological sense of justice that combines "respect for the otherness of beings and things and their right to continue to exist" with "respect and concern for people" (Boff 1997: 77). Boff hopes this is possible because his Christian faith teaches that God will make it possible. He theologically argues that when human beings turn toward the world, they will find themselves closer to the world's Creator.

Combining eco-justice and an environmental justice perspective, Boff asserts a theological unity between the human species and the rest of creation, but also pays attention to the struggles of particular communities wrestling with injustice and degradation in his own country. Boff finds powerful ideas in the Christian tradition, ideas that he hopes can motivate the entire human race; but he also works to organize local Christian communities in his native Brazil to save the Amazon.

Thinkers and activists like Boff raise the possibility that eco-justice and environmental justice can coexist, but the two ideas nevertheless remain distinct. Recognizing these distinctions is an essential step in observing the many diverse ways religion has engaged environmental issues, and helps to clarify how religious communities can engage these issues in the future.

Case study: comparing the *Earth Charter* and the *Principles of Environmental Justice*

Two documents that bring environmental issues into direct conversation with justice are the *Earth Charter* and the *Principles of Environmental Justice*. Comparing them can help to illuminate the distinctions and connections between eco-justice and environmental justice and the relevance of religion to both.

The product of ten years of cross-cultural, international discussions, the *Earth Charter* was completed in 2000. It offers "a shared vision of basic values to provide an ethical foundation for the emerging world community ... a common standard by which the conduct of all individuals, organizations, businesses, governments, and transnational institutions is to be guided and assessed." This document is addressed to every human being on the planet, and argues that we are one community with each other and all other creatures.

The *Charter* begins with this preamble:

> We stand at a critical moment in Earth's history, a time when humanity must choose its future. As the world becomes increasingly inter-dependent and fragile, the future at once holds great peril and great promise. To move forward we must recognize that in the midst of a magnificent diversity of cultures and life forms we are one human family and one Earth community with a common destiny. We must join toge-ther to bring forth a sustainable global society founded on respect for nature, universal human rights, economic justice, and a culture of peace. Towards this end, it is imperative that we, the peoples of Earth, declare our responsibility to one another, to the greater community of life, and to future generations.

The *Charter*'s final sentence also emphasizes a commitment to environmental and social justice, ending with this hope: "Let ours be a time remembered for the awakening of a new reverence for life, the firm resolve to achieve sustainability, the quickening of the struggle for justice and peace, and the joyful celebration of life."

The Principles of Environmental Justice were written collectively by participants at the First National People of Color Environmental Leadership Summit, convened in 1991 by the United Church of Christ's Commission for

Racial Justice. The Summit helped to bring momentum to a large number of new, grassroots environmental justice organizations, and to give a national voice to the environmental concerns of communities of color, who felt their perspectives were not recognized by the mainstream environmental movement.

The Principles begin with the following preamble:

We, the people of color, gathered together at this multinational People of Color Environmental Leadership Summit, to begin to build a national and international movement of all peoples of color to fight the destruction and taking of our lands and communities, do hereby re-establish our spiritual interdependence to the sacredness of our Mother Earth; to respect and celebrate each of our cultures, languages and beliefs about the natural world and our roles in healing ourselves; to insure environmental justice; to promote economic alternatives which would contribute to the development of environmentally safe livelihoods; and, to secure our political, economic and cultural liberation that has been denied for over 500 years of colonization and oppression, resulting in the poisoning of our communities and land and the genocide of our peoples.

The delegates at the Summit agreed upon 17 principles, which cover a wide range of topics: they affirm, for instance, the "ecological unity and the interdependence of all species," oppose the "destructive operations of multinational corporations," and demand "the cessation of the production of all toxins, hazardous wastes, and radioactive materials."

You can read the entirety of the Principles of Environmental Justice online at www.ejrc.cau.edu/princej.html, and the *Earth Charter* at www.earthcharterinaction.org.

Discussion questions

1 What are the primary concerns of each of these documents? Where are their concerns similar, and where are there differences?
2 How is humanity's relationship to nature or the earth depicted in each? Which do you find more urgent? Why?
3 Where do you find appeals to "justice" (directly or indirectly) in the *Earth Charter* and the *Principles of Environmental Justice*? For each document, would you characterize the appeal as more like "eco-justice" or "environmental justice" as you have come to understand these terms?
4 Where do you see religious language or ideas in each of the documents? Can you distinguish differences in the ways they approach, discuss, or reference religion and spirituality?

Notes

1 A third concept, "ecological justice," has also emerged. For some activists and scholars it is coterminous with "environmental justice," while for others (e.g. Baxter 2005) it refers more specifically to the justice that is due to nonhuman nature.
2 For more on the religious roots and environmental implications of Chavez's work in the UFW, see especially Levy (1975) and Dalton (2003).
3 For more information on Hurricane Katrina and environmental justice, see Barnshaw and Trainor 2007; Bullard and Wright (2009); Pastor *et al.* (2006).
4 The journal began publication in 1981 under the title *The Egg: A Journal of Eco-Justice*, and its name was changed to *Eco-Justice Quarterly* in 1993. For Gibson's own history of the organization, the journals, and the core idea behind both, see "Introduction to the Journey" in Gibson (2004).
5 Another Brazilian theologian, Ivone Gebara (1999), has similarly connected Christian theology with environmental problems in Brazil (particularly in the urban slums), and added an ecofeminist attention to the gender injustice inherent in these situations.

References

Barnshaw, J. and T. Trainor (2007) "Race, Class, and Capital amidst the Hurricane Katrina Diaspora," in D. Brunsma, D. Overfelt, and J.S. Picou (eds) *The Sociology of Katrina: Perspectives on a Modern Catastrophe*, Lanham, MD: Rowman & Littlefield.

Baxter, B. (2005) *A Theory of Ecological Justice*, New York: Routledge.

Boff, L. (1995) "Liberation Theology and Ecology: Alternative, Confrontation, or Complementarity?" in L. Boff and V. Elizondo (eds) *Ecology and Poverty: Cry of the Earth, Cry of the Poor,* Maryknoll, NY: Orbis Books.

——(1997) *Cry of the Earth, Cry of the Poor,* Maryknoll, NY: Orbis Books.

Boff, L. and C. Boff (1987) *Introducing Liberation Theology*, trans. P. Burns, Maryknoll, NY: Orbis Books.

Bullard, R.D. (1994) *Dumping in Dixie: Race, Class, and Environmental Quality*, 2nd ed., Boulder, CO: Westview Press.

Bullard, R.D. and B. Wright (eds) (2009) *Race, Place, and Environmental Justice after Hurricane Katrina: Struggles to Reclaim, Rebuild, and Revitalize New Orleans and the Gulf Coast*, Boulder, CO: Westview Press.

Bullard, R.D., P. Mohai, R. Saha, and B. Wright (2007) *Toxic Wastes and Race at Twenty: Grassroots Struggles to Dismantle Environmental Racism in the United States*, Cleveland: United Church of Christ Justice and Witness Ministries.

Carson, R. (1962; reprint 1994) *Silent Spring*, New York: Houghton Mifflin.

Chávez, C. (1969) "Letter from Delano," available at http://www.farmworkermovement. org/essays/essays/Letter%20From%20Delano.pdf (accessed December 8, 2009).

Colten, C.E. (2000) "Too Much of a Good Thing: Industrial Pollution in the Lower Mississippi River," in C.E. Colten (ed.) *Transforming New Orleans and Its Environs: Centuries of Change*, Pittsburgh: University of Pittsburgh Press.

——(2005) *Unnatural Metropolis: Wresting New Orleans from Nature*, Baton Rouge: Louisiana State University Press.

Conradie, E., C. Majiza, J. Cochrane, W.T. Sigabi, V. Molobi, and D. Field (2001) "Seeking Eco-Justice in the South African Context," in D. Hessel and

L. Rasmussen (eds) *Earth Habitat: Eco-Injustice and the Church's Response*, Minneapolis: Fortress Press.

Dalton, F.J. (2003) *The Moral Vision of César Chavez*, Maryknoll, NY: Orbis Books.

Dyson, M.E. (2004) *The Michael Eric Dyson Reader*, New York: Basic Citivas Books.

——(2006) *Come Hell or High Water: Hurricane Katrina and the Color of Disaster*, New York: Basic Civitas Books.

Edwards, B. (1995) "With Liberty and Environmental Justice for All: The Emergence and Challenge of Grassroots Environmentalism in the United States," in B. Taylor (ed.) *Ecological Resistance Movements: The Global Emergence of Radical and Popular Environmentalism*, Albany: State University of New York Press.

Evans, D., C. Kromm, and S. Sturgis (2008) *Faith in the Gulf: Lessons from the Religious Response to Hurricane Katrina*, Durham, NC: Institute for Southern Studies.

Gebara, I. (1999) *Longing for Running Water: Ecofeminism and Liberation*, trans. D. Molineaux, Minneapolis: Fortress Press.

Gibson, W. (ed.) (2004) *Eco-Justice: The Unfinished Journey*, Albany: State University of New York Press.

Lee, C. (ed.) (1992) *Proceedings: The First National People of Color Environmental Leadership Summit: The Washington Court on Capital Hill, Washington, D.C., October 24–27, 1991*, New York: United Church of Christ Commission for Racial Justice.

Levy, J.E. (1975) *César Chavez: Autobiography of La Causa*, New York: Norton.

Lipsitz, G. (2006). *The Possessive Investment in Whiteness: How White People Profit from Identity Politics*, 2nd ed., Philadelphia: Temple University Press.

McGurty, E. (2007) *Transforming Environmentalism: Warren County, PCBs, and the Origins of Environmental Justice*, New Brunswick, NJ: Rutgers University Press.

Ostrow, M, and T.K. Rockefeller, T.K. (producers and directors) (2007) *Renewal* [motion picture], Cambridge, MA: Fine Cut Productions.

Pastor, M., Jr., R.D. Bullard, J.K. Boyce, A. Fothergill, R. Morello-Frosch, and B. Wright (2006) *In the Wake of the Storm: Environment, Disaster, and Race After Katrina*, New York: Russell Sage Foundation.

Presbyterian Eco-Justice Task Force (1989) *Keeping and Healing the Creation*, Louisville, KY: Committee on Social Witness Policy of the Presbyterian Church (U.S.A.).

Rasmussen, L. (1996) *Earth Community, Earth Ethics*, Maryknoll, NY: Orbis.

Roberts, J.T. and M.M. Toffolon-Weiss (2001) *Chronicles from the Environmental Justice Frontline*, New York: Cambridge University Press.

Taylor, S.M. (2007) *Green Sisters: A Spiritual Ecology*, Cambridge, MA: Harvard University Press.

Timney, M.M. (1998) "Environmental Injustices: Examples from Ohio," in D. Camacho (ed.) *Environmental Injustices, Political Struggles: Race, Class, and the Environment*, Durham, NC: Duke University Press.

United Church of Christ Commission for Racial Justice (UCCCRJ) (1987) *Toxic Wastes and Race in the United States: A National Report on the Racial and Socio-Economic Characteristics of Communities with Hazardous Wastes Sites*, New York: Public Data Access.

Wright, B. (2003) "Race, Politics and Pollution: Environmental Justice in the Mississippi River Chemical Corridor," in J. Agyeman, R.D. Bullard, and B. Evans (eds) *Just Sustainabilities: Development in an Unequal World*, Cambridge, MA: MIT Press.

——(2005) "Living and Dying in Louisiana's Cancer Alley," in R.D. Bullard (ed.) *The Quest for Environmental Justice: Human Rights and the Politics of Pollution*, San Francisco: Sierra Club Books.

Further reading

Cole, L.W. and S.R. Foster (2001) *From the Ground Up: Environmental Racism and the Rise of the Environmental Justice Movement*, New York: New York University Press.

Hessel, D.T. (ed.) (1992) *After Nature's Revolt: Eco-Justice and Theology*, Minneapolis: Fortress Press.

Stein, R. (2004) *New Perspectives on Environmental Justice: Gender, Sexuality, and Activism*, New Brunswick, NJ: Rutgers University Press.

Chapter 13

Globalization

Lois Ann Lorentzen

> Globalization can apparently destroy democracy, create it, and be used by political entrepreneurs to manipulate democracy. This globalization must be a terrible, wonderful thing.
>
> (Michael Veseth 1998: 12)

Globalization, heralded as a "wonderful thing" leading to global prosperity and a unified planet, and a "terrible thing" bringing environmental collapse and the breakdown of local cultures, remains a highly contentious term. Its meanings are multiple and ambiguous, its effects the source of heated debate among scholars and media pundits. Although the term globalization is over-used, we cannot avoid it if we hope to engage seriously in contemporary scholarly and public debates.

Globalization, most broadly, is the integration of nation-states, cultures, economies, markets, and diverse peoples, into a global network or system. Many theorists emphasize the economic aspects and claim that globalization is the harnessing of local, national, and regional markets to the global through trade, flows of capital, technology, and financial investments. Beyond this general definition, it can mean:

1 an *economic agenda* that traverses the world, promoting market economies and enhancing trade in the service of capital growth;
2 an *ideology* representing values, cultural norms, and practices, seen by some as a superior worldview and by others as cultural hegemony;
3 a *corporate structure and mechanism* that may supercede the rule of nation-states and challenge or even threaten democracy;
4 a *global village*, the consequence of vast cultural exchanges, communication technologies, transportation, migrations, and a wide array of global interconnections, including the globalization of ideas; or
5 a *grassroots globalization* or *globalization from below* as witnessed in anti-globalization or pro-democracy movements emerging in resistance to economic and cultural globalization.

> (Eaton and Lorentzen 2003: 4)

Although little consensus seems to exist among globalization theorists, most claim that global connectedness, whether defined in economic, cultural, technological, or political terms, is the most important historical and social process affecting localities, states, and regions today. Globalization generally "refers to the economic and technological agenda that alters basic modes of cultural organizations and international exchange in many parts of the world" (Eaton and Lorentzen 2003: 4). The primary unit of analysis, then, must be the global system (Ó'Riain 2000). This chapter will examine often-contradictory claims made by globalization theorists, how globalization helps us understand contemporary religion, the link between globalization and the study of ecology, and the religion/globalization/ecology nexus as it plays out in one of the world's regions, Latin America. The concluding case study (pp. 194–99) demonstrates how globalization, religion, and environmental deterioration impact the lives of real people.

The claims of globalization

Globalization erodes the nation-state

According to some theorists, global financial markets, transnational corporations, and a global system of production and consumption all erode the nation-state. Cities such as London, New York, Tokyo, and Dubai are "global" cities and demonstrate the "emergence of interlinked global urban centers" that offer the "infrastructure and technological and human resources to coordinate and control the spatial dispersal produced by flexible accumulation" (Vásquez and Marquardt 2003: 45). The rise of the European Union and regional associations such as the North American Free Trade Agreement (NAFTA) further speaks to the relativization of the nation-state. Global processes of deterritorializaiton and reterritorialization have "undermined the viability of the nation state as a key analytical unit of modern social science" (Vásquez and Marquardt 2003: 36). Certainly any migrant will tell you that borders, citizenship, and the nation-state still matter. What globalization theorists claim, however, is that the state may no longer be the *primary* connection to the global, whether defined as market, culture, or polity.

Globalization redefines time and space

Increased global connectedness alters the human relationship to space and time. New technological and global communications mean we can be "here" and "there" or even everywhere simultaneously. I may physically move from Guatemala to Texas, but through Skype, email, Facebook, phone calls, and sending money and goods to family members, my daily life is global, or at least transnational. In the process, identity becomes delocalized. A statue welcoming visitors to San Salvador, El Salvador, is dedicated to *"hermanos lejanos"* (faraway brothers), signifying that you are here, part of the community and nation, even though you may physically live far away. British sociologist Roland Robertson (1994) refers to this phenomenon as *glocalization*, in which an individual, group, community, or social network may be simultaneously global and local. For glocalization theorists, sharp boundaries among the local, national, regional, and global blur and become one dimension.

The market drives globalization

Following the collapse of the Berlin Wall and the end of the Cold War, the global economic system became increasingly dominated by international capitalism. Financial markets experienced further integration. Major players such as the World Trade Organization pushed for open markets, and regional associations such as NAFTA and the European Union reduced or abolished trade restrictions to promote regional, if not global, economic interdependence. An "economic system operating along capitalist lines now encompasses most regions of the world" (Lechner and Boli 2000: 2). Globalization's critics claim that the unfettered market of globalization is but the "new *lingua franca* of finance capital, as well as the continuation of Western neocolonialism, now carried out by other means" (Hopkins *et al.* 2001: 2).

The market only partially defines globalization

Critics note that globalization theorists tend to "privilege economic and technological explanations and to downplay questions of agency, historicity, and social construction of meaning" (Vásquez and Marquardt 2003: 45). Yet even theorists who believe that the economy is the primary force driving globalization agree that cultural, political, technological, religious, and other dimensions are also important. The United States faces the largest wave of migration in its history, which is having a profound impact on the ethnic and racial composition of the country. One million legal immigrants enter the United States annually (consistent since the early 1990s), as well as roughly 500,000 undocumented persons; the United States now boasts a population that is nearly 12 percent foreign born. The cultural impact on both the United States and sending countries cannot be overstated. A young Colombian migrant in San Francisco may attend yoga classes on Tuesday night and Bollywood dance instruction on Wednesday, in the process constructing a new hybrid cultural identity.

Globalization is not new. Globalization is new

Europe embarked on a process of globalization as early as the sixteenth century, seeking to open markets and promote trade in far-flung corners of the globe. One can certainly make the claim that a world system character-ized by a core (Europe) and periphery existed five centuries ago. Globaliza-tion is merely the new word for colonialism. Later neocolonial projects encouraged by the United States further promoted globalization. The late nineteenth and early twentieth centuries witnessed both trade and expansion and huge waves of migration, surpassed only by that of the 1990s to the present. Yet, even theorists who agree that globalization is not new agree that the pace and density of today's processes are qualitatively different. Improved technologies and transportation connect people in ways unim-aginable a mere fifty years ago; financial investments and global trade con-tinue at a dizzying pace. As more and more remote localities enter the global capitalist system and are connected via internet and television, the world increasingly feels like one place.

Globalization is a wonderful thing

According to its celebrants, globalization allows more and more people to receive endless benefits from the worldwide exchange of capital. Global monetary institutions and financial elites "praise the increases in export commodities and trade, the participation in global wealth, and what they see as democratic civic processes" (Eaton and Lorentzen 2003: 4). Advances in communication mean that those involved in local struggles can more easily receive international assistance. Globalization thus makes it possible to pro-mote democracy, champion global human rights, protect biodiversity and bring international pressure to bear on numerous environmental causes, join struggles for the rights of women and gays, and develop any number of trans- and supra-national movements. Famously, the Zapatistas in Chiapas, Mexico, conducted an "e-(re)volution" using the internet as a "medium that makes possible mass participation and therefore has emancipatory potential" (Morellos 2007: 58). Information technology allowed the Zapatista struggle to be witnessed by a global audience. The local became global, the global responded by putting pressure on the state in service of the particular. Globalization, according to Walter Mignolo, may paradoxically create the conditions for "barbarian theorizing" in which "subaltern communities within the nation state create transnational alliances beyond the state to fight for their own social and human rights" (Mignolo 1998: 44).

Globalization is a terrible thing

Globalization's critics see its effects as overwhelmingly negative, including "deforestation, depletion of fisheries, propagation of infectious diseases, destabilization of national economies, homogenization of cultures, destruc-tion of national film industries, extinction of local languages, sexual tours, and exile and migration" (Hopkins *et al.* 2001: 3). The concentration of capital with global, hegemonic regimes increases economic inequalities both globally and within nation-states. The elite and the rich prosper while social violence increases, poor working conditions abound, and the environment is destroyed as global markets seek to expand at all costs. Political theorists such as Benjamin Barber criticize neoliberalism as the ideology behind globalization. Barber (1995) contends that globalization is an anti-democratic process given that corporations and the imperatives of the market control the political realm. Social theorist George Ritzer (2004) laments the increased consumption and cultural homogenization of globalization, terming this hegemonic tendency "McDonaldization."

> Destroyer of democracy? Path to global prosperity? Source of barbarian theorizing? Promoter of human rights for all? Homogenizer of culture? These "extravagant images of globalization" should caution us to proceed with analytic care as we consider the complicated intertwining of globalization, nature, and religion.
>
> (Veseth 1998: 157)

The most important debates among globalization's theorists, critics and advocates center on whether globalization is primarily destructive or beneficial. Economic globalization's advocates and institutions "praise the increases in export commodities and trade, the participation in global wealth, and what they see as the stabilizing of democratic civic processes" (Eaton and Lorentzen 2003: 4). On the other end of the continuum are anti-globalization theorists and movements such as the World Social Forum. The Forum attempts to bring non-governmental organizations, civil society, and popular social movements together to resist and transform what they see as the destructive elements of globalization. They believe that neoliberalism turns "all of life into a commodity" (Duchrow 2005: 609). Where proponents of globalization see increased wealth, critics see "ever-increasing poverty, exclusion, social degradation, violence, ecological destruction and the decline of democratic participation of the people, not only in the impoverished but also in the rich countries" (Duchrow 2005: 609).

The fierce and often contentious debate as to whether globalization is primarily beneficial or harmful has at its core radically differing views of the neoliberal economic model. The "Washington consensus" promotes neoliberal ideology, deregulation, privatization, open markets and free trade. The United States actively encourages other countries to follow this model, as do institutions such as the World Trade Organization, the International Monetary Fund, the G8, and the World Bank. Critics of the model see the neoliberal ideology underlying globalization as preparing the way for corporations to "rule the world" (Korten 1995). Transnational corporations and financial elites are able to move goods and capital without interference from governments in a world whose ultimate goal is capital accumulation.

Globalization's interpreters, whether critical or supportive of the neoliberal model, agree that it has been "driven both by a self-conscious projection of the economic integration of a world market and by technology, especially information technology" (Coleman 2005: 12). Its economic and technological agenda "alters basic modes of cultural organization and international exchange" (Eaton and Lorentzen 2003: 4). The dizzying pace of information technology, historic levels of global migration, rapidly increasing trade among nations, all underscore that globalization is occurring at breakneck speed. Although some interpreters argue that globalization is not new, most affirm that "our current patterns of rapid economic globalization are distinctive in many ways and global communication networks have transformed us in ways that happened in no earlier period" (Tucker 2005: 88).

13A

What would you identify as the most important debates and disagreements about globalization? Are there any claims about globalization that you think would be widely accepted by most who use the term?

Globalization and nature

Global warming, contaminated lakes and rivers that cross borders, air pollution, a diminished ozone layer; certainly we can make the case that increased globalization directly impacts (and harms) nature. Mining and oil companies based in rich countries roam the earth to extract the resources that fuel an ever-expanding global economy. An insatiable global hunger for beef leads to logging throughout Central America and the Amazon. Soil erosion, logging, mining, ranching, and the polluting of water sources force rural peoples into desperate struggles to survive. Displaced from their lands, they migrate to urban slums where they find inadequate sanitation services, contaminated air, polluted water, and minimal shelter.

The very term "global warming" demonstrates that our new global consciousness includes nature. Many environmental problems, such as acid rain, tropical deforestation, and air pollution, are truly global in scope and as such demand global solutions. Nature itself seems to conspire against the nation-state. The science of ecology shows us that interdependence characterizes ecosystems. If we think of the world as an ecosystem, it makes sense that actions that may seem local have global implications. An environmental problem is considered to be global when it may potentially affect us all, including nonhuman nature. Greenhouse gas emissions and high rates of energy consumption tend to be localized in rich countries; however, the effects of these trends are global and include "the flooding of coastal areas; the sinking of island nations; more frequent and violent storms; further deterioration of ecosystems; disruption of life cycles of flora; and changes in the migrating patterns of birds, fish and mammals" (Tucker 2005: 93). Thus, solutions to environmental challenges must also be global. If the world's fisheries are being depleted, all nations must pledge to curtail massive commercial exploitation. If deforestation further contributes to global warming and loss of habitat for animals, all must pledge to consume less meat, demand shade grown coffee, and share the price of forest protection.

13B

Which environmental problems would you identify as clearly global? Which as clearly local or regional? How do you judge between these categories?

Once again, globalization theorists differ in the assessment of the harms and benefits of globalization processes. Those who point to harm claim that economic globalization has a direct relationship to environmental degradation in far-flung corners of the planet. This occurs as rich countries directly invest in less affluent countries and in the process build factories that pollute, participate in sloppy extraction of resources, exploit oil reserves with little concern for the surrounding environment, and clear-cut forests for beef, coffee, and lumber for insatiable northern appetites. Global capitalism depends on the exploitation of natural (as well as human) resources.

Furthermore, the global economic system has encouraged less affluent nations to incur debt as they attempt to keep pace with countries at the core. The massive debt accumulated by countries on the periphery leads to structural adjustment, rearranging an economy so that vital social services and environmental protection measures are cut in order to service debt. Structural adjustment programs have historically been demanded by the institutions that are seen as key drivers of economic globalization (the International Monetary Fund, the World Bank, and the World Trade Association). Furthermore, the style of development historically favored by these institutions encouraged mega-projects, such as large dams, which further hastened environmental deterioration.[1]

Economic globalization is not solely to blame for grave ecological damage. Cultural globalization, led by the United States, provides an ideology of consumption and waste. The United States remains the world's leader in the marketing of mass culture. This mass culture both encourages consumption and influences patterns of consumption (Roberts and Thanos 2003: 26). Increased consumption demands more resources; when products demanded are non-local, further environmental damage results due to resource extraction, manufacturing costs, and transport. Coca-Cola truly does "make the world go round" in this cycle of consumption and destruction.

Those who see environmental benefits to globalization paint a very different picture. They see the beginnings of a "new social order in the relative costs and benefits of organic farming, ecotourism, certification of extractive products, green/blue (collar) labeling, globalized standards for transparency and 'fair trade,' an end to toxic dumping, defense of environmental victims and indigenous rights, and development programs based on local needs and initiatives" (Helvarg 2003: x). Groups like Greenpeace, Friends of the Earth, the Forestry Stewardship Council, the Interfaith Coffee Program, and countless others encourage large procurers on the path to sustainability. Third World environmental activist groups like Oil Watch in Ecuador and the Malaysia-based Third World Network speak to the growth of grassroots globalization harnessed to nature's well-being (Karliner 2000: 35). Environmental activist Joshua Karliner points to the vibrant movement in India against the negative impacts of globalization that unites "farmers, fisherfolk, union workers, urban dwellers and others" in "protest against transnational corporate penetration of the Indian economy" (2000: 36). A global civil society that operates between "states and markets" continues to grow. This global society identifies, publicizes, and tries to solve environmental problems (Lechner and Boli 2000: 372).

Much discourse about the environment by nature-loving people in the USA masks the way in which the nonhuman world is commodified and consumed. Although pro-environment attitudes have increased over the past few decades, critics argue that little of this support for an abstract environmentalism has translated into effective action in changing how people consume and how the economy is organized. The vitality of Western capitalism has been based on the massive externalization of ecological costs of production. This context, in which ecological costs are exported, allows those in affluent countries to mask the commodification of nature even as affective connections to nature are celebrated.

Jennifer Price, in "Looking for Nature at the Mall: A Field Guide to the Nature Company," writes:

> if the Nature Company sells over 12,000 products, it is hawking a small handful of large ideas. What does nature mean? The meanings that Americans have traditionally invested in "nature" are keystones of modern middle class culture. The Nature Company is a market bazaar for the meanings of nature. Here you can buy pocket Waldens and John Muir field hats to enjoy nature as wilderness. Here nature is also a destination for "adventure." What meanings of nature does it market and whose nature is on sale here?
>
> (Price 1996: 190)

Nature in the 1980s and 1990s United States became a therapeutic resource. Price claims that such marketing is about responding to quasi-religious middle class meanings of nature. The products sustain "middle class ideas of nature that soften the harsh materialism and artificiality of modern capitalist society while they also sustain, through the creation of artifice, the capitalist over consumption of resources" (Price 1996: 201).

Globalization and religion

The *Globalization Reader*, a compilation of essays by top theorists, makes no mention of religion. Yet, religion and globalization are profoundly intertwined. Can we speak about religion without noting that it may have laid ideological foundations for globalization? Can we ignore the globalizing role of the Catholic Church as it spread across the world? Does globalization itself further the spread of religion as it challenges the idea of the nation-state? Or, can religion provide powerful resources and means of resistance for those suffering from the destructive elements of globalization (Hopkins *et al.* 2001)? Given the preceding questions, it is shocking that "within scholarly debate in human sciences, world systems, transnationalism, and globalization, the role of religion remains understudied and under theorized" (Csordas 2009: 1). Religion is a critical component in the cultural-ideological-practical dimension of any global social system, and religious phenomena form a "significant part of the consciousness of the postmodern world system" (Csordas 2009: 19).

The ways scholars position the terms religion/globalization indicate our theoretical turn. When we write *religion and globalization*, economic globalization tends to be seen as the primary analytic domain; readers understand that we are exploring religion in the context of a globalized economy. According to Csordas, in this construction, the dominant ideological engine is neoliberal economic theory. Religion becomes a reaction to neoliberal ideology and global economics, as opposed to being a strong social and cultural force in its own right (2009: 2). Other scholars take this a step further by using metaphors of the market to describe religion. They write of a spiritual marketplace in which religious actors compete for clients and commodities in a crowded religious bazaar (e.g. Finke and Stark 1988).

On the other hand, writing about the *globalization of religion* or *globalized religion* offers analytic advantages by signaling an expansion beyond contemporary economics. This approach recognizes that globalized religions are not new. The Iberian Catholic church may be considered an early example of "hyperglobalization." In Latin America, transnational religious groups such as the Society of Jesus (Jesuits), Franciscans, and Dominicans "permanently altered the cultural landscape of Latin America," paving the way, many would claim, for economic and political conquest (Lorentzen 2001: 93–94).

Theorist Thomas Csordas (2009) notes four ways that the *globalization of religion* is taking place:

1 *Local religious imaginations take up encroachment of the global economy.* Countless examples exist of local religions incorporating global symbols, from the use of Coca-Cola in traditional indigenous rites in Chiapas, to Colgate's sponsorship of *kolam* (ritual drawings made of rice) in India, to the mass conversion to Christianity of the Urapmin in remote West Sepik Province, Papua New Guinea (Lorentzen 2001; Nagarajan 2001; Robbins 2009).

2 *The growth of pan-indigenous movements.* Indigenous peoples worldwide, although still poorly recognized within their respective nation-states, have banded across borders for activism, promotion of human rights, protection of sacred spaces, and cultural exchanges. Csorda writes: "Thus we are presented with the existence of a Hopi reggae society in which the residents of the ancient mesas embrace a kindred Rastafarian spirituality" (2009: 7).

3 *A reverse globalization in which religions spread from the margins to the core.* The Brazilian Santo Daime flourishes in the Netherlands, Yoruba-based religions are no longer limited to a "Black-Atlantic" cultural zone, and yoga is practiced in all parts of the globe (Csordas 2009: 8).

To further complicate our analysis, what if we consider *Globalization itself as a religion*, as some theorists do? Note that this relates "religion" and "globalization" in a new way, identifying *globalization as religion*. Theologian Dwight Hopkins makes the claim that the "globalization of monopoly financed capitalist culture is itself a religion" (Hopkins 2001: 8). Its god is the concentration of wealth, it is transcendent in that it has no ultimate allegiances to nations or institutions, and its theological anthropology sees human value as defined by consumption. It is a "global church with neoliberal economics as a kind of canon law" (Csordas 2009: 9).

Other chapters in this volume claim that free market economics and environmentalism have religious elements or can be understood as religion. Similarly, it might be helpful to think of globalization as a religion. Hopkins writes:

> Religion is a system of beliefs and practices comprising a *god* (which is the object of one's faith), a *faith* (which is a belief in a desired power greater than oneself), a *religious leadership* (which determines the path of belief), *religious institutions* (which facilitate the ongoing organization of the religion), *theological anthropology* (which defines what it means to be human), *values* (which set the standards to which the religion subscribes), a *theology* (which is the theoretical justification of the faith),

and *revelation* (which is the diverse ways that the god manifests itself in and to the world).

(Hopkins 2001, 9, italics added)

What would happen if we analyzed globalization as a religion and asked ourselves: What are the gods, faith, leadership, institutions, anthropology, theology, and revelation of globalization? We might conclude that private property holds absolute status, that the International Monetary Fund and the World Bank are "religious-like" institutions, and that the ideal human accumulates capital and possesses commodities (Hopkins 2001: 13). If we think of globalization as a religion we can bring insights of other religious traditions to bear on it. We might find that few religions allow "for the basic values of capitalism like greed, egoistic individualistic competition, consumption and a limitless accumulation of wealth at the cost of people and the Earth" (Duchrow 2005: 700). Religious traditions may provide the resources to counter the ideological claims made by globalization advocates.

13C

Why might it be helpful for scholars to think of globalization as a religion? How does this relate to claims, discussed in other chapters, that free market economics or environmentalism have religious elements or can be understood as religions?

Religion and globalization, globalization of religion, globalized religion, the religion of globalization: Who would think that word order and preposition placement could make such a difference in critical thinking about the globalization/religion nexus?

To further complicate matters, religion may *further* processes of globalization. The Charismatic Catholic movement and Pentecostal Christianity have grown worldwide over the past two decades. Although Pentecostal Christianity creates hybrid forms of religious practice in a grand array of cultural contexts, according to some scholars the aspiration is for a universal culture and a "master narrative of salvation history" (Csordas 2009: 90). Religious groups may also promote practices and ideologies that actively *resist* economic globalization. Liberation theology, for example, actively opposes economic globalization and the neoliberal model. The vibrant, nonviolent, antiglobalization movement in India, noted earlier, grounds itself in *satyagraha* (soul force), the religious philosophy and strategy of Mahatma Gandhi. Religion may also actively *engage* the reality of globalization. The Council for the Parliament of the World's Religions, the Pluralism Project at Harvard University, and other interfaith and inter-religious projects, for instance, attempt to actively engage diverse forms of religious expression on a global scale (Hopkins *et al.* 2001: 7).

Obviously a simple, unitary approach to the complicated field of religion and globalization is inappropriate. Perhaps, as Csordas suggests, it is most productive to "understand globalization as a multidimensional process with religion, pop culture, politics, and economics as intimately intertwined as they are in lives of actors responsible" (2009: 3).

I wrote earlier that religious traditions assist us in countering the ideological claims made by globalization. Religious groups provide alternative worldviews to that offered by neoliberal ideology. They can provide inspiration, hope, and spaces for environmental action. Mary Evelyn Tucker and John Grim write that, "[w]hile in the past none of the religions of the world have had to face an environmental crisis such as we are now confronting, they remain key instruments in shaping attitudes toward nature" (2000: xvii). Many environmental movements around the globe are rooted in religious traditions. In Brazil, the Roman Catholic Church's Landless Movement is arguably the most active player on behalf of peasants displaced by deforestation and land grabs. The Sarvodaya Movement of Sri Lanka, rooted in Mahayana Buddhism, has a political agenda that includes "protection of the environment, biodiversity, the use of appropriate technology" (Gottlieb 2006: 489). The environmental justice movement in the United States came out of work by the United Church of Christ. Increasingly religious groups acknowledge their moral responsibility to resist environmentally destructive practices of globalization.

13D

What influence can religious groups have on global environmental and economic issues? What influence should they have?

The globalization/religion/environment nexus in Latin America

Species extinctions currently occur at least 100 times more often than the rates identified in fossil records, great areas of the planet are deforested, powerful governments and companies push for increased resource extraction from lands of the poor, safe drinking water becomes difficult to find. Many see the preceding problems as brought on by the ideology and rapacious appetite of globalization. The British newspaper the *Guardian*, for instance, claims that "The US cult of greed is now a global environmental threat" (January 20, 2010). Increasingly these profound environmental damages are seen as religious issues, whether caused by a "cult of greed" or by the theological anthropocentrism of the Judaeo-Christian tradition as famously described by Lynn White, Jr. (1967).

Religious leaders such as Pope Benedict XVI decry the exploitation of the planet's resources and the disproportionate impact of environmental harms on the poor. He claims that the Catholic moral theological doctrine of "respect for life" demands protection of the natural world as well as human beings (Benedict XVI 2009). Fourth-World theorists employ theoretical concepts derived from indigenous belief systems to explain patterns of violence perpetrated on the land and native peoples, claiming that aboriginal nations fit neither old models of the nation-state, nor new norms and structures of globalization (Roberts and Thanos 2003: 172). Engaged Buddhism interprets teachings and practices in light of environmental degradation, in part by challenging the consumerist culture that is spreading around the world. In each case, a religious response to environmental degradation is implicitly also a response to globalization.

This intersection of religion, globalization, and environment is apparent in Latin America, the most urban of all regions in the developing world. Garbage, contaminated water, lack of access to food, and polluted air are daily realities for Latin America's urban poor. Eighty percent of the illnesses in Latin America and one-third of the deaths are due to contaminated water (Roberts and Thanos 2003: 99). Latin America provides a classic example of severe environmental damage caused by globalization processes, in both historical and contemporary/postmodern forms. Christianity initially provided an ideology justifying both colonial and later capitalist expansion. Now, a variety of religious traditions yield both theoretical and activist resources to provide alternative models to unchecked economic globalization.

Contact began with a clash of religio-cosmological worldviews. Indigenous religions were many and diverse, yet most shared worldviews in which nature remained central in myth, narratives, and rituals; the sacred literally permeated everyday life (Lorentzen with Leavitt-Alcántara 2006). The Roman Catholic Church generally allied itself with governments and the wealthy, providing ideological support for economic expansion, extraction of resources, and trade. The growth of liberation theology since the late 1960s, however, has marked a major change in the Latin American church's response to the needs of the poor. Liberation theology claims that God sides with the most oppressed. Increasingly liberation theologians realized that the oppression of the poor and the destruction of nature were linked. Liberation theology spread and became a global movement promoting, in part, an ecological understanding as a paradigm for interpreting social realities. Ricardo Navarro, director of the Centro Salvadorenno de Tecnologíia Apropriada (CESTA), claims that polluting rivers through the excessive use of pesticides is a social sin, equal to denying food to people through unjust economic and social structures: Both cause death. The violation of nature is a religious offense.

Eco-theology in parts of the Latin American Catholic Church led to resistant praxis (engaged practice). The Pastoral Land Commission of the Catholic Church in Brazil, for instance, has long worked to protect fishing habitat, preserve the Amazon jungle, and gain land for peasants. The Environmental Movement of Olancho, a coalition of religious leaders and subsistence farmers in Honduras, opposes uncontrolled commercial logging. Their leader, Father José Andres Tamayo, regularly receives death threats and at least one of the group's activists has been killed in this eco-religious struggle.

Pan-indigenous activism also grows throughout Latin America. The Zapatista uprising in Chiapas, Mexico, for example, united "traditional" indigenous peoples, Roman Catholics, and evangelical Maya, in order to protest the imperatives of the global economy as expressed in the North American Free Trade Agreement (Lorentzen 2001). Maya in Guatemala protest oil drilling in Lake Petén; the Kogi of Colombia struggle to protect their sacred mountain. Declarations from the World Conference of Indigenous Peoples consistently promote a pan-Indian religious perspective tied to the defense of natural resources.

Latin America provides us with a classic case. Conflicting religious worldviews collided in the sixteenth century "New World." Actors throughout the continent promote an ecological global consciousness and models for environmental religious activism. As demonstrated by the case study below, the story still unfolds.

Case study: what's yours is mined[2]

Alicia listened to sounds of splashing water from her rock perch. Her two-year-old son jumped from boulder to boulder as the family's clothes dried in the sun. Eight months pregnant, Alicia enjoyed the rhythm of life in her tiny village tucked high in the mountains of northern El Salvador. Walking home, she carried her laundry as her son skipped ahead of her. Without warning, shots rang out, instantly killing Alicia and the child she carried inside her, and also wounding her son.

What could Alicia's murder have to do with theoretical discussions about globalization, religion and globalization, globalization and nature, and the globalization/environment/religion nexus? Kidnappings, torture, death threats, international treaties and tribunals, foreign companies, local environmental activists, the United States, the Salvadoran Roman Catholic Church, and even Pope Benedict XVI play a role in this true story. How did a remote area of El Salvador become embroiled in a global struggle pitting local farmers against corporations and international legal bodies? As this case unfolds we will view the drama of globalization, nature, and religion played out in sparsely populated northern El Salvador.

The context

> In many countries or regions in the south, the environmental destruction
> has reached such levels that what were once considered gifts from God,
> like air, water or food, are now the main sources of death. In El Salvador
> for example, the leading causes of death are infectious respiratory dis-
> eases, coming from air pollution, and gastrointestinal diseases coming
> from water and food pollution. In other words, the most dangerous
> things that a human being can do in El Salvador are to breathe air,
> drink water, or eat food.
>
> (Navarro 2005: 1467)

El Salvador, the Western hemisphere's smallest and most densely populated
country, faces what some term *ecocidio* or ecocide. El Salvador's extreme
environmental vulnerability has many causes. Long years of military dicta-
torships were followed by a brutal 12-year civil war in which chemical war-
fare encouraged by United States military advisors made large tracts of land
uninhabitable. A monoculture agricultural model, reckless industrialization,
and overpopulation have also played their part. Eighty percent of El Salvador's
natural vegetation has been eliminated, less than 3 percent of the original
forest remains, and 77 percent of the soil is severely affected by erosion and
low fertility—due, in part, to pesticides and other chemicals. Forty-six percent of the population lack potable water, 75 percent go without sanitary
services, one-fifth of the population has insufficient food, and 80 percent of those
under five years of age are malnourished. Salvadorans live with daily doses
of air pollution, contaminated water, respiratory diseases, floods, mudslides,
water shortages, cholera, dengue fever, and inadequate nutrition.

Cabañas is a hilly region in north central El Salvador. The department
(state) is the second poorest in El Salvador; over 55 percent live under the
poverty line. Local farmers eke out a living raising sugar cane and beans.
According to the United Nations Development Programme, Cabañas boasts
the worst score on the Human Development Index, a composite measure
that takes into account life expectancy, per capita income, education, and
other indicators. Little Cabañas is also the site of the December 26, 2009
murder of Dora "Alicia" Sorto Rocinos and of a powerful environmental
movement.

The company and the community

Pacific Rim, a mining company based in Vancouver, Canada, began exploring for gold and silver in northern El Salvador in 2002. The Ministries of the
Economy and Environment, under President Francisco Flores, invited the
company to El Salvador and issued exploration permits for a volcanic chain
with gold and silver in the north of the country. Mining had been rare in El

Salvador, but that changed when gold prices tripled after 2001. Pacific Rim assured its shareholders that they had discovered a rich vein of bonanza gold.

Pacific Rim claims that the company and its subsidiaries are "environmentally and socially responsible gold mining and development companies" (2010). The local community, on the other hand, claims that when exploration at the El Dorado site began, local water sources dried up. Pacific Rim offered an Environmental Impact Assessment for public review, yet only one printed copy could be found in all of El Salvador. Robert Moran, an independent, nonpartisan hydrogeologist, reviewed the case in 2005 (Moran 2005) and concluded that Pacific Rim's assessment lacked important data and testing processes.

Environmental experts, including Moran, confirmed local farmers' fears. The cyanide used to extract gold and silver could contaminate water and soil. The amount of water the extraction process would use in a day— 900,000 liters—is the same amount a local family would use in twenty years. Two percent of the profit made would stay in El Salvador, and very little of that in Cabañas. The El Dorado mine, as well as the 25 additional sites explored by Pacific Rim, posed grave environmental and health risks.

The movement

The first resistance came from residents of Trinidad, Cabañas, when their wells dried up following test drilling by Pacific Rim. Locals quickly formed the Environmental Committee of Cabañas to educate the community about the health and environmental risks of cyanide contamination from mining. Local concerns sparked a nationwide movement, La Mesa Nacional Frente a la Minería (the National Forum Against Mining), composed of environmental activists, religious leaders, human rights workers, and local peasants. La Mesa claims that mine exploitation deposits high levels of cyanide in water sources and that water shortage and contamination affects the production of corn, beans, and rice. The anti-mining movement gained popularity; a poll by the University of Central America (2007) showed that 62 percent of Salvadorans oppose gold mining.

The Salvadoran government refused to grant extraction permits to Pacific Rim and the company ceased operations at the El Dorado mine in 2008. President Antonio Saca opposed the mine and the current President, Mauricio Funes, continues the government's opposition. Presidents and legislators from the ARENA party (the right) and the FMLN (the left) remain united in their opposition to extraction by Pacific Rim.

This opposition does not come without a price. Three anti-mining activists have been murdered since opposition to Pacific Rim began. Gustavo Marcelo Rivera Morena, a vocal opponent of Pacific Rim Mining Company, disappeared on June 18, 2009; his tortured body was discovered in a well on June 30. In July, the priest Luis Alberto Quintanilla survived a kidnapping and assassination attempt. In August, Ramiro Rivera Gomez, the vice-president of the Environmental Committee on Cabañas, was shot eight times in the legs and back. He survived and was put under 24-hour police protection, but was nevertheless killed by gunmen on December 20, 2009. A 14-year-old girl with him was also wounded. A week later, Dora "Alicia" Sorto Recinos, who had been an outspoken critic of the El Dorado gold mine and a member of the Environmental Committee of Cabañas, was also shot and killed.

The escalating violence, assaults, and death threats center on Pacific Rim: those murdered have all been prominent anti-mining activists. While local authorities chalk the murders up to common crime, the country's human rights ombudsman is pursuing the case, President Funes has called for an investigation, and the Inter-American Commission on Human Rights is demanding that the Salvadoran government provide protection for environmental activists in the region. Nevertheless, as of June 2010, no one has been convicted of any of the murders.

The church

Local religious leaders quickly became involved in the anti-mining struggle. The Episcopal Conference of Roman Catholic Bishops of El Salvador (CEDES) chastized Pacific Rim for valuing gold over human life. The bishops published a statement in May 2007 clearly outlining the official Salvadoran Church position. An excerpt follows:

> Our small country is the place where God the Creator called us to life. We also wish to pronounce ourselves against (mining) before it is too late. The reasons of our concern are the following ones: 1. It has been demonstrated that this type of operation causes irreversible damage to the environment and to the surrounding communities. 2. People suffer grave health problems due to the large amounts of cyanide used in the extraction of gold and silver. 3. Water is used in the extraction process of these minerals. (This water) would be inevitably contaminated, beginning an irreversible process of polluting subsoil water and the rivers that little by little would spread to a great part of the national territory. 4. The pollution would also have grave consequences for the flora and the fauna, extending also to agriculture, cattle and fish. 5. In a country so small and populated as ours, the negative effect would be multiplied. No material advantage can be compared with the value of the human life.
>
> (CEDES 2007)

Archbishop Fernando Sáenz LaCalle affirmed the church's rejection of mining, appearing in February 2008 before the Salvadoran Assembly. The Bishops requested that the United States Conference of Catholic Bishops present their opposition to mining to the United States Millennium Challenge

Account, which funds a development project near the mine. Archbishop LaCalle, during a visit to the Vatican, reported to Pope Benedict XVI that mining was one of the gravest problems facing El Salvador. He stated, "It is not right to risk the health of the population and damage the environment so that a few who do not live here can take 97% of the juicy profits, but they leave us with 100% of the cyanide" (LaCalle, quoted in DiarioCoLatino.com 2007). Pope Benedict himself criticized mineral exploitation at the World Youth Day in Sydney, Australia, saying, "There are also scars which mark the surface of our earth, erosion, deforestation, the squandering of the world's minerals and ocean resources in order to fuel an insatiable consumption" (Benedict XVI 2008).

International law and agreements

In 2007 the Pacific Rim Mining Company, in accordance with El Salvador's mining law, filed an Environmental Impact Study with the Salvadoran Ministry of Natural Resources and Environment to obtain a mining extraction concession for its El Dorado project in Cabañas. The Salvadoran government denied the application and Pacific Rim ceased its operations at El Dorado in 2008. Pacific Rim then began arbitration proceedings against El Salvador with the World Bank's International Center for Settlement of Investment Disputes on April 30, 2009.

The company claims that El Salvador violated the investments rules of the U.S.–Dominican Republic Central American Free Trade Agreement (DR-CAFTA), which El Salvador signed in 2006. The agreement allows multi-national companies the right to sue for cash compensation when their profits have been undermined by measures that are considered expropriation. Canada is not a signatory to DR-CAFTA, so technically Pacific Rim is not allowed to sue the Salvadoran government. However, the company routed the lawsuit through Pac Rim Cayman, a subsidiary based in Reno, Nevada, and hired a U.S. firm to lobby the U.S. government. According to a press release, the company will be suing El Salvador for "hundreds of millions of dollars" for "multiple breaches of international and Salvadoran law" (Pacific Rim 2009). According to CEO Tom Shrake, "While we regret having to take this action, we fully intend to pursue the Company's rights vigorously. Sadly, it is not just the rights of Pac Rim that are being compromised, but the rights of all Salvadorans and future foreign investors" (Pacific Rim 2009). Pacific Rim claims that El Salvador violated the spirit of nondiscrimination because the nation allows domestic companies to pollute while denying that privilege to Pacific Rim. They are suing for "profit infringement." Arbitration at the World Bank between El Salvador and the Pacific Rim Mining Company began on May 31, 2010. The hearing is taking place at the International Center for Settlement of Investment Disputes in Washington, DC. A settlement is expected by September 2010.

El Salvador, a poor country, may lose millions of dollars badly needed for public services and government programs. The government claims that it is merely doing what governments should do—protecting its people from harm. The case may set a precedent. As Michael Busch writes, "At stake is a question that affects all nations: Can private interests (foreign interests) trump national sovereignty under international law?" (2009: 1).

Conclusion?

Pacific Rim files a costly suit against El Salvador in the World Bank. El Salvador signed an international trade agreement that allows such a suit. Pacific Rim, a Canadian company, files through a U.S. subsidiary. A poor country musters financial resources to defend itself on a global stage. Local peasants fight a large foreign company. The Roman Catholic Church, at local, national, and international levels, becomes involved in a local mining case. A mining company and a poor country face off in the World Bank. Local communities, the Roman Catholic Church, and the Salvadoran government are united in their opposition to the opening of the El Dorado mine. Three environmental activists are murdered.

The local, the state, the global, the environment, religion, and foreign corporations remain intertwined in tiny Cabañas, El Salvador. The outcome is yet to be decided.

Discussion questions

1 The case is about a remote area in El Salvador. In what ways is it a local case? In what ways is it global?
2 How do the various definitions of globalization come into play here? Which of the claims about globalization made in this chapter do you see as relevant? Which seem to be challenged?
3 Does this case study suggest that globalization is good, bad, or both? Are there alternative cases you can think of that would give a different impression of globalization?
4 How might liberation theology be relevant to this case study? How could a liberation theologian respond to it?

Notes

1 In fairness, it should be noted that the trend now is away from mega-projects. The World Bank for example, did not provide funding for China's infamous Three Gorges Dam.
2 I am very grateful to Salvador Leavitt-Alcantara for familiarizing me with this case. He provided me with information, websites, and data about this local environmental struggle and its global dimensions.

References

Barber, B. (1995) *Jihad vs. Mcworld*, New York: Random House.

Benedict XVI (2008) "Address to Young People," available at http://www.vatican.va/holy_father/benedict_xvi/speeches/2008/july/documents/hf (accessed February 2, 2010).

——(2009) *Caritas in Veritate*, available at http://www.vatican.va/holy_father/benedict_xvi/encyclicals/documents/hf_ben-xvi_enc_20090629_caritas-in-veritate_en.html (accessed February 9, 2010).

Busch, Michael (2009) "El Salvador's Gold Fight," *Foreign Policy in Focus*, available at http://www.fpif.org/articles/el_salvadors_gold_fight (accessed February 4, 2010).

CEDES (Episcopal Conference of Roman Catholic Bishops of El Salvador) (2007) "Let's Take Care of Everyone's Home," available at http://www.crispaz.org/news/list/2008/0612.html (accessed February 3, 2010).

Coleman, J. (2005) "Making the Connections: Globalization and Catholic Social Thought," in J. Coleman and W.F. Ryan, (eds) *Globalization and Catholic Social Thought*, Maryknoll, NY: Orbis Books.

Csordas, T. (ed.) (2009) *Transnational Transcendence: Essays on Religion and Globalization*, Berkeley: University of California Press.

Duchrow, U. (2005) "Globalization," in B. Taylor (ed.) *The Encyclopedia of Religion and Nature*, London: Thoemmes Continuum.

Eaton, H. and L. Lorentzen (eds) (2003) *Ecofeminism and Globalization: Exploring Culture, Context, and Religion*, Lanham, MD: Rowman & Littlefield.

Finke, R. and R. Stark (1988) "Religious Economies and Sacred Canopies: Religious Mobilization in American Cities, 1906," *American Sociological Review* 53: 41–49.

Gottlieb, R. (2006) "Religious Environmentalism in Action," in R. Gottlieb (ed.) *The Oxford Handbook of Religion and Ecology*, Oxford: Oxford University Press.

Helvarg, D. (2003) "When the People Lead," in J. Roberts and N. Thanos (eds) *Trouble in Paradise: Globalization and Environmental Crises in Latin America*, New York: Routledge.

Hopkins, D. (2001) "The Religion of Globalization," in D. Hopkins, E. Mendieta, L. Lorentzen, and D. Batstone (eds) *Religions/Globalizations: Theories and Cases*, Durham, NC: Duke University Press.

Hopkins, D., E. Mendieta, L. Lorentzen, and D. Batstone (eds) (2001) *Religions/Globalizations: Theories and Cases*, Durham, NC: Duke University Press.

Karliner, J. (2000) "Grassroots Globalization: Reclaiming the Blue Planet," in F. Lechner and J. Boli (eds) *The Globalization Reader*, Oxford: Blackwell Publishers.

Korten, D. (1995) *When Corporations Rule the World*, West Hartford/San Francisco: Kumarian Press/Berrett-Koehler Publishers.

DiarioCoLatino.com (2007) "La jeraquía católica ratifica su rechazo en El Vaticáno," available at http://www.diariocolatino.com/es/20080312/opiniones/53010 (accessed February 6, 2010).

Lechner, F. and J. Boli (eds) (2000) *The Globalization Reader*, Oxford: Blackwell Publishers.

Lorentzen, L. (2001) "Who Is an Indian: Religion, Globalization, and Chiapas," in D. Hopkins, E. Mendieta, L. Lorentzen, and D. Batstone (eds) *Religions/Globalizations: Theories and Cases*, Durham, NC: Duke University Press.

Lorentzen, L. with S. Leavitt-Alcántara (2006) "Religion and Environmental Struggles in Latin America," in Roger Gottlieb (ed.) *The Handbook of Religion and Ecology*, Oxford: Oxford University Press.

Mignolo, W. (1998) "Globalization, Civilizing Processes, and the Relocation of Languages and Cultures," in F. Jameson and M. Miyoshi (eds) *The Cultures of Globalization*, Durham, NC: Duke University Press.

Moran, Robert (2005) "Technical Review of the El Dorado Mine Project Environmental Impact Assessment (EIA), El Salvador," available at http://www.miningwatch. ca/en/technical-review-el-dorado-mine-project-environmental-impact-assessment-eia-el-salvador (accessed February 3, 2010).

Morellos, H. (2007) "E-(re)volution: The Zapatistas and the Emancipatory Internet," *A contra corriente: A Journal on Social History and Literature in Latin America* 4 (2) (Winter): 54–76.

Nagarajan, V. (2001) "(In)Corporating Threshold Arts: *Kolam* Competition, Patronage and Colgate," in D. Hopkins, E. Mendieta, L. Lorentzen, and D. Batstone (eds) *Religions/Globalization: Theories and Cases*, Durham, NC: Duke University Press.

Navarro, R. (2005) "Salvadoran Reflection on Religion, Rights, and Nature," in Bron Raymond Taylor (ed.) *The Encyclopdia of Religion and Nature*, London and New York: Continuum International.

Ó'Riain, S. (2000) "States and Markets in an era of Globalisation," *Annual Review of Sociology* 26 (August): 187–213.

Pacific Rim (2009) "Pacific Rim Subsidiary Commences CAFTA Arbitration Proceedings Against Government of El Salvador," April 30, 2009 Press Release, available at http://www.pacrim-mining.com/s/News.asp?ReportID=364986 (accessed June 24, 2010).

——(2010) "Statement Regarding Recent Events in El Salvador," available at http://www.pacrim-mining.com/s/ES_Eldorado.asp (accessed June 24, 2010).

Price, J. (1996) "Looking for Nature at the Mall: A Field Guide to the Nature Company", in W. Cronon (ed.) *Uncommon Ground: Rethinking the Human Place in Nature*, New York: W.W. Norton & Company.

Ritzer, G. (2004) *The McDonaldization of Society*, Revised New Century edition, Thousand Oaks, CA: Pine Forge Press.

Robbins, J. (2009) "Is the *Trans*-in *Transnational* the *Trans*-in *Transcendent?* On Alterity and the Sacred in the Age of Globalization," in T. Csordas (ed.) *Transnational Transcendence: Essays on Religion and Globalization*, Berkeley: University of California Press.

Roberts, J. and N. Thanos (2003) *Trouble in Paradise: Globalizatin and Environmental Crises in Latin America*, New York: Routledge.

Robertson, R. (1994) "Globalisation or 'Glocalisation'," *Journal of International Communication* 1(1): 33–52.

Tucker, M.E. (2005) "Globalization and the Environment," in J. Coleman and W.F. Ryan (eds) *Globalization and Catholic Social Thought*, Maryknoll, NY: Orbis Books.

Tucker, M.E. and J. Grim (2000) "Series Foreword," in D.T. Hessel and R.R. Ruether (eds) *Christianity and Ecology: Seeking the Well-Being of Earth and Humans*, Cambridge, MA: Harvard University Press.

University of Central America (2007) "Encuesta sobre conocimientos y percepciones hacia la mineria en zonas afectadas por la incursion minera en El Salvador," available at http://www.uca.edu.sv/publica/iudop/Web/2008/finalmineria040208.pdf (accessed February 4, 2010).

Vásquez, M. and M.F. Marquardt (2003) *Globalizing the sacred: Religion across the Americas*, New Brunswick, NJ: Rutgers University Press.

Veseth, M. (1998) *Selling Globalization: The Myth of the Global Economy*, Boulder, CO: Lynne Rienner Publishers.

White, L. Jr. (1967) "The Historical Roots of Our Ecologic Crisis," *Science* 155(3767) (March 10): 1203–07.

Further reading

Franklin, S., C. Lury. and Stacey, J. (eds) (2000) *Global Nature, Global Culture*, London: Sage.

Hopkins, D., E. Menieta, L. Lorentzen, and D. Batstone (eds) (2001) *Religions/Globalizations: Theories and Cases*, Durham, NC: Duke Press.

Petrotta, M. (2009) "Congressional Brief: Mineral Mining in El Salvador," available at http://elsalvadorsolidarity.org/joomla/index.php?option=com_content&task=view&id=226&Itemid=65 (accessed February 9, 2010).

Vásquez, M. and M. Marquardt (2003) *Globalizing the Sacred; Religion across the Americas*, New Brunswick, NJ: Rutgers University Press.

Chapter 14

Place

Brian G. Campbell

Place matters

In recent years, there has been an increasing emphasis on place among those concerned about environmental issues. One of the most visible examples is the local food movement, which touts the value of eating with a sense of place, buying foods grown close to home, preserving heirloom plants adapted to local conditions, and celebrating local culinary traditions. Meanwhile, scholars from a variety of disciplines (geography, architecture, planning, anthropology, philosophy, religious studies, etc.) have taken a renewed interest in place as a fundamental aspect of life and a key intellectual concept. This chapter introduces a variety of critical perspectives and theories for thinking about place in the study of religion and ecology, with particular emphasis on phenomenology, bioregionalism, and cultural geography.

Like some of the other key terms in this book, place is an important concept in part because it is so common. When we meet someone new, one of the first things we share is where we are from. Our place helps define who we are and helps shape our experience of the world. Environmental issues are also always situated in particular places. So are religions. Perhaps because place is such a pervasive category, we often take it for granted, without thinking about what it means and why it matters. Place obviously refers to spatial relationships, describing a physical, geographical location: "Let's meet at my place," or, "I want to buy a hotel on Park Place." We also use place to refer to social relationships, especially one's position or rank in a social hierarchy: "That ought to keep her in her place," or "I finished in first place." Thinking critically about place demands sorting out the ways social and spatial relationships are often intertwined.

Both these senses of place are key to the study of religion and ecology. We have particular places that matter to us personally, sites that hold particular memories and meanings, and shape our ethical commitments. This is true collectively as well. American environmentalism, for example, traces its history through particular sites such as Walden Pond and Yosemite Park, Warren County, North Carolina and Love Canal, New York, or more recently the Alaska National Wildlife Refuge (ANWR) and New Orleans' Lower Ninth Ward. Religious traditions ground their concern for the natural world in particular places, whether these exist in sacred texts and myths (Eden, New Jerusalem) or as sacred sites (the Ganges). Religions also teach us how we should understand our place in the social sense, as humans in relation to one another and to the broader more-than-human natural and supernatural world.

The critical perspectives that follow stress the social and spatial aspects of place in different ways. As you consider these differences, think about how each approach defines this common and complex category. What does place mean for each and why does place matter? What aspects of religion does each approach emphasize? Rather than thinking about these approaches in the abstract, try to keep in mind particular places you care about. What are the strengths and weaknesses of each approach for thinking about those places, about particular religious beliefs and practices, and about particular environmental issues you can examine in place?

Phenomenology: perceiving and experiencing place

Phenomenology is a philosophical tradition that systematically examines the human experience and perception of the world. Rooted in the thought of Edmund Husserl, Martin Heidegger, and Maurice Merleau-Ponty, this approach seeks to describe the pre-theoretical, embodied experience of a place. Here, the human person is not a subject separate from the objectively real world. Instead, the human being is always already a "being-in-the-world" (from Heidegger's term *Dasein*), in-the-world in the sense not just of being spatially situated in a physical world of objects, but of being indivisibly involved in the world, a world we actively encounter with and through our ideas and values, perceptual and sensory capacities.

Over the last three decades, philosophers and geographers have applied the methods and ideas of phenomenology to issues of place and the environment. Humanistic geographer Yi Fu Tuan has developed a key distinction between space and place (Tuan 1977). While *space* is undifferentiated, abstract and empty, *place* is particular, familiar, endowed with meaning and significance. In much of western history, space has been treated as philosophically superior—an objective, universal container for all reality. Phenomenologists argue that place is always primary and deserves greater attention. In David Casey's words, "[t]o live is to live locally, and to know is first of all to know the place one is in" (Casey 1996: 18). Tuan develops a concept he calls "topophilia" to describe this "affective bond between people and place." This critical form of attachment shapes one's identity and one's capacity to care for the broader world (Tuan 1974).

Phenomenology aims to understand the essence of what makes a place a place, the particular qualities that give it a distinctive identity and facilitate such topophilia. We recognize places by their distinctive physical features: a well-worn, fading old sofa; a smooth, sloping granite dome. The essence of a place is not only a matter of features we passively perceive. We actively encounter place, with intentionality and with particular behaviors and practices: the sofa as the place where dad naps; the mountain as the place we climb to watch the Easter sunrise. Self-consciously or not, people make places significant.

Phenomenologist Edward Relph stresses that we also create "placeless" places, which lack the rich, authentic identity that gives rise to topophilia (Relph 1976). He argues that placelessness is a key ailment in the modern industrialized world. The landscape is sprawling with places built to look alike—strip malls, chain stores, and suburban developments. We build structures like airports, skyscrapers, and highways whose scale overwhelms us. We also invest in "other-directed" places, which appeal to outside tourists, spectators, and consumers rather than local people. Relph laments the "Disneyfication" and "museumification" of places, which idealizes them in ways that make them feel shallow and superficial. Relph's critique of the placelessness of mass, consumer culture is an invitation and a challenge to local communities, including religious communities. How can they preserve and produce more authentic places, drawing on their deeper traditions of place-making?

14A

Edward Relph and other phenomenologists of place are critical of mass-produced aesthetics, including pedestrian-friendly new urbanist developments and energy-efficient prefabricated buildings. What are the positive and negative consequences of mass-produced buildings and places like these? Can they promote an authentic sense of place and a sustainable lifestyle?

While Relph's work focuses primarily on architecture and the built environment, another group of thinkers have developed an explicitly ecological phenomenology focused on nature and place more broadly. These thinkers argue that the human experience of the more-than-human environment, the encounter with place, is the strongest foundation for environmental ethics and politics. This "eco-phenomenology" asserts that perception is *inter*-subjective and *inter*-corporeal. Philosopher David Abram writes:

> To touch the coarse skin of a tree is thus, at the same time, to experience one's own tactility, to feel oneself touched *by* a tree. And to see the world is also, at the same time, to experience oneself as visible, to feel

oneself *seen* ... We can perceive things at all only because we ourselves are entirely a part of the sensible world that we perceive! We might as well say that we are organs of this world, flesh of its flesh, and that the world is perceiving itself *through* us.

(Abram 1996: 68)

Abram situates the perceiving body within an ecological web and claims this interconnected perception defines the essence of our being-in-the-world: "we are only human in contact, and conviviality, with what is not human" (Abram 1996: ix). Abram highlights what is a key concept for many eco-phenomenologists: Merleau-Ponty's notion of "the flesh." Asserting that the human body is thoroughly intertwined with the "flesh of the world," eco-phenomenology rejects dualistic worldviews that imagine the human mind (soul, spirit, etc.) as something separate from the embodied, enfleshed places we inhabit.[1]

This perceptual interconnectedness provides a basis for an eco-phenomenological environmental ethic, a concern for nature emerging from the encounter with place. Properly attuned, we can see the natural world as Emmanuel Levinas invites us to see the human other: intimately, face to face, beautiful and vulnerable, a mirror of our own self.[2] Eco-phenomenology extends this ethic, inviting us to see the face of nature in each particular place. David Abram asserts:

the "new environmental ethic" toward which so many environmental philosophers aspire ... will not come through the logical elucidation of new philosophical principles and legislative structures, but through a renewed attentiveness to this perceptual dimension that underlies all our logics, through a rejuvenation of our carnal, sensorial empathy with the living land that sustains us.

(Abram 1996: 69)

Belden Lane's *Landscapes of the Sacred* is a phenomenological approach to the study of religion and the environment. Throughout the text, he uses his own personal experiences to highlight the "sensory exchanges" between people and place. Places are not passive material for cultural construction, but participate in a "dynamic reciprocity." He describes his experience in Utah's Canyonlands National Park:

Your first impression is one of being trapped at the end of the earth in a dry canyon carved by the distant memory of water. Slickrock winds its way along meanders traced by the forgotten music of swirling streams. The silence of the place is unnerving. That distracting echo you occasionally hear is but the sound of blood pumping through your own temples. But if you are patient, you become gradually attentive to the way aging juniper trees speak to the rock, how wind whispers along canyon walls and morning sunlight dances on yucca plants and Mormon tea. You flinch, startled as Raven, the Trickster, comes out of nowhere, soaring overhead with the audible, rhythmic beating of feathers on air. You begin slowly to move through the place as part of its own distinctive pattern.

(Lane 2002: 57)

Like the phenomenologists that inform his work, Lane stresses that the experience of place cannot be reduced to purely cultural or material factors. Every place, in the words of Edward Casey, "retains a factor of wildness, that is, of the radically amorphous and unaccounted for" (Casey 1996). In Lane's terms, we must leave room for the sacred, for the messy and inexplicable. He recognizes that we need multiple approaches to place, including bioregionalism and cultural geography, but he emphasizes that above all we need a phenomenological and poetic sensitivity, attentive to the voice of the place itself, speaking through our embodied experience.

Bioregionalism: re-inhabiting place

Like phenomenology, bioregionalism is concerned with the authenticity and integrity of places in a rapidly modernizing, urbanizing, globalizing world. Both perspectives highlight the potentially powerful bonds between people and place as a resource for environmentalism. We act ethically because we care about the place we call home. Phenomenology is a fundamentally intellectual tradition, concerned with how this connection to place shapes our experience of the world. Bioregionalism is a more grassroots movement that has developed intellectual, practical, and artistic responses to the environmental crisis, all emerging from the particulars of place.

Bioregionalism asserts that the most important response to the ecological crisis is to "reinhabit" place. To do this, we must rethink our sense of scale, sinking deep roots in the local environment we call home. Human communities must be transformed according to the ecological demands of their diverse local bioregions. Peter Berg, one of the key leaders of the movement, explains this term: "A bioregion is defined in terms of the unique overall pattern of natural characteristics that are found in a specific place. The main features are generally found throughout a continuous geographic terrain and include a particular climate, local aspects of seasons, landforms, watersheds, soils, and native plants and animals" (Berg 2002). The essence of place, from this perspective, lies in its particular pattern of ecological features.

This movement emerged among a small group of counterculture artists and activists in the San Francisco Bay Area in the late 1960s. Gary Snyder was one of the first to formulate the ideas of bioregionalism, and he has remained one of its most prominent voices. Snyder gained notoriety in the

1950s as a poet in the San Francisco Renaissance, distinctive for his explorations of wilderness, writing, Zen meditation, and Native American culture. Like many of his generation, this wanderer was eventually ready for deeper roots in place. After spending the bulk of the 1960s studying and practicing Zen in Japan, Snyder returned to California. He and his family settled down with a community of like-minded back-to-the-landers in the foothills of the Sierra Nevada Mountains. Since then, his poetry and essays have consistently addressed bioregional themes. In "The Place, the Region, and the Commons," Snyder writes, "Bioregional awareness teaches us in specific ways. It is not enough to just 'love nature' or to want to 'be in harmony with Gaia.' Our relation to the natural world takes place in a place, and it must be grounded in information and experience" (Snyder 1990: 39).

While we often define places by their political names and borders, bio-regionalism calls for places to be mapped according to their ecological identities and natural boundaries. Snyder calls his bioregional home the "Shasta Bioregion," part of "Turtle Island," his "old/new name for the con-tinent based on many creation myths of the people who have been living here for millennia" (Snyder 1974). In naming the continent in this way, Snyder recognizes the privileged place bioregionalists give to native cultures. Peter Berg writes, "people are also counted as an integral aspect of a place's life," and he calls for "present day reinhabitants" to learn from "ecologically adaptive cultures of early inhabitants" as they "attempt to harmonize in a sustainable way with the place where they live" (Berg 2002).

In a 1992 talk, Snyder stated, "I don't know if I'm an Indian or not. I do know that I'm a Native American. Here again is a Turtle Island bioregional point. Anyone is, metaphorically speaking a Native American who is 'born again of Turtle Island.' Anyone is a Native American who chooses, con-sciously and deliberately, to live on this continent" (Snyder 1999: 336). Leslie Marmon Silko and a number of Native American writers have criticized Snyder, and bioregionalism more broadly, for this appropriation of the term "native," calling it a "new version of cultural imperialism."[3]

Snyder and Berg developed bioregionalism in California, and the move-ment quickly spread through grassroots groups that sprang up around the country. Bioregionalism also spread through cultural historian Kirkpatrick Sale's *Dwellers in the Land*, which introduced its ideas to a wide audience and situated them in a centuries-old tradition of decentralized resistance to industrialization.[4] Sale asserts that wisdom emanates from the earth, calling us to be "dwellers in the land." This demands "once again comprehending the earth as a living creature" and "contriving the modern equivalent of the worship of Gaea [*sic*]." For him, this means not an occasional act of devo-tion, but a wholesale commitment to dwelling in the land. We must relearn the laws of nature and transform our lifestyle to fit the "immediate and specific place where we live" (Sale 1985: 41–42). Sale summarizes the bioregional alternative, one that touches every aspect of the social order, in Table 14.1.

Sale argues that the bioregional paradigm is superior because nature serves as the model for human civilization. We learn about our place through phenomenological experience, but also through disciplined scientific study, and together these reveal underlying natural laws as a guide for our social, economic, and political systems. Sale's argument rests on the assumptions that there are underlying natural laws and that healthy ecosystems tend toward equilibrium and unity, the sort of qualities that translate well into social policy. Many ecologists now challenge this assumption, instead asserting that natural systems are far more dynamic and chaotic (Lodge and Hamlin 2006; Worster 1993). The scientific facts on the ground do not so easily translate into values and norms to guide human society.

Thomas Berry was another key voice spreading bioregionalism, and his ideas have been especially influential for the study of religion and ecology, as discussed in Chapter 7 of this book. Berry's *The Dream of the Earth* at once focuses on the vast scale of the cosmic "universe story" and the particular context of the bioregion. Within this framework, Berry reimagines the whole of civilization, including religion, economics, and technology. He also proposes a total transformation of American college education to include not just education about the earth, but education from and through the earth itself. Higher education should be holistic, fostering ecological and spiritual wisdom, not through detached abstraction and analysis, but through direct experience with one's immediate environment (Berry 1988).

Berry's attention to both bioregional and cosmic scales points to an important challenge for thinking about place. How can we think and act locally, but also take seriously our place in broader global, even cosmic processes? Both phenomenology and bioregionalism prioritize the local,

Table 14.1 The bioregional alternative

	Bioregional paradigm	*Industrio-scientific paradigm*
Scale	Region	State
	Community	Nation/world
Economy	Conservation	Exploitation, change/progress
	Stability	World economy
	Self-sufficiency	Competition
	Cooperation	
Polity	Decentralization	Centralization
	Complementarity	Hierarchy
	Diversity	Uniformity
Society	Symbiosis	Polarization, growth/violence
	Evolution	Monoculture
	Division	

epistemologically and ethically. We know a place through direct, embodied experience. We care about a place because it is home. This commitment to the local is perhaps their greatest strength and greatest weakness, and one of the most important differences between phenomenology, bioregionalism, and cultural geography.[5]

14B

Look online for a copy of "Where You At? A Bioregional Quiz." How well do you know your bioregion? What additional bioregional wisdom would you add to tailor this quiz to your context?[6]

Cultural geography: power, difference, and global connections

Cultural geography focuses attention on global dynamics, and especially the ways global capitalism is transforming place. This approach examines not experience or ecology, but material practices and spatial structures that shape our relationship to one another and the environment. Cultural geography asserts that places cannot be taken for granted as "natural," with obvious boundaries and essential qualities, but, instead, that places are constituted and constructed through complex social, economic, and political processes. The goal in studying place is to understand and respond to these processes.

Influential cultural geographer David Harvey describes places as "permanences within the flux and flow of capital circulation" (Harvey 1996: 295). Harvey insists that it is precisely because of globalization's flux and flow that place has become such an important locus of popular and scholarly concern. We construct these "permanences" as sites of relative stability, meaningful and secure refuges in a rapidly changing world. Harvey describes the power of "militant particularism," especially among radical environmentalist and environmental justice groups, who resist the negative forces of globalization by appealing to their deep, distinctive, and often sacred bond with place.

Harvey warns, though, that such embrace of place is fundamentally conservative and reactionary. Efforts to protect and preserve place also serve to make permanent particular hierarchies of power and difference. He describes, for example, a neighborhood in the Baltimore suburbs that elected to become a gated community. Residents appealed to the sense of "place" as safe, familiar, and culturally coherent (and racially homogenous), over and against the specter of chaotic, uncontrollable, and racially mixed "space" (Harvey 1996: 291–93). Though environmental groups may have the best of intentions, their place-based politics often reinforce problematic structural inequalities of race and class.

Doreen Massey has a more optimistic view of what place can mean in a complex, pluralistic context. She calls for a "global" and "progressive" sense of place as an alternative to conservative notions of place, ranging from "reactionary nationalisms to competitive localisms, to sanitized, introverted obsessions with 'heritage.'" Massey develops this approach using her London neighborhood as an example. She argues that places are defined not by some essential, bounded identity, but by their distinctive combination of differences and their dynamic connections with the broader world. On her walk down a single street, Massey encounters people and products from all corners of the planet. Places in fact have quite permeable boundaries, with webs of social and material relations extending across vast expanses of time and space. She notes, "People's routes through the place, their favorite haunts within it, the connections they make (physically, or by plane or post, or in memory or imagination) between here and the rest of the world vary enormously." Places in fact have multiple identities that coexist, and diverse groups often contest these meanings. Massey also stresses the importance of seeing complex historical forces at play in the ways place is structured in the present. "It is (or ought to be) impossible even to begin thinking about Kilburn High Road without bringing into play half the world and a considerable amount of British imperialist history" (Massey 1993: 64–65). As powerful as this past is, it does not determine the future. Places actively construct and reconstruct their histories in response to contemporary challenges.

Globalization creates new configurations of time and space, with constantly changing networks and flows of highly mobile information, capital, and people. Culturally geography calls us to think globally, but it is not enough to simply recognize that we're all connected or that environmental issues affect the whole planet. Individuals and groups exercise very different kinds of power over these global issues and changing patterns. Massey experiences globalization quite differently from the Arab immigrant she encounters at the newsstand. The global economy recognizes and rewards a certain cosmopolitan class, while marginalizing others. Massey argues that we must be attentive to the power dynamics among these various groups, not only at the local level, but in the ways people engage global structures and processes. Each place has an embedded "power-geometry," which reflects and reinforces social differences like race, class, gender, and citizenship (Massey 1993: 61).

Harvey argues that too often environmental politics is grounded in romantic feelings toward nature and place rather than careful analysis of social, political, and economic structures, local and global. He acknowledges the "depth and intensity of feeling" people have in "intimate and immediate relations to nature," but he warns that precisely because phenomenological experience of the immediate environment feels so "authentic," it tempts us to ignore larger material processes and structures (Harvey 1996: 313–14). Just as Marx warns against the "fetishism of commodities," Harvey warns against the fetishism of the local and the fetishism of nature. Echoing the concerns of environmental justice activists, he critiques mainstream environmentalism for prioritizing the places in nature that feed our romantic appetite for pristine wilderness while ignoring the health of other ecosystems and places, especially urban environments.[7] Who has the power to shape which places get access to environmental benefits like parks, public transit, clean air and water? Which places get stuck with environmental burdens like waste facilities, dirty industries, and mega-highways? Cultural geography calls us to pay attention to the ways place is constructed, reflecting particular ideas of nature, but also making particular social ideologies and inequalities seem natural. Paying attention to nature, especially in a diverse urban context, requires more than simply paying attention to what is immediately observable. Rather than taking spatial and social relationships for granted, this approach challenges us to investigate how the landscape came to be structured the way it is today.

14C

Draw a map of the place you call home. How are differences like race, class, religion, and ethnicity reflected in the spatial structure of the place? What sorts of boundaries mark the areas where different groups live, work, or socialize? What do you know about the history of how these communities came to be located in this way? What do you know about where environmental burdens and benefits are located in this place? Do you see connections between these social and environmental patterns?

Adrian Ivakhiv's (2002) *Claiming Sacred Ground: Pilgrims and Politics at Glastonbury and Sedona* provides one model of religion and ecology scholarship that incorporates the perspectives of cultural geography along with phenomenology and bioregionalism. This ethnographic study examines the "spatial practices" or "practices of place" of New Age pilgrims: hiking, meditation, visualization, chanting, 'chakra activation,' invocation or channeling of guides or spirits, and the arrangement of stone or rocks in medicine wheels and the conducting of ceremonies within them. Grounding his research in two prominent pilgrimage sites, Ivakhiv stresses the multiplicity of competing practices that develop at a given place. He demonstrates that New Agers' practices must be interpreted within the context of "interpretive disputes with other groups, and broader sets of socioeconomic relations." At Glastonbury and Sedona, Forest Service bureaucrats, tourism promoters, real estate developers, Native Americans and Evangelical Christians produce their own senses of place, often contesting one another's practices and politics. Ivakhiv argues that, in addition to these local ways place is contested, New Age pilgrims also challenge the perspectives and practices of transnational capitalism and science. They create competing ways of knowing nature and alternative economies. Like Belden Lane, Ivakhiv is attentive to the textures of place and his own embodied experience as an ethnographer, but he also stresses the necessity for analyzing the immediate, local aspect of place as dynamically situated within complex global flows of culture and capital (Ivakhiv 2002: 191–93).

Religion, place, and the environment

Religion scholars have long stressed the importance of place. Mircea Eliade argues that sacred space orients all of reality. The sacred "irrupts" in a particular place, making it the *axis mundi*, the center and origin of the world, the zone of absolute reality, radically set apart from everything profane (Eliade 1954). Subsequent scholars stress the social processes and politics underlying this mapping of the sacred. Jonathan Z. Smith argues that constructing a place as sacred center simultaneously constructs other places as profane, religiously and politically marginal. The mapping of the sacred is always a mapping of social power (Smith 1987: 104).[8] David Chidester and Edward Linenthal focus on the "symbolic labor" by which sacred space is constructed—the "choosing, setting aside, consecrating, venerating, protecting, defending and refining" of sacred spaces. They argue that because sacred space asserts a particular symbolic and social order, it is inherently contested. Sacred spaces mark "hierarchical power relations of domination and subordination, inclusion and exclusion, appropriation and dispossession" (Chidester and Linenthal 1995: 17).

These contrasting approaches within religious studies mirror the approaches outlined above, and raise some of the same questions about how we should think about place. What defines a place as sacred? In what ways is this sacredness a cultural phenomenon (constructed through particular stories, practices, and politics), a natural phenomenon (produced by experiencing the distinctive features of the place itself), or a supernatural phenomenon (a religious reality, which cannot be reduced)? Where should we focus our attention when studying place: locally or globally, on the perceiving person or the broader cultural context? What tools and sensitivities are most helpful for understanding the nature of place: the perspectives of social or natural sciences, or the aesthetic capacities of the poet?

Scholars of religion and ecology have begun to wrestle with these questions and to utilize some of these varied approaches to place. In doing so, they are expanding the focus to examine religion and place, not only at exceptional sacred sites, but also in the everyday practices that express concern for the natural world. Sarah McFarland Taylor describes how environmentally activist Roman Catholic nuns are "reinhabiting" their bioregions and greening their religious traditions and practices (Taylor 2007). Rebecca Kneale Gould examines homesteaders who cultivate spiritual and sustainable lifestyles by dwelling in one place and learning to live in harmony with the natural environment (Gould 2005). Both scholars highlight the ways seemingly mundane practices like growing and eating food can express deep senses of spirituality and connection with place. They argue that such everyday actions are important expressions of religious and ethical commitment, especially in relation to the environment. To understand religion and environmentalism, we must pay attention to how individuals and communities orient themselves in place through such on-the-ground practices.

14D

What insights do each of these approaches to place offer as you think about your school's campus? What is the essence of the place? How is it embedded in a particular bioregional context? How are power and difference structured spatially? What is the relationship between your campus and global flows of information, capital, human and natural resources? How has your education been shaped by these particulars of place?

Whether examining dramatic, contested sacred sites like Stone Mountain (in the case study below) or everyday, domestic spiritual practices like eating locally, the approaches outlined in this chapter provide multiple ways to analyze the importance of place. As we confront increasingly complex environmental issues, with local and global causes and effects, we need these contrasting approaches to place. We must learn to think both spatially and socially about the environmental challenges we face. This means thinking carefully about scale, power, and difference. It means paying attention to what we sense directly, in our bodies, and to the forces and flows that are hidden from view.

Case study: Stone Mountain: a sacred site, commodified and contested

The world's largest piece of exposed granite, Stone Mountain is the most dramatic landmark among the gently rolling hills of the Georgia piedmont and now the sprawling suburbs of Atlanta. It has long been a place where surrounding communities have negotiated their relationships with one another and with the natural world. Stone Mountain also has a long history as a sacred place. Atop the mountain, early indigenous groups erected several large stone formations whose purpose is now a mystery. Creek and Cherokee leaders used the peak for political gatherings and religious rituals.

Stone Mountain was later transformed into a different kind of sacred site, a memorial to the Confederacy and its "Lost Cause." In the 1920s, renowned sculptor Gutzon Borglum began carving enormous images of Robert E. Lee, Jefferson Davis, and Stonewall Jackson right into the granite dome. Promoter E. Lee Trinkle described Stone Mountain as "consecrated ground that God himself has raised up," a "mecca of glory," a "sanctuary of truth," and a "sermon in stone," where the South's "golden age ... defied the future" (Trinkle 1923). In 1915, William J. Simmons chose Stone Mountain as the place to reawaken another potent symbol of Southern identity, the Ku Klux Klan (KKK), marking this new beginning with a complex weaving of racial and religious symbolism, including the Klan's first cross-burning. The KKK spread and splintered, but for decades the group continued to return to Stone Mountain for its annual pilgrimage, the "Klonvocation."

This sacred site is also a highly commercialized tourist destination, where visitors flock to enjoy both nature and Southern nostalgia. In 1958, the state of Georgia purchased Stone Mountain to preserve its natural wonder and cultural meaning, but also with the stated purpose of generating revenue. Over the next decade, at the height of the civil rights movement, the state completed the Confederate carving and, inspired by the popularity of *Gone With the Wind*, erected an antebellum style plantation in the meadow below. To increase its "authenticity," officials hired actress Butterfly McQueen, who had played house slave Prissy in the movie version, to greet visitors. The state also enhanced Stone Mountain's "natural" qualities, constructing a large lake and adding a driving loop, scenic railroad, campground, picnic shelters, hiking trails, petting zoo, horseback riding academy, and game ranch.

In 1998, the state privatized the management of the park, partnering with Herschend Family Entertainment, a Christian company that operates Dollywood and a number of theme parks in Branson, Missouri. Herschend soon began construction of a $100 million theme park celebrating the "fun side of the Southern story." Herschend also developed new nature attractions, the most remarkable being the "Coca-Cola Snow Mountain," which features "real snow in Atlanta." The attraction was scheduled to open in 2007 but shut down after public outcry over the wastefulness of generating 200 pounds of freshly made snow out of county water each day during a severe drought. The following year, with public reservoirs still dangerously low, the attraction opened with water from Stone Mountain's own lake, run through a filtration system to make sure the snow is clean and white, just like real snow.

Figure 14.1 Stone Mountain's quarries provided granite for confederate memorials throughout the South. By 1915, the United Daughters of the Confederacy envisioned the mountain itself as an icon of the Lost Cause, and they led efforts to promote and pay for the massive memorial.

Source: Poster courtesy of the Stone Mountain Collection; Manuscript, Archives and Rare Book Library, Emory University.

Like other sites of natural and cultural significance, Stone Mountain is a place where divergent public values, memories and meanings come in contact and come into conflict. Before carving the Confederate memorial, sculptors removed what remained of Native American stone formations. After the state took ownership, authorities tried to remove the Klan's increasingly controversial imprint on the place. In 1962, they restricted Klan access to the park, prompting a struggle between state troopers—with clubs and teargas—and a crowd of hooded Klansmen, who eventually forced their way to the mountain for what they called a "religious ceremony."

The Klan continued to gather annually on private land at the base of the mountain until the 1990s, when a growing number of African-Americans in this booming Atlanta suburb asserted their power to inscribe new meanings at Stone Mountain. In 1994, a black civic group sponsored an integrated community-wide picnic at Leila Mason Park, adjacent to the private land where the Klan continued to gather for its annual Klonvocation and cross-burning. What was long a place of exclusion and hate, they now claimed as a place of harmony and integration.

In 1997, Chuck Burris was elected the first African-American mayor of the town of Stone Mountain, which surrounds the park. He struck a deal with the daughter of former mayor and KKK Imperial Wizard James Venable, agreeing to keep her father's name on a city street if the family would stop hosting Klan rallies on its property. A year later, Burris purchased Venable's house. The first thing he did when moving in was to hang a picture of Martin Luther King on the bedroom wall. King too had subverted the racist history of this place. In 1963, from the steps of the Lincoln Memorial, he ascended to the climax of his most famous speech saying, "Let freedom ring from Stone Mountain of Georgia." Fully aware of the Klan history and Confederate commemoration, King declared the sacred significance of this as a place not fixed in a racially segregated past, but ushering in a future of justice and equality. In 2000, Burris dedicated a "Freedom Bell" in the heart of Main Street as a kind of counter-monument representing King's vision.

These groups draw on religious resources to contest the cultural legacy of the place. Others challenge ideas of nature at Stone Mountain. A small, evangelical ministry called "Creation Science Defense" uses geologic evidence embedded in the granite of Stone Mountain to demonstrate that the earth is quite young. They publish a field guide and lead fieldtrips for home-schoolers, promoting a biblical environmental ethic of human dominion and care for creation. Another group, the psychics and energy workers of the "First Georgia Dowsers," also offers an alternative to mainstream scientific ideas of nature. Through careful attention to patterns of earth energy, they identify places of disharmony, often caused by past pollution and violence. They focus their psychic energy to heal the earth.

Each morning at 6 a.m., a group of devoted hikers meets to climb Stone Mountain. The mountain has special memories for this gathering of long-time, white residents of the town. They are the heart and soul of the "Friends of Stone Mountain" watchdog group that has challenged the continued construction here. One member explained, "I am not a tree hugger, but ... I will always fight for the park." Another continued, "We connect with places with a tendency that some people don't understand. It's a Southern thing. You fight even though you know you can't win. You're fighting after it's lost, and you'll fight after you know it's hopeless" (Smith 2003). Here, Lost Cause values memorialized at Stone Mountain provide the model for protecting the sacred site from the profane forces of commercialization and development. These groups challenge the way nature is represented and managed at Stone Mountain, asserting alternative histories and practices of reverence and care. They strategically claim the power of their intimate local, personal, and spiritual connections to place.

Discussion questions

1 Based on this short case study, which groups do you think should have the power to make decisions about how Stone Mountain park is managed?
2 In what sense would you say this mountain is a "natural" place? What about "sacred?"
3 Most visitors to Stone Mountain Park have no knowledge of the Klan's history at the site. There is a small, but easily missed photograph in an out-of-the-way corner of the museum, but otherwise the park seems to hope this bad memory will simply be forgotten. Is such a strategy of erasure the most appropriate solution, or should the park do more to acknowledge its checkered past? What do you think is the best way to deal with this uncomfortable aspect of the place's identity?

Notes

1 Philosopher Monika Langer (2003) develops this idea of the flesh.
2 Christian Diehm (2003) elaborates this eco-phenomenological ethics of encounter, drawing on the work of Emanual Levinas.
3 For a more detailed discussion of this debate, see Gray (2006).
4 Some within bioregionalism criticized *Dwellers in the Land* as overly intellectual, not reflecting the anarchic, activist strands of the movement. For more on the charged responses to Sale's book, see Aberley (1999).
5 A number of scholars have proposed models of bioregionalism that account for this global scale. Mitchell Thomashow (1999, 2002) develops a "cosmopolitan bioregionalism." Adrian Ivakhiv (2002) calls for a "nonessentialist bioregionalism," that includes "an ethical and critical appreciation of difference of plurality, and a non-essentialist understanding of place which recognizes the ambiguity and mutability of borders and cross-border movements, territorialities and deterritorializations."
6 "Where You At?" was developed by Leonard Charles, Jim Dodge, Lynn Milliman, and Victoria Stockley, and originally published in *Coevolution Quarterly* 32 (Winter 1981): 1.

7 Robert Bullard has written extensively on environmental justice and the politics of place. See, for instance, Bullard (2007); Bullard and Wright (2009). Historian William Cronon (1996) has also been an influential voice in the debate over wilderness as a privileged place in environmentalism. Many others have joined in this "wilderness debate," as can be seen in two anthologies: Callicott and Nelson (1998); Nelson and Callicott (2008).
8 Smith proposes two basic structures of spatiality in religions, the "locative" and "utopian." The former is characteristic of closed, static systems that affirm and celebrate the sacred order of the cosmos, often ritually producing correspondingly ordered, bounded physical spaces. Here, the greatest threat to the sacred is vast, open, chaotic space that lies beyond the bounds of the ritually ordered sacred. Smith contrasts this with the utopian vision of space, which sees highly structured space as static and oppressive. Here, the sacred lies beyond the social structure, and individuals strive for freedom by escaping the bounded, ordered social space. See Smith (1978).

References

Aberley, D. (1999) "Interpreting Bioregionalism: A Story from Many Voices," in M.V. McGinnis (ed.) *Bioregionalism*, New York: Routledge.

Abram, D. (1996) *The Spell of the Sensuous: Perception and Language in a More-Than-Human World*, New York: Pantheon Books.

Berg, P. (2002) *Bioregionalism (a Definition)*, San Francisco Diggers Archives Online, available at http://www.diggers.org/freecitynews/_disc1/00000017.htm (accessed September 19, 2009).

Berry, T. (1988) *The Dream of the Earth*, San Francisco: Sierra Club Books.

Bullard, R.D. (2007) *The Black Metropolis in the Twenty-First Century: Race, Power, and Politics of Place*, Lanham, MD: Rowman & Littlefield.

Bullard, R.D. and B. Wright (2009) *Race, Place, and Environmental Justice after Hurricane Katrina: Struggles to Reclaim, Rebuild, and Revitalize New Orleans and the Gulf Coast*, Boulder, CO: Westview Press.

Callicott, J.B. and M.P. Nelson (1998) *The Great New Wilderness Debate*, Athens, GA: University of Georgia Press.

Casey, E. (1996) "How to Get from Space to Place in a Fairly Short Stretch of Time: Phenomenological Prolegomena," in S. Feld and K.H. Basso (eds) *Senses of Place*, Santa Fe, NM: School of American Research Press.

Chidester, D. and E.T. Linenthal (1995) "Introduction," in *American Sacred Space*, Bloomington: Indiana University Press.

Cronon, W. (ed.) (1996) *Uncommon Ground: Rethinking the Human Place in Nature*, New York: W.W. Norton & Company.

Diehm, C. (2003) "Natural Disasters," in C. Brown and T. Toadvine (eds) *Eco-Phenomenology: Back to the Earth Itself*, Albany: State University of New York Press.

Eliade, M. (1954) *The Myth of the Eternal Return*, New York: Pantheon Books.

Gould, R.K. (2005) *At Home in Nature: Modern Homesteading and Spiritual Practice in America*, Berkeley: University of California Press.

Gray, T. (2006) *Gary Snyder and the Pacific Rim: Creating Countercultural Community*, Iowa City: University of Iowa Press.

Harvey, D. (1996) *Justice, Nature, and the Geography of Difference*, Cambridge, MA: Blackwell Publishers.

Ivakhiv, A.J. (2002) *Claiming Sacred Ground: Pilgrims and Politics at Glastonbury and Sedona*, Bloomington: Indiana University Press.

Lane, B.C. (2002) *Landscapes of the Sacred: Geography and Narrative in American Spirituality*, Baltimore, MD: Johns Hopkins University Press.

Langer, M. (2003) "Nietszsche, Heidegger, and Merleau-Ponty: Some of Their Contributions and Limitations for Environmentalism," in C. Brown and T. Toadvine (eds) *Eco-Phenomenology: Back to the Earth Itself*, Albany: State University of New York Press.

Lodge, D.M. and C. Hamlin (2006) *Religion and the New Ecology: Environmental Responsibility in a World in Flux*, Notre Dame: University of Notre Dame Press.

Massey, D. (1993) "Power-Geometry and a Progressive Sense of Place," in Jon Bird (ed.) *Mapping the Futures: Local Cultures, Global Change*, London and New York: Routledge.

Nelson, M.P. and J.B. Callicott (2008) *The Wilderness Debate Rages On: Continuing the Great New Wilderness Debate*, Athens, GA: University of Georgia Press.

Relph, E.C. (1976) *Place and Placelessness*, London: Pion.

Sale, K. (1985) *Dwellers in the Land: The Bioregional Vision*, San Francisco: Sierra Club Books.

Smith, B. (2003) "The Battle for Stone Mountain; Watchdog Group that Opposed Rent Cut Undeterred by Setback," *Atlanta Journal-Constitution*, July 31, DeKalb, 1JA.

Smith, J.Z. (1978) *Map Is Not Territory: Studies in the History of Religions*, Leiden: Brill.

——(1987) *To Take Place: Toward Theory in Ritual*, Chicago: University of Chicago Press.

Snyder, G. (1974) *Turtle Island*, New York: New Directions Publishing Corporation.

——(1990) *The Practice of the Wild: Essays*, San Francisco: North Point Press.

——(1999) *The Gary Snyder Reader: Prose, Poetry, and Translations, 1952–1998*, Washington, DC: Counterpoint.

Taylor, S.M. (2007) *Green Sisters: A Spiritual Ecology*, Cambridge, MA: Harvard University Press.

Thomashow, M. (1999) "Toward a Cosmopolitan Bioregionalism," in M.V. McGinnis (ed.) *Bioregionalism*, New York: Routledge.

——(2002) *Bringing the Biosphere Home: Learning to Perceive Global Environmental Change*, Cambridge, MA: MIT Press.

Trinkle, E.L. (1923) "Address by Governor E. Lee Trinkle of the Commonwealth of Virginia on the Occasion of the First Carving on the Stone Mountain Confederate Memorial at Stone Mountain, Ga., June 18, 1923," Stone Mountain Collection, Manuscript, Archives and Rare Book Library, Emory University, Atlanta.

Tuan, Y. (1974) *Topophilia: A Study of Environmental Perception, Attitudes, and Values*, Englewood Cliffs, NJ: Prentice-Hall.

——(1977) *Space and Place: The Perspective of Experience*, Minneapolis: University of Minnesota Press.

Worster, D. (1993) *The Wealth of Nature: Environmental History and the Ecological Imagination*, New York: Oxford University Press.

Further reading

Janz, Bruce (n.d.) "Research on Space and Place," at http://pegasus.cc.ucf.edu/~janzb/
place/home.html. (For a comprehensive list of readings and resources.)
Cresswell, T. (2004) *Place: A Short Introduction*, Malden, MA: Blackwell Publishers.
(Offers an accessible survey of the concept from the perspective of geography.)
Freeman, D.B. (1997) *Carved in Stone: The History of Stone Mountain*, Macon, GA:
Mercer University Press. (For a more general, book-length history of Stone
Mountain.)
Hale, G.E. (2003) "Granite Stopped Time: Stone Mountain Memorial and the
Representation of White Southern Identity," in C. Mills and P.H. Simpson (eds)
*Monuments to the Lost Cause: Women, Art, and the Landscapes of Southern
Memory*, Knoxville: University of Tennessee Press. (The best critical, scholarly
treatment of Stone Mountain's history.)
McGinnis, M.V. (ed.) (1999) *Bioregionalism*, New York: Routledge. (For more on
bioregionalism.)
Morse, M. (1999) "The Changing Face of Stone Mountain," *Smithsonian* 29: 56–67.
(Gives a good sense of the shifting racial landscape of the town, including profiles
of Mayor Burris and the "6 a.m. mountain climbers".)
Thayer, R.L. (2003) *Lifeplace: Bioregional Thought and Practice*, Berkeley:
University of California Press. (For more on bioregionalism.)

To learn more about Stone Mountain visit the website of the privately man-
aged park (http://www.stonemountainpark.com/) or the state agency, the
Stone Mountain Memorial Association (http://www.stonemountainpark.org/).
Another useful internet resource is "Shades of Gray: The Changing Focus of
Stone Mountain Park," which includes a timeline, primary documents, and
historic images. The site was produced as a class project by University of
Virginia American Studies students Matthew G. Muller, Corey W. McLellan,
and Charles F. Irons (http://xroads.virginia.edu/~ug97/stone/home.html).

Afterword

Teaching indoors, but not business as usual

Laurel Kearns

While many of the complicated questions about religion and ecology raised in the preceding chapters remain unanswered, one conclusion seems clear: We cannot continue business as usual. We cannot behave as if what we know has no effect on how we then act. We cannot leave that knowledge in the textbook or in the classroom; we must encourage each other to act on what we have learned. If we fail to encourage one another to act on and in the world, then we have failed to do our job. We have merely replicated the historical/traditional—and mistaken—Western division between knowledge and action, between theory and praxis, and between mind and body. We have just continued this problematic trend by creating a seeming split between scholarship and activism.

Yet activism is, in a way, *what we do every day when we teach and learn*. Even if we are teaching about seventeenth-century Dutch "Still Life" paintings or nineteenth-century Russian literature, professors teach because we think that what one knows makes a difference, because we hope that students will take what they have learned and somehow think, act, and live differently in the world. This desire to go beyond knowledge for knowledge's sake has always been true of teaching "religion," whether in the context of religious studies and theology in colleges or, even more explicitly, in seminaries and theological schools. Teaching about religious worldviews and practices directly engages Paul Tillich's notion of "ultimate concerns" that has been discussed intermittently throughout this volume.

The analysis of individual, congregational, cultural, and broad, cross-cultural "ultimate concerns" cannot be, and should never be, limited to abstract, conceptual analysis in the classroom. Sociologist Nancy Nason-Clark, who researches religion and domestic violence, makes a similar assertion when she states:

> [S]cholarship devoid of social activism is like a car that is never driven for fear of an accident, a house too clean for guests, a restaurant preparing for service but never finalizing its menu, a church so busy with programs that it cannot help hurting men and women.
>
> (Nason-Clark 2001: 11)

While Nason-Clark is talking about studying violence toward humans, the work of studying the relationship between religion and ecology also includes understanding the connection between religions and the violence we have committed against the earth and all its creatures, the future generations of all living creatures and the larger planetary systems—or, in the words of some religious traditions, the whole of the creation.

Why are we in the classroom, after all? The authors in this volume have given you a clear idea of why they are in the classroom, and they invite you to wrestle with the implications of what you have learned from this book. When we teach and learn about environmental issues, we are always aware that it is, indeed, troubling knowledge that we are conveying. We know that our scholarship and teaching cannot be somehow removed from the larger issues of the world. I don't know anyone who teaches in environmental studies, or in the emerging field of "religion and ecology," who doesn't care passionately about the future of the planet and all of its inhabitants. In this book, we directly address the question of what humans (in various religious and cultural contexts) value most in the world, how those values profoundly affect the life and health of the planet on which we depend, and how the environmental context in which religion is practiced profoundly shapes it. Moreover, we examine not only recognizable "environmental" issues, but also those various cultural and religious worlds of meaning that provide the larger contexts of meaning that give shape to everyday values and actions.

As scholars and teachers, we need to make clear the connections between what is learned in the classroom and what we can then do outside of it, always recognizing that different people may make different connections and go in many different ways. Is not part of why we study and teach religion and ecology that we hope to motivate each other to do something, to care, to speak up? It is the job of education to help us see the ways that we can connect what we learn with the larger world, to shape our futures. As ethicist Anna Peterson concludes in her powerful essay in *EcoSpirit*:

> Here is the hope that our ideas can matter in a new way and help shape future ways of living on the earth. We can help create the grounds, though not the inevitability, of a new relationship between ideas and practice, a new "walk" and a new "talk." This hope is related to the knowledge that if we can change in this way, walk in this direction, so might others, and another kind of life—not only of thought—may be possible.
>
> (Peterson 2007: 62)

We hope that what is learned most from this volume is this interconnectivity of all issues, that ecology cannot be divorced from what we value most and how we then live our lives. Nor can environmental issues be separated from our justice concerns about the treatment of people and communities of color, or of those in poverty, or of women (Baugh, Chapter 10) and children, or of those who are oppressed and disadvantaged in any society. From these concerns, we see connections to the treatment of animals (Aftandilian, Chapter 9), the destruction of ecosystems, the destruction of forests, the leveling of mountains (Witt, Chapter 3)—all things that are seen to be of "use" to those with more power, who are mainly interested in maintaining that power.

The future of the planet's ecology is directly affected by the interconnectedness and injustices of the world's globalized economic system, as Laura Hartman examines (Chapter 11). As she mentions, the root word for ecology and economy is the same, the Greek word for household, *oikos*; it is also the root word of the term ecumenism (which refers to bettering the relations within one religious "house," such as among Christians, or between religions). Simply put, we cannot separate our actions in one part of the "household" from its effect on the rest of the household. Ecological, economic, and religious/ethical rules and understandings for "the planetary household" need to be examined *together* to further our understanding of sustainability, as Willis Jenkins (Chapter 8) and others in this volume have attempted to do. Instead of replicating the fragmentation, bifurcation, and opposition that so often characterize the prevailing understanding of our global situation, our approach must move in a more accurate, responsible, and "organic" direction. Knowledge can and should lead to social responsibility and to contributions to the common good.

In the academy, this approach is often known as engaged scholarship, and the field of "religion and ecology," as the authors in this book have demonstrated, is a clear example of such scholarship. But this book is about more than conveying the conversations and insights of a developing scholarly field in a classroom context. As the editors comment in their introduction: "If religion is to be relevant to our time, it needs to respond to the reality of environmental degradation. If faith traditions and spiritual practices are to fulfill their role as moral guides, they need to reflect on the ethical implications of these trends and to lead people of faith to more just and sustainable lives. Religion must respond to the reality of environmental degradation." We are clear that the work we do in the academy is ultimately intended to benefit, assist, and challenge those outside academic institutions.

The work of scholars on environmental justice and eco-justice is an outstanding example. By collecting data, looking for patterns, and making connections, scholars help local residents and activists, as well as voters and policy makers, see the broader picture. The path-breaking study by the United Church of Christ on "Toxic Wastes and Race" and the two follow-up studies are excellent examples. By working with and writing about different environmental justice or eco-justice struggles (Bohannon and O'Brien, Chapter 12) and successful movements to address environmental degradation and environmental racism, scholars make others aware. They both inspire and provide useful knowledge for those seeking to understand and address similar issues in other contexts. And by gathering together data and making them available to the general public, as does the Environmental Justice Resource Center at Clark Atlanta University, scholars and researchers help to empower people to change things for the better. Those working on eco-justice, the connection between religious concerns and justice for all earth's inhabitants discussed in this volume, also illustrate this engaged scholarship, which is facilitated by institutions like the Forum on Religion and Ecology.

Further, as environmental and eco-justice scholars so clearly demonstrate, this is a two-way street; the work of those "on the ground" who experience injustice, or who are actively seeking to address the spiritual and environmental crisis we find ourselves in, should inform our scholarship and our teaching. Authors in this volume such as Rebecca Kneale Gould, Mark Wallace, Mary Evelyn Tucker, and John Grim are further examples of scholars whose work with people in religious and activist communities informs their research, and who work with activists to bring about a better future for the planet. My own work of more than two decades of learning from those in religious environmental movements and organizations profoundly shapes my scholarship, my teaching, and my engagement with the world. I cannot sit idly by in my office in the forested campus of Drew University while knowing about the toxicity and degradation of so much of urban New Jersey, the diminishment of ecosystems, the "global weirding," as Thomas Friedman calls it, of the planet, and not have it affect my teaching, my scholarship and my activism.

At the same time as I am arguing that teachers need to challenge the reluctance in the academy and in the classroom to connect scholarship with action, and to encourage their students to be more activist, I imagine the student's impatience, just wanting to do something immediately and not spend so much time reading and learning. It is not at all hard to imagine, as I have been that student many a time. The authors of this book are familiar with the desire to use what we know, to be more activist after becoming frustrated with those who don't want to know the full scope of the environmental crisis, or those who sort of know but don't care, or who know and can't be bothered because it interferes with their comfortable lifestyles, or who know and are afraid to risk disrupting the power dynamics. This is just as true in the academy as in our everyday lives, and we work to transform our institutions, our professional societies, our disciplinary guilds. It is what led us to become scholars—to better understand the complex dynamics of religious worldviews and practices, the frequent gap between ideas and action, and then to translate that into our teaching, scholarship, and the motivation to challenge business as usual. The student's urge to do something now is understandable and laudable. We are, after all, talking about our students' future and can only hope that they want to do something to affect it.

Yet in wanting action on issues, students and activists can brush off understanding the complexity of issues and contexts. Just as scholarship devoid of praxis is a luxury, activism without taking advantage of what scholars know is often well meaning but misguided, or even careless. Understanding the issues, the stakeholders, the power dynamics, the operative worldviews, and how they shape the framing and counter-framing of what needs to be done makes action all the more effective. So a balance must be struck, because to be an activist without some understanding of systems, of worldviews, of behavioral psychology, of the intricate related-ness of ecosystems, is ultimately to be less effective. This broader under-standing comes in part from the classroom and scholarship, but needs to be balanced by also listening deeply and learning from others who are actively trying to do something. That is why case studies (such as Witt's (Chapter 3) and Finnegan's (Chapter 6)) and cooperation with people in non-profits, government agencies, and grassroots groups such as those men-tioned throughout this volume are an important part of the classroom and scholarship.

This is one earth, filled with interlocking, interconnected ecosystems of which we are a part; the weather and climate respect no boundaries of nation or class or ecosystem; the air we breathe and the water that we—and all creatures—depend on for life are not givens, but can be toxic and life threatening and can come from sources far beyond our control. Once we fully take into account these realizations, the well-known phrase "think globally, act locally" becomes think locally and act locally because, of course, it is all global in the end (Lorentzen, Chapter 13). Similarly, we must think globally and act globally, because it is eventually also all local (Campbell, Chapter 14).

Business as usual maintains this bifurcation between local and global, between scholarship and activism; it maintains the status quo that wants us to forget that we are all producers of the social world and that the current societal systems and cultural patterns exist because we created them and we participate in continuing their existence. Particularly in the US, we have much work to do to avoid being complicit. Too many tend to dismiss any future concerns because we all benefit right now from consuming more than our share, from continuing, or trying to return to, the business as usual that contributed to our planetary crisis. In the academy, we must resist the com-fortable complacency of doing scholarship that is divorced from a concern and responsibility for the world, of not risking anything for fear of being labeled less of a scholar or student because we are activist. If we do not resist, we continue business as usual. If the planetary context in which we all live and breathe is endangered, then surely it is relevant to anything and everything we teach and learn. It is hard enough that we mainly teach and learn indoors, divorced from the world of wonder that Deane-Drummond and Sideris discuss (Chapter 5), often without windows on the larger world.

We certainly cannot afford to maintain the ivory tower and be even more removed from what happens in it. So, please, no more business as usual.

References

Nason-Clark, N. (2001) "Making the Sacred Sage: Woman Abuse and Communities of Faith," in N. Nason-Clark and M.J. Nietz (eds) *Feminist Narratives and the Sociology of Religion*, Walnut Creek, CA: AltaMira Press.

Peterson, A. (2007) "Walking the Talk: A Practice Based Environmental Ethic as Grounds for Hope," in, L. Kearns and C. Keller (eds) *Ecospirit: Religions and Philosophies for the Earth*, New York: Fordham University Press.

Further reading

Kearns, L. (1996) "Saving the Creation: Christian Environmentalism in the United States," *Sociology of Religion* 57(1): 55–70.

——(2002) "Greening Ethnography and the Study of Religion," in J. Spickard, S. Landres, and M. McGuire (eds) *Beyond Personal Knowledge: Reshaping the Ethnography of Religion*, New York University Press.

Glossary

These definitions are intended for students, and will be helpful as you consider the questions and ideas raised in this textbook. It is important to note, however, that this glossary is not exhaustive in two senses. First, there are many more terms relevant to the study of religion and ecology that are not included here, either because of limited space or because the editors are skeptical that a brief definition is useful. Second, each term is defined as it is used in this book, but a careful reading of the chapters will clearly show that these are controversial and complicated ideas which must be thought about rather than simply and conclusively defined.

For more detailed discussions of these and many other concepts in the field, we recommend you consult two encyclopedias: the *Encyclopedia of Religion and Nature*, edited by Bron Taylor (Continuum, 2005), and the *Encyclopedia of Sustainability, Volume 1: The Spirit of Sustainability*, edited by Willis Jenkins (Berkshire, 2009).

(The numbers in parentheses at the end of an entry refer to the chapters in which the terms occur.)

Animism A belief system that attributes a "soul" or "spirit" to all things, often including a belief that all are interconnected through a single spirit that inhabits and unifies the entire natural world. (2)

Anthropocene A proposed name for the current geological epoch, in which human beings have profound influence upon the future of life and ecosystems. (8)

Anthropocentrism A moral stance that takes the human species as the center of value, distinguishing this species from other creatures and assuming that human beings should be primarily or exclusively concerned about the well-being of other humans. (5, 9)

Biodiversity The variety of life, generally measured in terms of the diversity of genes within a species, species within an ecosystem, and ecosystems within the planetary system. The drastic contemporary reduction in this variety is a key dimension of contemporary environmental degradation. (2, 7, 12)

Bioregionalism   A movement calling people to reinhabit particular places, which advocates commitment to understand, remain in, and protect a specific region and its environmental features. (14)

Climate change   In one sense, a natural phenomenon, as the earth's atmospheric system is constantly in flux and global weather trends are always influenced by such changes. In contemporary usage, however, climate change more commonly refers to the unprecedented and rapid changes that industrial human activity is causing in the climate (anthropogenic climate change), particularly through the greenhouse effect. These changes include warming of the average temperature on earth, melting of the polar ice caps, and more severe droughts and storms throughout the world. (4)

Commodification   Treating a person, a place, or an object as an economic resource. This often entails assuming that the only or primary value of something is the value for which it can be bought or sold. (13)

Consumerism   The trend in wealthy human societies toward increased production and procurement of goods and services. When widespread in a culture, shopping becomes a dominant form of recreation and the society's well-being is believed to depend upon ever-expanding consumption. (11)

Cosmology   An explanation of how the universe works, how it came to be, and how human beings fit within it. A cosmology can be based on a religious tradition, a scientific study, or both. (7, 11)

Creation   A reference to the natural world as a whole that stresses its unity and coherence by implying that it is the work of a divine energy or purpose, a creator. (2, 7, 12)

Creation spirituality   A form of worship and belief that takes the material world, viewed as creation, as the primary source, site, and purpose of religious ritual and morality. (7)

Cultural geography   A study of places and the concept of place that pays particular attention to global capitalism as an influential force changing the ways space is constructed through social, economic, and political processes. (14)

Death of nature   An argument that modern science's attempt to reduce its subjects to their smallest constituent parts leads people to see the natural world as full of independent, disconnected, and therefore "dead" matter. This is contrasted with a more organic view of the natural world frequently associated with pre- and postmodern thought. (See also *End of nature*) (2, 4)

Dominion   A theological belief that humanity has been placed in a position of authority over the rest of creation; an understanding of the world as designed to be subject to humanity. (2, 14)

Dualism   A way of understanding something that distinguishes two, and only two, distinct categories within it, i.e. understanding humanity as male and female, a society as rich and poor, a culture as white and nonwhite, sexuality as straight and gay, creatures as human and non-human. Critics argue that such division inevitably creates a hierarchy, raising one category and denigrating the other. (10)

Ecocentrism   A moral stance that takes ecosystems as the basis and center of value, seeking to protect and sustain the conditions necessary for the interconnected coexistence of life within a system. This is a proposed alternative to anthropocentrism. (5, 8)

Ecofeminism   An activist stance and an interdisciplinary scholarly perspective committed to developing alternatives to male-dominated human societies and to preserving the health and integrity of ecosystems. Eco-feminism is based on observed connections between the oppression of women and the abuse of the natural world and on proposed connections between the solutions to these two problems. (4, 7, 10)

Eco-justice   A theological ideal that emphasizes the unity of environmental and social morality, assuming that other people and other creatures should be treated justly and that a singular moral stance toward both is possible. (7, 8, 12)

Ecological economics   A movement within economics which takes ecological principles seriously and so calls for basic changes in the assumptions economists make, the goals they work toward, and the tools they use to measure economic health and success. (7, 11)

Ecology   In one sense, a branch of biological science focused on understanding organisms in the context of their living and nonliving environments, studying the connections between evolving life-forms and the world around them. In another sense, ecology is a morally instructive system of interconnections, a claim about the interrelated character of nature that has instructive lessons to teach all people. (4, 5)

Economics   The study of how people acquire and manage the materials they need to live. As an academic discipline, economics measures complex systems of supply, demand, production, distribution, and consumption in human societies. (11)

Ecotheology   A study of the intersections between theological ideas (beliefs about the sacred and religious life) and environmental issues. This term is most explicitly used by Christian and Jewish theologians, but has also been applied to those who develop environmentalist ideas out of any religious tradition. (2, 5, 11)

End of nature   The belief that there is no more "pure" nature (that has not been modified by human beings) due to the pervasive, global impact of human technologies. While the "death of nature" refers to a change in the way human beings understand the natural world, the end of nature refers to a change in the way the world itself functions. (See *Death of nature*) (4)

Environmental degradation An umbrella term describing the many negative impacts that human behaviors and technologies have had on the rest of the natural world. (1, 4, 7)

Environmental injustice The unjust distribution of environmental harms, by which the poor, people of color, women, and other minority groups experience the negative effects of environmental degradation more severely, are often deprived of access to environmental amenities, and have less influence on decisions about how a human culture will relate to its natural environment. (12)

Environmental justice (EJ) A movement of activists who oppose environmental injustice. This movement began in reaction to higher incidences of cancer and birth defects due to the use of toxic chemicals and siting of hazardous wastes in minority communities, and has expanded to study and oppose the many ways poor and marginalized peoples suffer the worst effects of environmental degradation. (7, 12)

Environmental racism The environmental injustices of waste siting, neighborhood structure, political policies, and infrastructure that particularly impact people of color. (12)

Environmentalism The political, activist, and academic movement that takes as its central concern ecological well-being, sustainability, or the care of a particular ecosystem. (1, 4, 7)

Eschatology A theological inquiry about the "end times," which can refer to the end of a current cultural system or the end of the entire cosmos. (11)

Essentialism The belief that the true identity of an individual or a group hinges upon an unchanging, central characteristic, whether that be a soul, genetics, or any other single concept. This term is often discussed in debates about whether or not gender categories are socially and historically constructed or biologically determined. (10)

Ethology The study of animal behavior, which seeks to understand both the diversity of the animal world and the similarities between the ways humans and other animals behave. (9)

Feminism Taking female standpoints as the critical lenses through which to examine all of reality. Most forms involve a critique of patriarchy, the male-centered and ordered worldviews and institutions that mark contemporary societies. This term also refers to an activist movement for women's liberation over the last century. (10)

Fourth world Indigenous communities that often live within and among "first-world" peoples. (13)

Gender A set of qualities, characteristics, and norms used to identify the difference between the sexes in any given society. There is substantial debate among academics and activists about whether these qualities and characteristics are somehow natural and essential, or are entirely socially constructed. (10)

Globalization   The expansion of networks of exchange and connection that link people across cultural, national, and geographic boundaries. Economic globalization usually refers to the worldwide reach of free-market style capitalism; cultural globalization often refers to the worldwide reach of certain art, entertainment, information, and religions. (Introduction, 10, 13, 14)

Glocalization   A characteristic of contemporary societies and contemporary issues in which the differences between "local" and "global" are ambiguous and/or in flux. (13)

Immanent   In theology, the idea that God or the Divine is in and with this world rather than distinct from it. The opposite of transcendent. (Introduction, 1, 2)

Incarnation   The materialization or actualization of an idea, concept, or reality; literally, becoming flesh. In Christian thought, this refers to God becoming human in the person of Jesus Christ. (2)

Interconnectedness   An attention to the ways events or actions are linked with one another. Many environmentalists draw moral lessons from the interconnections of ecosystems, the earth as a system, and/or the entirety of the universe. (4, 7)

Interdependence   A view of interconnectedness that emphasizes the ways everything and everyone is in some way contingent on the existence of others; nothing can exist on its own. This is a central tenet of many traditions within Buddhism, and is often developed into a critique of Western individualism by those who learn from those traditions. (7)

Justice   A commitment to ensuring that every member of a community has fair and equitable access to resources and equal participation in communal decision-making processes. Most discussions of justice also involve a commitment to rectifying the situation of community members who have the fewest resources and/or the least power in decision-making. (8, 10, 12)

Liberation Theology   A movement, especially within Christian theology, that privileges the perspective and concerns of the poor and the oppressed in making theological claims or ethical decisions (10, 12).

Liminal   The status of a person, place, or situation that is in transition or straddles two different states of being, and therefore is characterized by ambiguity, danger, and/or power. (9)

Lived religion   The way in which religion and religious practices manifest in the daily lives of practitioners. The "lived religions" approach is also a method that some religious scholars use to study the phenomenon of religion, often placed in direct opposition to the study of religious "worldviews." (Introduction, 3)

Mindfulness   A concept and practice that focus on training the mind to be aware of the interdependent nature of all reality and the interconnected nature of actions. Buddhist religious practice asserts that mindfulness leads to more ethical behavior. (11)

Nature A vastly complicated term with many different meanings. In some cases, it refers to everything that is not human. In others, it refers to the entire process of ongoing life, including humanity. In still others, it refers to the chemical, physical, and/or biological makeup of an entity, e.g. "It is in her nature to love glossaries." (4, 5)

Neoliberalism A belief system and/or economic theory that emphasizes the importance of the private sector over the public, the power of free markets to solve problems, and the benefits of successful business to the rest of society. (13)

Nonviolence A personal discipline and political strategy that develop alternatives to violence. Also known as *ahimsa*, a term drawn from Hinduism, nonviolence became a very important part of the Gandhian revolution in India and in the Civil Rights movement in the United States. (7, 11, 12)

Oikos Greek for "house." Found in the roots of *eco*logy ("words about the house"), *eco*nomy ("management of the house"), and *ecu*menism ("inhabited world," emphasizing religious unity). (4, 11)

Panentheism A term used by religious scholars to discuss the relationship between God and the world. Literally, "all in god," this position suggests that all of the world/universe exists within God (God is therefore immanent to the world) but that the world does not exhaust the reality of God (Godself is also therefore transcendent to the world). (2)

Pantheism A term used by religious scholars to discuss the relationship between God and the world. Literally "all is God," this position suggests that "world" and "god" are the same thing. In other words, divinity is totally immanent to the world. (2)

Phenomenology A branch of philosophical analysis that takes human experience as the beginning point for knowing and understanding reality. Two central ideas are that the world is as we experience it through our five senses and that we can have "raw experience" of nature without imposing history, tradition, culture, and reason upon those experiences. (7, 14)

Planetarity Awareness that all of the earth's inhabitants share the planet as their singular home and common ground in an enormous and ever-expanding universe. (7)

Practices The actions and behaviors of human beings in their lived contexts. Religious scholarship that focuses on practices often takes a particular interest in studying how communities or individuals actively interact with their religious traditions (rather than studying the traditional texts or beliefs of a religion) and/or an interest in how religious and social norms are reinforced through the ways in which they are acted out by people. (Introduction, 14)

Praxis Action that demonstrates, carries out, and expresses a theoretical awareness. This term bridges the traditional divide between theory and practice. (13)

Religious studies The academic study of how religions or religious phenomenon influence and are influenced by their social or environmental contexts; often placed in contrast to theology. (Introduction, 1, 2)

Sabbath See *Shabbat*.

Sacred Most simply, that which is separate from the profane or the everyday. Sacredness is ascribed to places, objects, persons, or times that people associate with the divine, that which is beyond or greater than the human, and/or a uniquely important event. (1, 2, 14)

Scale Deliberate attention to how the scope of one's vision affects what one sees. For instance, a human body can be studied at the microbiological level, as a person within their immediate environment, or as an inhabitant of planet Earth. Used in ecology and many other scientific disciplines. (4, 14)

Sex The biological makeup of a person's reproductive organs; a physical reality, in contrast to the cultural reality of gender. (10)

Sexuality The way a person defines her or himself as a sexual being. Often specifically refers to sexual preference, e.g. heterosexuality, homosexuality, or bisexuality. (10)

Shabbat A day of rest commemorating the seventh day of creation in Jewish and many Christian traditions. The Sabbath has been utilized by many religious environmentalists as a symbol for our need to give the earth a time for rest for restoration and renewal. (2, 11)

Shari'a The religious obligations of Islamic law. Also used to identify a politically enforced legal system based on those religious obligations. (6, 8, 11)

Sheikh A spiritual master, teacher, and guide in the Muslim tradition who is part of a lineage of teachers. (6)

Speciesist A form of prejudice based on the assumption that human beings are uniquely important and that the perspectives and interests of other species are unimportant or secondary. (9)

Stewardship The belief that humans have been given the responsibility (usually, by a creator/God) to take care of the earth. Some environmentalists call for stewardship as the basis of environmentalist morality, while others worry that this approach is problematically anthropocentric. (3, 8)

Subscendence The belief that the divine is fully present in the earth, making everything sacred. This is a direct contrast to transcendence. (2)

Sufism The mystical form of Islam, concerned with direct knowledge of God. Sufi Muslims usually belong to an order that follows a sheikh and practices a ritual of remembrance (*dhikr*) particular to their community. (6)

Sunni   A group within Islam which identifies itself as part of the *Ahl al-Sunna wa 'l-Jamā'a* (the People of the Custom and Community). The majority of Muslims are Sunni. (6)

Sustainability   Most basically, a way of living and using resources that does not degrade the ability of future generations to continue a culture's way of life. A "strong" concept of sustainability would also emphasize the necessity of preserving ecosystems, endangered species, and the like. (7, 8)

Sustainable development   The attempt to preserve the environment and improve societies through the advancement and growth of economic prosperity. (7, 8)

Teleology   A theological inquiry into, or belief related to, the direction of history, e.g. a belief in continual human progress. Teleology is distinct from eschatology in that it is not solely concerned with "end times." (11)

Theological anthropology   A basic understanding of human nature with particular emphasis on what fundamentally motivates people, how and whether people can change, and what most basically shapes a person's character. More specifically, this often refers to how we view humanity in light of our understandings of the divine. (11)

Theology   The study of the divine and its ramifications for how we understand humanity, the religious community, human culture, and the world as a whole. More broadly, theology can also signify constructive and critical work within any religious tradition. (Introduction, 2)

Transcendence   The belief that God or the divine resides in a place separate from (and, usually, superior to) the physical world. (Introduction, 2)

Universe story   A new religious narrative, associated especially with Teilhard de Chardin (1881–1955) and Thomas Berry (1914–2009), based on the interconnected, evolutionary progress of creation and humanity's particular role as a reflective, conscious creature. (7, 14)

Wilderness   Those parts of the world that are perceived to be untouched by humanity. (4, 10)

World religions   A category that emerged in nineteenth-century Europe to encompass the most prevalent religious traditions on the planet, minimally including Judaism, Christianity, Islam, Buddhism, and Hinduism. Much work in religion and ecology has focused on the environmental import of an expansive list of world religions, including a 10-volume book series published by the Forum for Religion and Ecology. (Introduction, 7, 11)

Worldview   A set of basic assumptions through which one views reality, usually shared among members of a community and often heavily influenced by religious traditions. (Introduction, 1, 2, 7, 8)

Index

Abram, David 33, 205–6
ahimsa 156–57, 161, 233
Albanese, Catherine 58, 85
Ammar, Nawal 25–26
animals 56, 66–67, 88–89, 108–10,
    112–29, 156
animism 33–35, 40, 61, 125–28, 228
anthropocene 104, 228
anthropocentrism 65, 193, 228 230
Appalachia 41–46, 170–71

Bacon, Francis 67
Bekoff, Marc 67, 114, 121
Berg, Peter 207–8, 219
Berry, Thomas 53, 63, 82–84, 92–93,
    120, 125, 209, 219, 235
Berry, Wendell 148, 152, 161, 162
Bible 2, 7, 24, 29, 33, 37, 59–60, 116,
    122, 131, 154–55
biocide 81
biodiversity 3, 21, 35, 52, 68–69, 86, 96,
    101–2, 110, 172–75, 184, 192, 228
bioregionalism 203–12, 218–21, 229
Boff, Leonardo 87, 174–76
Brundtland Report 99
Buddhism 5, 18, 26, 28–31, 85, 88, 94,
    135, 149–50, 157, 192–93, 200, 232, 235
Bullard, Robert 85, 168–70

Cabañas, El Salvador 194–99
Callicott, J Baird 84
Cancer Alley 165
Carson, Rachel 66–67, 141, 164
Chavis, Benjamin 169–70
Chávez, César 164–66
Chipko movement 107
Christianity 14–15, 31, 33–38, 44–45,
    59–61, 63, 65, 71, 85, 115–19,
    134–36, 148–56, 171–75; Anglican
    90; Evangelical 7, 24, 38, 44, 59–60,
    217; Pentecostal 191; Presbyterian
    171, 179; Roman Catholic 37, 90,
    139, 164–66, 189, 191–94, 197–99;
    United Church of Christ 167–68, 173
climate change 3, 32–35, 52–53, 57–58,
    68–69, 72, 93, 108, 110–11, 229;
    see also global warming
Cobb, John 85, 107, 152, 155
colonization 14, 56, 177, 184
commodification 105, 185, 188–91, 212,
    214–18, 229
Confucianism 53, 149–50
consumerism 68, 71, 86, 140, 147,
    150–51, 157, 161, 193, 205, 229
cosmology 82–84, 100, 152, 229
Council of All Beings 119, 124, 126, 128
creation 7, 33–34, 65, 93, 95, 98, 99–100,
    113, 115, 117–18, 122–24, 135, 208,
    223, 229; in Christianity, 25,
    32–35, 44, 59, 82, 121, 123–24, 148,
    154, 161, 171–73, 175, 179, 227;
    Yuchi account, 122–23; *see also* nature
creation spirituality 82–85, 135, 229
creationism 217
Cronon, William 57–58
Csordas, Thomas 189–92
cultural geography 203, 207,
    210–13, 229

Daly, Herman 87, 106, 107,
    152–53, 155
Daly, Mary 130
dark green religion 61, 63, 94; *see also*
    light green religion
Darwin, Charles 49, 65–66; *see also*
    evolution

Dawkins, Richard 67, 70
Dayempur Farm 73–76
de Chardin, Teilhard 83, 235
deep ecology 84, 119, 126
DeWitt, Calvin 59–61, 117
dominion 37, 117–18, 123, 217, 229
dualism 132, 134–39, 230
Durkheim, Emile 17–18, 19–22

Earth Charter 85, 92, 99, 100, 111, 176–78
Eaton, Heather 85, 131, 138, 181–86
ecocentrism 65–66, 107, 230
eco-justice 68, 87, 90, 93, 102, 163–80,
    224–25, 230
eco-kosher see kosher
ecofeminism 63, 125, 130–39, 141,
    144–46, 179, 200, 230
ecological economics 82, 87, 93, 111,
    152–56, 160, 161, 230
ecology 5, 43, 49–62, 64–71, 141, 182,
    223–24, 230; definitions of 49, 58–62,
    64–72, 147; history of 49–51, 64, 141;
    science of 51–52, 54–55, 186;
    worldview defined by 52–55, 66–68,
    142, 156–57; see also nature
economics 49, 82, 87, 93, 111, 112,
    147–62, 189–92, 209, 230
ecotheology 69, 89, 155–56, 172,
    194, 230
Ehrlich, Paul 91
ethology 120, 231
environmental activism 7–9, 41–44,
    52–54, 131–32, 158–60, 168–71,
    194–99, 222–27
environmental degradation 1–4, 8, 18,
    21–22, 25, 28, 38, 51, 53, 59–62,
    82–84, 101, 154, 158, 163, 171–75,
    187, 193, 224, 231
environmental despair 35–37, 39, 69
environmental injustice 53, 68,
    163–79, 231
environmental justice (EJ) 63, 107, 111,
    145–46, 163–80, 192, 210–12, 219,
    224–25, 231
Environmental Protection Agency
    (EPA) 43
environmental racism 166, 168–71, 178,
    180, 224, 231
environmentalism 5, 21–22, 26, 58, 67,
    82, 90–94, 107, 126, 171, 174, 179,
    188, 190–91, 200–203, 207, 212–14,
    219–20, 227, 231

eschatology 152–53, 231
essentialism 136–37, 231
ethics 25, 67–68, 81, 84, 88, 91, 108–10,
    171–73
evolution 5, 7, 32, 49–50, 66, 83–84, 94,
    114–18, 135

feminism, 130–46, 179, 230, 231;
    see also ecofeminism
Foltz, Richard 25–26, 118, 121
Food Not Bombs (FNB) 158–60
Forum on Religion and Ecology
    (FORE) 5, 82–92, 124, 160, 225
fourth world 193, 231
Francis of Assisi, Saint 116

gaia hypothesis (gaian, gaia) 94, 135,
    145, 208
Gandhi, Mahatma 156–57, 165,
    191, 233
Gardner, Gary 91
Gebara, Ivone 131
Geertz, Clifford 18–22
gender 130–46, 231–32
Genesis Farm 90
Gibson, Larry 42, 45
Gibson, William 171
global warming 35–36, 38, 186–87;
    see also climate change
globalization, 4, 8, 89, 131, 138,
    143–46, 153, 157–58, 161, 164,
    181–201, 210–11, 232
glocalization 158, 160, 183, 232
Gottlieb, Roger 22, 33, 85, 115, 118,
    156, 192
green sisters/green nuns 90, 94, 139–40,
    145, 172, 179, 220
Griffin, Susan 132

Haeckel, Ernst 49–50, 64
halal 156, 158, 160–61
Harvey, David 210–12
Harvey, Graham 33–35, 40, 85, 120
Hessel, Dieter 60–61, 85
Hinduism 14, 28, 29, 31, 88, 135, 149,
    162, 233, 235
holism 54
homesteading 26, 40, 140, 144, 220
homo economicus 152–53, 157
Hopkins, Dwight 190
Huerta, Delores 164
Hurricane Katrina 165–68

idolatry 149, 155
immanent 2, 16, 20, 37, 132–34, 232–33
incarnation 35–37, 71, 232
indigenous religions 2, 5, 27, 33–34, 56,
    84–88, 90, 92, 103, 113–17, 120–21,
    126, 175, 188, 190–94, 215, 231
interconnectedness 4, 51–55, 59–60,
    206, 224, 232
interdependence 2, 36, 53, 83, 177, 183,
    186, 232
International Society for the Study of
    Religion, Nature and Culture
    (ISSRNC) 89, 145
intrinsic value 100, 107
Islam 2, 5, 15, 25–29, 34, 88, 118, 121,
    126, 149, 156, 161, 234, 235; and
    farming 73–77; and fishing 108–10;
    Sunni 73–77, 235.
Ivakhiv, Adrian 212–13

James, William 30–33
jubilee 149, 154–55, 160–61
Judaism 5, 22, 25, 29–31, 33, 36–38, 88,
    135, 145, 149–50, 161, 235
justice 21–22, 32, 38, 85–87, 100–108,
    129, 134, 142–43, 163–78, 217,
    223–25; defined 163, 172, 232; as
    virtue 64; see also eco-justice and
    environmental justice

karma 149
kashrut 156, 162
Kaza, Stephanie 85, 157
Keller, Catherine 85
khilafa 109–10
King, Martin Luther, Jr. 33, 165, 217
kosher 118, 128, 156, 160; see also
    kashrut

liberation theology 178, 191–93, 199, 232
light green religion 61; see also dark
    green religion
Limits to Growth 98–99, 111
Linzey, Andrew 117–18
lived religion 6–7, 232
Love Canal 132, 203
Loy, David 151, 158
Luther, Martin 119

Marx, Karl 6, 19–21, 212
Massey, Doreen 211
McDaniel, Jay 85

McFague, Sallie 31–39, 85, 134–36,
    155–56
McKibben, Bill 57–58, 66, 69
Merchant, Carolyn 36, 133–34; see also
    death of nature
Millennium Development Goals 86–87,
    91, 93
mindfulness 157, 232
Misali Ethics Project 108–10
mountaintop removal 41–46

Naess, Arne 84
National Council of Churches (NCC) 90
nature 2, 5–6, 28–37, 40, 64–77, 186–89,
    205–12, 215–18; death of 36, 40, 133,
    145, 229–30 definitions of 55–63, 64–66,
    233; end of 57, 63, 69, 72, 201, 230;
    reverence for 28, 33–34, 67, 193; as a
    social construction 130–41, 188–89;
    as world beyond human influence
    55–58; see also creation, ecology
nature religion 31, 58, 62, 85, 93
neoliberalism 185–86, 189–93, 233
nonviolence, 125, 156–61, 233

oikos 49, 147–48, 158, 160, 224, 233

Pacific Rim Mining Company,
    195–99
Page, Tovis 138, 141
panentheism 35, 233
pantheism 34, 37, 233
pesticide 37–38, 164–65
Peterson, Anna 223
phenomenology 203–21, 233
place 28, 35, 39, 43, 75, 103, 138,
    203–21, 229
planetarity (planetary) 53, 63, 81, 92,
    94, 101, 108, 134, 153, 223–34
politics 131, 211–13
pollution 21, 38, 43, 53, 81, 85, 86, 151,
    165–66, 179, 180, 186, 195, 197
pragmatism 105–7
praxis and theory 222–27
Principles of Environmental Justice 169,
    176–77

Qur'an 2, 25, 109, 118, 121

Racism 136, 165–71, 178, 180,
    224, 231
Rasmussen, Larry 85, 100, 169

religion 1–26, 27–39; definitions of
    14–22, 27, 29–30; and nature 5–6, 29,
    40, 89, 141, 200, 228; and science 63,
    101; study of 23–26, 41–45
religious studies 4, 23–25, 122, 128,
    222, 234
Renewal 90, 161, 166
Rockefeller, Steven 85, 100
Rolston, Holmes, III 84
Ruether, Rosemary Radford 60–62, 85,
    134–35

sabbath/shabbat 39–40, 150, 154–55,
    158, 234
Schumacher, E. F. 156–58
Sen, Amartya 106
Shabbat/Sabbath 39–40, 150, 154–55,
    158, 160, 234
Shari'a 108–9, 149, 234
sheikh 73, 234
Shinto 14
Shiva, Vandana 133–34
Smith, Jonathan Z. 14, 20, 213
Snyder, Gary 85, 207–8
Speth, James Gustav 191
spirituality 29, 32, 61, 76, 92, 100, 119,
    135, 139, 143, 214, 229
stewardship 44, 109, 118, 159, 188, 234
Stone Mountain 214–18, 221
subscendence 35, 234
sustainability 92, 96–112, 152, 174, 176,
    224; defintions of 87–88, 235; history
    of 97–100; "strong" and "weak" 105
sustainable development, 87, 91–92,
    99–100, 235
Suzuki, D. T. 16–17, 19–21

Taylor, Bron 61, 85, 89
Taylor, Dorceta 137
Taylor, Sarah McFarland 90, 139, 172, 214
teleology 152–53, 235
theism 34–35, 70–71, 233
theological anthropology 190, 235

theology 23–24, 64–65, 117–18, 134–35,
    151, 155–56, 172–74, 235; feminist
    31, 131–32, 134–35; liberation
    174–76, 191–93, 232; natural 71;
    prosperity 151
Thoreau, Henry David 36, 39, 58
tikkun olam 150
Tillich, Paul 14–17, 19, 20–21, 27–28,
    30–32, 222
Torah 30, 36, 38, 40
Toxic Wastes and Race 167, 169, 178,
    179, 224
transcendence 16, 20, 35, 37, 132, 235

United Farm Workers (UFW) 144,
    164–65, 173, 178
United Nations 86, 88, 111, 195
Universe Story 82–84, 209, 235
University of Florida 89
usury 149, 155

virtues 49, 64–65, 67, 70

Waskow, Rabbi Arthur 31–34, 37, 39,
    40, 118, 128
Weber, Max 13–14, 26, 150, 162
West Virginia Council of Churches
    43–46
White, Lynn, Jr. 59, 63, 193, 202
wilderness, 2, 57–58, 130, 141, 188,
    212, 235
Wilson, E. O. 68, 91, 95
wisdom 59–60, 64–65, 68–70, 76, 157,
Women and Life on Earth (WLOE)
    142–46
wonder 35, 53, 65–72, 81, 111, 121,
    215, 226
World Council of Churches (WCC)
    98–100
world religions 8, 14, 29, 85, 88, 90, 235
worldview 6–8, 18–19, 30–34, 51–52,
    61, 88, 99, 133–34, 152, 193–94, 206,
    222, 225–26, 235